T0405739

Semantic Digital Libraries

Sebastian Ryszard Kruk • Bill McDaniel
Editors

Semantic Digital Libraries

Sebastian Ryszard Kruk
National University of Ireland
Digital Enterprise Research Institute
Lower Dangan
Galway
Ireland
sebastian.kruk@deri.org

Bill McDaniel
National University of Ireland
Digital Enterprise Research Institute
Lower Dangan
Galway
Ireland
bill.mcdaniel@deri.org

ISBN 978-3-540-85433-3 e-ISBN 978-3-540-85434-0

Library of Congress Control Number: 2008934757

ACM Computing Classification (1998): H.3, H.5, I.2

Cover design: KünkelLopka, Heidelberg

Printed on acid-free paper

9 8 7 6 5 4 3 2 1

springer.com

I dedicate this book to my gorgeous wife,

Ewelina,

who stayed with me

through ups and downs

ever since

semantic digital libraries

came in to our lifes and brought us

to the far edge of Europe

Sebastian Ryszard Kruk

This book is dedicated to

my lovely wife,

Linda,

who has seen me through

thick and thin, good and bad

and who will, apparently,

follow me anywhere in the world

Bill McDaniel

Preface

The Archchancellor turned the pages carefully.
They were well illustrated.
The Librarian knew his wizards.
The Science of Discworld, Terry Pratchett

Sebastian Kruk:

In 2002, the Polish government initiated the creation of a national digital library that would deliver cultural heritage to each household through the Internet. At that time, I was focusing my research on information retrieval, supported by the upcoming technologies of the Semantic Web. It was Prof. Henryk Krawczyk from Gdansk University of Technology who helped me to align my research with the growing demand for digital library management systems. As a result, my Master's Thesis presented a prototype of a semantic digital library called Elvis-DL.

Two years later, I was invited by Prof. Stefan Decker to continue my research on semantic digital libraries in the newly set up Digital Enterprise Research Institute in Galway, Ireland; soon after which Elvis-DL became JeromeDL and opened a new chapter of my research on semantic digital libraries. Two years ago, after the first *Tutorial on Semantic Digital Libraries* that we gave at JCDL 2006, I met Bill and we started implementing the semantic digital libraries vision, particularly JeromeDL, in the context of eLearning. The project got more momentum when my team was recently re-joined by Mariusz Cygan, who became the main architect and developer of JeromeDL.

Along the way, I collaborated with many people who influenced and helped me to put the domain of semantic digital libraries into shape. To mention only a few who's help I appreciate the most: Prof. Daniel Schwabe, Bernhard Haslhofer, Predrag Knezevic, Sandy Payette, Dean Kraftt, and Traugott Koch.

Bill McDaniel:

For me my adventures in electronic libraries began in the 1970s working in the UK with, and extending the capabilities of, IBM mainframe libraries that are used for source code storage and DataPoint minicomputer full text indexing methods. After returning to US in the early 1980s, I built electronic libraries and full text index access methods using VSAM under a variety of mainframe operating systems. These libraries were used in commercial software application products where it was required to store documents that are coded in IBM GML and in high speed printer data streams for intelligent document assembly systems. My second generation design included links to other documents and metadata tags that are attached to the documents for search purposes.

Throughout the 1990s, I worked with unstructured data in the form of documents coded for composition, which ultimately encoded in Adobe Acrobat PDF. This work emphasized the value of tagged databases, interdocument linking, and the possibilities of hyperlinking text elements. But the new computing systems and PCs had no good library support for managing such document collections, for indexing the text, or for searching related and interlinked documents intelligently.

In 1999, I became aware of the Semantic web and did some experiments of my own and turned to building initial semantically powered products. But the web did not have the structure for the easy tagging of documents. HTML was too limiting and XML was just getting started. Semantics required more time for maturation.

By the early 2000s, when I joined Adobe, the chicken and egg problem of metadata acquisition was obvious I spent much of my time there working on building an automatic metadata entity extraction system while researching the possibilities of semantically powered systems.

Joining DERI in 2006, I met Sebastian and learned about JeromeDL, the semantic digital library project here. In my capacity as eLearning project executive, I have been able to see the semantic digital libraries emerging and the underlying challenges being met. At the same time, the potential of libraries which could interlink documents, books, users, and other entities on a semantic level, interoperating with a multitude of other systems, has become apparent. This book is a fascinating collection of papers about these possibilities, the work already completed, and the things to come.

For me, it is a chance to see the long term vision of documents and their intricate potential become more fully realized. I hope every reader takes away as much insight from these chapters as I have gained by helping to gather and edit them.

Dear reader, the book you hold in hand now is a result of the work of many people who saw the potential of applying semantic web and social networking technologies to digital libraries domain. It is an outcome of ongoing research in that newly established domain of discourse and of an intensive development of open source projects like FEDORA, BRICKS, Greenstone, SIMILE, and JeromeDL.

We hope you will enjoy reading as much as we enjoyed researching, developing, and finally delivering this book.

Galway, Ireland,
July 2008

Sebastian Ryszard Kruk
Bill McDaniel

Contents

List of Contributors

David Bainbridge
Department of Computer Science
University of Waikato
New Zealand
davidb@cs.waikato.ac.nz

John G. Breslin
Digital Enterprise Research Institute
National University of Ireland
Galway, Ireland
john.breslin@deri.org

George Buchanan
Department of Computer Science
University of Swansea
United Kingdom
g.r.buchanan@swansea.ac.uk

Mariusz Cygan
Digital Enterprise Research Institute
National University of Ireland
Galway, Ireland
mariusz.cygan@deri.org

Maciej Dabrowski
Digital Enterprise Research Institute
National University of Ireland
Galway, Ireland
maciej.dabrowski@deri.org

Jakub Demczuk
Digital Enterprise Research Institute
National University of Ireland
Galway, Ireland
jakub.demczuk@gmail.com

Gilles Falquet
Centre Universitaire d'Informatique
University of Geneva
1227 Carouge, Switzerland
falquet@cui.unige.ch

Slawomir Grzonkowski
Digital Enterprise Research Institute
National University of Ireland
Galway, Ireland
slawomir.grzonkowski@deri.org

Adam Gzella
Digital Enterprise Research Institute
National University of Ireland
Galway, Ireland
adam.gzella@deri.org

Bernhard Haslhofer
Department of Distributed
and Multimedia Systems
University of Vienna
Vienna, Austria
bernhard.haslhofer@univie.ac.at

Annika Hinze
Department of Computer Science
University of Waikato
New Zealand
hinze@cs.waikato.ac.nz

Predrag Knežević
Freelancer Consultant
Darmstadt
Germany
pedjak@gmail.com

Ewelina Kruk
Digital Enterprise Research Institute
National University of Ireland
Galway, Ireland
ewelina.kruk@deri.org

Sebastian Ryszard Kruk
Digital Enterprise Research Institute,
National University of Ireland,
Galway, Ireland,
sebastian.kruk@deri.org

Bill McDaniel
Digital Enterprise Research Institute
National University of Ireland
Galway, Ireland
bill.mcdaniel@deri.org

Luka Nerima
Centre Universitaire d'Informatique
University of Geneva
1227 Carouge, Switzerland
nerima@cui.unige.ch

Markus Reis
Austrian Research Centers
Research Studio Digital Memory Engineering
Vienna, Austria
markus.reis@researchstudio.at

Dagobert Soergel
College of Information Studies
University of Maryland
College Park, MD, USA
dsoergel@umd.edu

Katarzyna Stankiewicz
Gdansk University of Technology
Narutowicza 11/12
Gdansk, Poland
kst@zie.pg.gda.pl

Marcin Synak
Gdansk University of Technology
Narutowicza 11/12
Gdansk, Poland
msynak@wp.pl

Adam Westerski
Digital Enterprise Research Institute
National University of Ireland
Galway, Ireland
adam.westerski@deri.org

Ian Witten
Department of Computer Science
University of Waikato
New Zealand
ihw@cs.waikato.ac.nz

Tomasz Woroniecki
Digital Enterprise Research Institute
National University of Ireland
Galway, Ireland
tomasz.woroniecki@deri.org

Jean-Claude Ziswiler
Centre Universitaire d'Informatique
University of Geneva
1227 Carouge, Switzerland
ziswiler@cui.unige.ch

Introduction

Bill McDaniel and Sebastian Ryszard Kruk

1 Some History

As we look forward to the emergence of semantic digital libraries, it is good to consider their origins and sources in traditional digital libraries. A short examination of their definitions and applications will prove fruitful. It will provide a base for our later examination of the implications of adding semantic power to the digital library concept.

Digital libraries have been around for quite some time. Wikipedia[1] references Greenstein and Thorin to define a digital library: "*A digital library is a library in which collections are stored in digital formats (as opposed to print, microform, or other media) and accessible by computers*" [79].

Originally, they were designed to contain objects for operating systems to use; linked object code libraries, source code libraries, compiled object code for reuse by multiple programs. They emerged from a consideration of the needs of the OS to find and load components but a recognition that existing file systems were too limited to support these activities in a timely fashion.

The essential structure that emerged remains even today; a directory of library members which provides names and other metadata for the objects contained followed, in the same dataset or file, by the actual binary for each object referenced by a directory member.

The details are different for each type of library, of course, but the essential nature of a digital repository for named objects remains. Typically, digital libraries are artifacts constructed on top of more fundamental data storage structures supported directly by the OS. Very few OSs support a library as a low level data structure.[2] Instead, they are based on relative record accesses, indexed sequential access methods, or relational databases.

[1] `http://en.wikipedia.org/wiki/Digital_library`

[2] IBM DOS and VSE did not support libraries as fundamental. Neither do Windows, OS X, or flavors of Unix. IBMs AS400 uses a relational database as its core file system which *might* be construed as a type of digital library, but typically digital libraries are still defined on top of that database. The best example is

One of us created a digital library access method in the early 1980s based around the IBM Virtual Storage Access Method and its relative record dataset architecture. It was called VLAM, the Virtual Library Access Method.

This digital library (DL) was intended to provide several services which traditional access methods did not: long names, BLOB storage, document storage, rapid directory search, inter-object links, and a great deal of meta-data. Later, an indexing method was invented to allow full text indexing of the objects for sophisticated search and retrieval. This was a hashed bitmap index known as the Holographic Index Access Method (HIAM).

2 Todays Libraries

Digital libraries (DLs) have grown since that time in both numbers and uses with specialized applications and implementing very sophisticated data structures. More and more of them are created on top of personal computer operating systems such as Unix, Linux, or Windows. Many are implemented on top of relational database systems such as Oracle, DB/2, or SQL Server. Most recently, the emergence of open source operating systems and database engines with enterprise level features and reliability has created a significant movement toward digital libraries implemented on top of Linux and MySQL.

The attraction of relational databases for library creators is the built-in capabilities of easily creating, storing, and searching large quantities of meta-data for library objects. Directories can be distributed across orthogonalized tables and the associated metadata can be isolated so as to improve search performance. However, the cost is one of licensing and installing an RDBMS (Relational Database Management System) to achieve this.

The availability of relatively high powered database engines such as MySQL makes this possible, but still involves the installation of the MySQL engine on the server. If the library system is localized on each users machine, this replication is an obstacle. Certainly, if the system is server based as more and more are, then the use of an RDBMS for a digital library is easier.

Consequently, many digital libraries are still implemented using only OS-provided storage services. This, of course, implies the creation of new code bases that implement storage algorithms, indexing, garbage collection, update processing and the myriad other storage components necessary for such a systems implementation.

Because of this many digital libraries are implemented directly on the OS file system, with separate files used for each object, a special set of index files, and directory files which contain metadata for each object. This approach has several drawbacks. A multi-file system is more vulnerable to corruption and

the IBM MVS (now z/OS) support of Partitioned Datasets (PDS) which *is* a fundamental operating system access method. However, it is severely limited in flexibility and not easy to use.

synchronization problems. File system access is typically slower than accessing objects within a single file because of OS file open and close logic.

There are, of course, several open source access methods and even digital library platforms which can be used to speed up the deployment of a digital library. But it is still necessary to craft and tune a digital library for specific applications to gain the maximum benefit for applications and users accessing the contents of the library. One such set of tuning requirements emerges when the digital library is to be a semantic digital library.

3 Semantic Digital Libraries

For the most part, digital libraries are searchable either through their directory structure or via a full-text index to allow searching of the contents of their objects. The directory scan facility provides a mechanism for answering such queries as, "*list all objects alphabetically*" or "*list all objects created since 13/05/2000*".

The full text index search extends this to such queries as "*list all objects containing the words automatic transmission*" or "*list objects not containing the name Joe Bloggs*".

But there is no way to support a query such as, "*list all objects which are related to the subject of haute cuisine*", particularly if the term "*haute cuisine*" never appears in the digital library. This is where the addition of semantics to a library can be useful. Semantic information, represented by metadata attached to each object and by one or more ontologies to provide semantic context for searches, can be used to resolve just such queries. The additional flexibility and search capability represented by such a technique make a semantic digital library much more valuable than a traditional DL for an average user.

Incorporating semantic data and processing into a DL involves the attachment of metadata to objects in such a library and providing user access to semantically powered search engines. The metadata is, typically, expressed in Resource Description Framework (RDF) syntax and consists of relationships expressed in grammatical triples consisting of a subject, a predicate, and an object. For example, a triple about a document may be "`Letter to Joe`" "`is-a`" "`PDF`" where "`Letter to Joe`" is the subject, "`is-a`" is the predicate and "`PDF`" is the object. Such a triple would indicate that the library object named Letter to Joe is a PDF file.

Such semantic data and the acyclic graphs that are represented by it are not natural structures for searching and retrieval by standard tools such as relational databases or ISAM style access methods. In particular, indexing, retrieval, and graph traversal remain problematic processes from the standpoint of speed and performance. Much research has gone into improving the performance of semantic search and retrieval and the performance is beginning to scale to enterprise levels. There is still much to be done, however.

4 Applications and Solutions

Semantic Digital Libraries (SemDLs) offer a new level of flexibility, interoperability, and connectedness for digital repositories. These repositories are growing in number at an ever accelerating pace. The need and the opportunity for advanced search and retrieval capabilities are great. As much as 80% of the information already stored on the Internet is unstructured data, locked up in documents, photos, html pages and other formats.

In addition, the interrelationships between all this information is implicit, largely locked up in our human languages and shared experience. Only through the use of sophisticated linguistic analysis could these sources of information be resolved and patterns of interrelationships be discovered. Semantics add these capabilities. Ontologies provide both a known vocabulary and a formalized set of interrelationships that permit the search algorithms an understanding of the unstructured data and metadata they traverse. So queries about haute cuisine can be resolved to include documents that discuss cooking, baking and fusion when those terms are used in a context to imply one another.

One of the most significant capabilities offered by semantic technologies is the ability to encode and decode profile information about users in a semantically powerful way. Encoding (e.g., in RDF) diverse and detailed information such as a users location, food preferences, attitudes, transport methods, goals, aspirations, and other facets of a user personality and situation allows semantic search engines to derive a set of rules for configuring other search results appropriately.

Applications for these abilities include health care where semantics can resolve patient symptom descriptions into a search result providing the proper treatment for an obscure and obscurely described set of symptoms.

Social networking sites such as Flickr and MySpace become more valuable the more connections can be made between their users and content. As users are self-tagging, using tags that make sense to them but not necessarily to others, a search and link mechanism needs to able to resolve different terms and concepts. The use of semantic ontologies coupled with the metadata tagging provide this. A user of these systems can be placed much more richly into a network with explicit and implicit linkages.

Learning systems can use a SemDL to store course descriptions and rules for creating programs of learning that are tailored to each user. This is one of the applications that benefits tremendously from the availability of detailed user profiling.

Archiving systems can be improved by using a SemDL to encode more metadata about stored digital objects than traditional archive systems. The result is an archive that is more useful later when its contents are searched by different users who may not know much about the contents or may encode queries using different syntax and semantics than originally anticipated.

5 Conclusions

Semantic Digital Libraries (SemDLs) offer the opportunity to expand the usefulness of digital libraries which will probably contain the worlds majority of data in the future. Semantics makes unstructured data, particularly, a truly machine usable, machine navigable resource.

In the rest of this book we will look at SemDLs in detail, examining their applications, the solutions they provide, and the problems they solve.

Not to be overly pollyannaish, however, we will also look at the limits of SemDLs, the outstanding problems regarding scalability and usability, as well as some applications where adding semantics to the library offers no improvements or enhancements.

This book is organized fairly loosely and, as a collection of papers and essays from others, can be read in any order. However, we have organized the contributions into five categories to bring some sense of pattern to the subject.

Part One introduces the reader to the two primary concepts which the rest of the book bring together. Digital libraries are introduced and explored in the first paper while the notion of the Semantic Web and Ontologies are introduced in the second paper. Finally, John Breslin takes the reader through the expansion of the Web from 1.0 to the current Web 2.0 embodying some semantics then onward into the future Web 3.0 where social semantic spaces become deeply embedded in the day to day life of everyone on the web.

Part Two begins to marry these concepts of Digital Libraries and Semantic Web together to define and elucidate Semantic Digital Libraries for the reader. We start the section off with an examination of the goals of bringing these two ideas together and follow up with an examination of the architecture of Semantic Digital Libraries. Finally, this part concludes with an examination of the vision of Semantic Digital Libraries as vital tools for the long term preservation of information.

Part Three examines Ontologies and their role in bringing Semantics to life. Two papers explore different usage scenarios for ontologies. The first chapter in this section looks at using ontologies to classify publications in a bibliographic manner and to make different ontologies in this space interoperate using semantic technologies. The second chapter examines the use of ontologies to define social networks and the role of libraries in architecting and driving such communities.

Part Four examines three prototype Semantic Digital Libraries. JeromeDL is described with its emphasis on social semantics. BRICKS is described from its pivotal role in defining Semantic Digital Library architecture. Lastly the Greenstone libraries are described. These three exemplars of Semantic Digital Libraries provide the reader with an excellent overview of both the architectural evolution and the divergent uses Semantic Digital Libraries can be put to.

Part Five concludes the book with a look at the future uses of Semantic Digital Libraries. The first chapter examines Hyperbooks and how Semantic

Digital Libraries will organize, manage, and make them more generally available and useful. The next chapter looks at Digital Document Archiving, and the value Semantic Digital Libraries can bring to the process of archival, search, and retrieval as more and more documents remain online for the foreseeable future. The next chapter looks into the uses of Semantic Digital Libraries and social networks for the future. Finally, we conclude with a short examination of the probable future directions Semantic Digital Library research will take.

This book should provide a solid grounding in the principles, research, design, architecture, and implementation of Semantic Digital Libraries and their uses. We hope readers take away a solid sense of the power of these new libraries and their potential.

Acknowledgement

This material is based upon works supported by Enterprise Ireland under Grant No. ILP/05/203 and by Science Foundation Ireland Grant No. SFI/02/CE1/I131.

Part I

Introduction to Digital Libraries and Semantic Web

Digital Libraries and Knowledge Organization

Dagobert Soergel

This chapter describes not so much what digital libraries are but what digital libraries with semantic support could and should be. It discusses the nature of Knowledge Organization Systems (KOS) and how KOS can support digital library users. It projects a vision for designers to make and for users to demand better digital libraries.

What is a *digital library*? The term "Digital Library" (DL) is used to refer to a range of systems, from digital object and metadata repositories, reference-linking systems, archives, and content management systems to complex systems that integrate advanced digital library services and support for research and practice communities. A DL may offer many technology-enabled functions and services that support users, both as information producers and as information users. Many of these functions appear in information systems that would not normally be considered digital libraries, making boundaries even more blurry. Instead of pursuing the hopeless quest of coming up with the definition of *digital library*, we present a framework that allows a clear and somewhat standardized description of any information system so that users can select the system(s) that best meet their requirements. Section 2 gives a broad outline for more detail see the *DELOS DL Reference Model* [133].

1 A Vision of Digital Libraries

At its best, a digital library

- Integrates access to materials with access to tools for processing materials (DL = materials + tools);
- Supports individual and community information spaces through functionality for selection, annotation, authoring/contribution, and collaboration.

The remainder of this section elaborates on this vision, starting with a use case that illustrates advanced DL functionality (see Table 1).

1.1 Use Case Illustrating Advanced DL Functionality

Table 1. Use case/scenario. Writing a proposal for a drug prevention program

The director of a drug-free community coalition works on developing a prevention project and the funding for it. Signing on to the AOD (Alcohol and Other Drugs) DL, she begins by browsing the prevention section of the thesaurus hierarchy to get a structured overview of various prevention approaches (see Table 2).

From the thesaurus scope notes, some approaches seem particularly applicable to her community, so she follows the links to more in-depth explanations. Back from the thesaurus she follows a link from JG10.4.6 *prevention through education* to a funding program announcement. She opens the guidelines for submitting proposals and copies a proposal template into her private space (shown in another window) and fills in some text and copies some text (which is transferred with its source).

From the program announcement, she follows a link to projects funded previously and further to project reports and evaluations. She comes across the unfamiliar term *triangulation* and clicks on it to see the thesaurus entry, which gives an explanation and the hierarchical context.

In another document she highlights the phrase *prevention program evaluation* to initiate a cross-database search in her own system and three external databases. She copies four references with abstracts to her private space and adds some (public) semantic tags that capture what these documents can contribute to the proposal. (Later she will return to these, select one for detailed reading (using a reading tool that lets her quickly identify important paragraphs), and add more notes and quotes to her emerging proposal.)

From the program announcement, she follows a link to relevant research, selects some articles, and tags them with elements of her proposal outline. One of the papers compares the effectiveness of several prevention curricula. She follows a link to the top-rated curriculum and from there finds further reviews and some discussion of resources required.

She still needs demographics of her community; she uses a tool to query census data and produce a table with the data she needs. She also needs funding sources for the required local match, so she searches two external databases and incorporates the results into her proposal.

Now she completes the first draft with annotations as to why a piece is included or why certain language is used. She emails two board members and a city staff member for comments, giving them access to her private space. Upon receiving their revisions (with changes tracked) and comments, she produces the final version and uploads a pdf to the agency's submission system.

Table 2. Prevention approach hierarchy. Excerpt, only selected annotations

Code	Term
JG	prevention approach
JG10	. Individual-level prevention
JG10.2	. . Individual- vs. family-focused prevention
JG10.2.2	. . . Individual-focused prevention
JG10.2.4	. . . Family-focused prevention
JG10.4	. . Prevention through information and education
	SN Information and education directed at individuals to Influence their knowledge, beliefs, and attitudes towards AOD and their AOD use behavior.
	ST *prevention through persuasion*
	NT+JH2 health information and education
	BT+N communication, information, and education
	RT MP18.2.8.8 demand reduction policy
	+ND16.8 information event
	+T demographic characteristics
JG10.4.2	. . . social marketing prevention approach
	SN Using techniques from product marketing to influence the acceptability of a social idea or cause by the members of a group, or to influence attitudes, beliefs, (and behaviors such as drug use) with the goal of effecting social change.
	RT +JE6 prevention campaign
	+MI6 cultural sensitivity
	+MR2 marketing
	+JE6 mass media
JG10.4.4	. . . Prevention through information dissemination
JG10.4.6	. . . Prevention through education
	SN This approach aims to improve critical life and social skills (decision making, refusal skills, critical analysis, and systematic and judgmental abilities). Where appropriate, index the subject matter.
	ST *educational prevention approach*
	NT JH2.2.2 health promotion in the classroom
	BT +NF education and training
	RT MP18.2.8.16 harm reduction policy
	+NF16.2 AOD education
JG10.4.6.4	. . . . Prevention through youth AOD education
JG10.4.6.6	. . . . Prevention through parent AOD education
JG10.4.6.8	. . . . Drinking and driving education
JG10.4.8	. . . Peer prevention
JG10.8	. . Prevention through spirituality and religion
JG10.10	. . Prevention through public commitment
JG12	. Environmental-level prevention
JG14	. . Social policy prevention approach
JG12.4	. Multi-level prevention

1.2 Challenges for Digital Libraries

To achieve the broad vision of enabling access to any data (information, knowledge, answer, digital object), digital libraries face many challenges, among them:

- Searching for text, images, sound, and composite objects – multimedia search.
- Semantically enhanced search to improve retrieval from free text and image content and to better exploit user-assigned tags.
- Search across many languages – multilingual search.
- Search across many systems – syntactic and semantic interoperability.
- Finding answers, not just documents; reasoning and inference.

Of course, there are also challenges of physical and semantic preservation (interoperability over time) and of hardware and software implementation, such as P2P and grid.

Another major theme in this vision of a comprehensive digital library or information space is *integration*:

- Integrate many presentation formats.
- Integrate libraries, archives, and museums; also databases and other information systems.
- Integrate reading/viewing/listening, database access, processing data, and authoring/creating.
- Integrate publishing and communication platforms.

This integration will result in a unified environment in which users can carry out all their work – work tasks and information/communication tasks, reading and authoring. The user need worry only about doing tasks, **not** about accessing different kinds of information formats and systems, selecting task-specific applications, or sharing information between applications [203].

1.3 Illustrative Advanced DL Functions

In advance of Sect. 3, Table 3 gives a glimpse of advanced digital library functionality organized into three major themes:

1. Document presentation, interactive documents, learning objects
2. Tools for working with documents and data, and
3. Tools for creating documents

Table 3. Advanced digital library functionality

(1a) Present documents in new ways:

- Display the structure of hypertext documents as a graph.
- Show high-level overviews with drill-down to text, then to data and detail of methods; for example, graphical representation of the flow of ideas in a document, or concept maps showing the relationships between ideas in a document.
- Use moving video, sound, and animation to make ideas come alive.
- Let user control views of 3-D objects (rotate, select cross sections).
- Highlight named entities in the text, such as person names in a news reader.
- Integrate presentation approaches, multimedia.
- Provide alternate versions for different readers
  - By difficulty, such as an introduction to statistics with/without calculus;
  - By language (with automated translation as needed);
  - A spoken or braille version for the blind;
  - Same data as text, table, or graphic – adapt to the reader's cognitive style.

(1b) Present documents interactively:

- Make mathematical formulas and procedure descriptions live (executable). For example, a document may present an economic model with links to the software and economic data sets so that the reader can run the model.
- Make the reader an active participant:
  - Interactive fiction; presenting questions or problems to be solved, with the answer determining further presentation;
  - Simulations involving the reader; for example, a simulation of pricing decisions in a business textbook or an adventure game.

(2a) Provide tools for working with documents:

- Links from text terms to a thesaurus show hierarchical context and definition.
- Fine-grained search of text databases; find specific passages or facts within documents, incl. the document under study (s.a. information extraction below).
- Annotation and social tagging tools. Private and public annotation.
- Authoring tools. Integrate reading/viewing/listening and authoring/creating.
- Tools for working with images and sound documents.

(2b) Provide tools for working with data:

- Tools for importing data from tables in text.
- Tools for information extraction: Extract statements from text and insert them into a database (entity identification, relationship extraction).
- Tools for reasoning over a database.
- Tools for statistical processing.
- Tools for running a model over a set of data (economic or biological simulation).
- Tools for analyzing large instrument-collected data sets (e.g., gene chip data).
- Sequencing individual modules into processing chains to be run repeatedly.

(continued)

Table 3. (continued)

(3) Provide new ways of creating documents

- Support producing documents by combining text, image, and sound modules already in the digital library ("writing in the large", virtual documents produced by a script).
- Auto-compile personalized documents; for example, a personalized textbook on statistics, taking a reader with a given subject interest and mathematics background from her present state of knowledge to her desired state of knowledge. Such documents could be implemented as paths through a hypertext, using prerequisite strands of concepts, such as in the AAAS Atlas of Science Literacy (see Table 12).
- Documents from data:
  - Text generation, graphs, visualization. Extreme case: automatically analyze instrument-generated data and then compose a paper reporting the results.
  - Web pages live with a database

1.4 Some Examples of Digital Libraries and Digital Library Software

Table 4 shows some examples of digital libraries that among them illustrate some of the functions listed. The table is arranged from more conventional DLs that focus on facilitating access to documents to DLs with more functionality. Most of these have some kind of subject directory users can browse, and some of them have most of their content contributed by users.

There is a wide range of software systems supporting the creation and maintenance of digital libraries; the examples in Table 5 illustrate the range. Content management software offers much DL functionality with a focus on collaborative content production and versioning, often including semantic-based search. Enterprise search software is also in this general arena; it often comes with powerful features supporting semantic search, such as linguistic processing, entity and relationship extraction, and automatic classification.

2 Characteristics of a Digital Library

Many ask "What is a digital library?", but the more important question is "What combination of system components and features best supports a user's work and other needs?". Rather than giving a definition of "digital library", this section discusses some typical characteristics of digital libraries and information systems in general, arranged by

- Collection,
- User community served,
- Purpose,
- Specific functions and services.

Table 4. Examples of digital libraries (DLs)
Arranged roughly from more conventional DLs to DLs with more functionality

ACM DL ScienceDirect	Many professional associations (here the Association of Computing Machinery) and publishers (here Elsevier) have a DL of their journals, books, and reference works. Free access to bibliographic data, paid access to full text. portal.acm.org/dl.cfm sciencedirect.com
ICDL	International Children's Digital Library Focuses on digitizing children's books from around the world, making them findable through child-centered criteria, and facilitating online reading. icdlbooks.org
The Shoah VHA	52,000 videotaped interviews with Holocaust survivors, thesaurus of 4,000 subjects and 45,000 names of places, periods, people, etc. usc.edu/schools/college/vhi click Archive > About The Archive > The Visual History Archive
NSDL	National Science Digital Library (US). Support for education & collaboration nsdl.org
Connexion	A user-created DL of educational material; small knowledge chunks (modules) that can be organized as courses, books, reports. cnx.org
Wikipedia	Collaboratively constructed collection of anonymous encyclopedia articles wikipedia.org
Louvre	A museum Web site seen as a digital library containing both images and text, often with interactive features louvre.fr
Perseus	A rich network interconnecting places and sites, buildings, art objects (all represented by images), people, texts, words, ... Virtual walks through historical places. perseus.tufts.edu
Tufts University	An interesting array of DL-related tools uit.tufts.edu/at/?pid = 24, uit.tufts.edu/at/?pid = 24, dca.tufts.edu/tdr/pr/index.html

The characteristics are multi-faceted and often measured on a continuum. Any digital library or other information system can be described by a profile expressed in terms of these characteristics.

At the core of a digital library is a collection:

1. Typically a collection of digital objects that are of interest in their own right (primarily for reading, listening, viewing by people, but also for use by programs) rather than merely pointing to other objects. Examples:
   - A collection of digitized books (as opposed to just an online catalog),
   - A collection of biographies (as opposed to a personnel database),
   - A collection of oral histories,
   - A collection of software modules (on the margin of what many would consider a DL).

Table 5. DL software systems

Focusing on digital repository functions	DSpace (dspace.org)
	Fedora (fedora.info), see Tufts University, Table 4
Wider spectrum of DL functionality	Greenstone (greenstone.org)
	OpenDLib (opendlib.com/home.html)
	DELOS DLMS (Digital Library Management System, see delos.info, search for DLMS, more at dbis.cs.unibas.ch/delos_website/delosdlms.html). A software environment for integrating many tools
Content management	IBM DB2 Content Manager (www-306.ibm.com/software/data/cm/cmgr/mp)
See list in Wikipedia	Oracle Content Management SDK (oracle.com/technology/products/ifs/index.html)
	Documentum (documentum.com) Vignette (vignette.com)
	DRUPAL (drupal.org), Joomla! (joomla.org) (open source, managing Web sites)
Enterprise search	IBM's OmniFind (www-306.ibm.com/software/data/enterprise-search)
	Verity (verity.com)
	Convera's RetrievalWare (convera.com/solutions/retrievalware/default.aspx)
	Endeca (endeca.com), one of the growing breed of facet-based search engines

2. Typically, a collection for which items are carefully selected and acquired. Selection implies weeding, as some objects become less useful with age.
3. Typically, a collection which is curated; minimally, objects are preserved.

The collection of a DL can be described along many dimensions, among them

- Types of information objects included (text, images, sound recordings, learning objects);
- Origin of information objects by place and time;
- Content coverage of the information objects
  - Language of text objects
  - Subject domain
  - Place and time coverage.

The types of materials in the collection can also be characterized with respect to their suitability for given user groups and purposes (see below).

A DL that provides just a collection with access to known items is called a *digital repository*. Repository functions include document acquisition, safe storage and preservation, version control, finding known documents, and document presentation.

A digital library must manage composite documents, and the functionality it provides here is a DL characteristic. Composite documents can be quite complex, often including components in several media (multimedia documents), where the components are information objects in their own right. Components may be annotations. A composite object could be an entire database. (With native XML databases, the boundary between "document" and "database" has become completely blurred.) So a DL may offer, within one integrated environment, search for documents, search within documents, and search within one or more databases (as these terms are usually understood). A repository needs a *document model* [41, 78] to manage these complexities, such as the XML-based Document Object Model (DOM) (see Wikipedia), or the Fedora Digital Object Model [136].

Even DIALOG (dialog.com), a service that provides search of over 600 databases, qualifies as a DL: it provides access to bibliographic databases that link to the full text of documents, full-text databases, and substantive databases with data on companies, chemical compounds, etc.

A DL can be characterized by the user community it serves along any number of demographic characteristics, such as age, level of education, subject specialty, or membership in an organization. Users can be both consumers of services and contributors if the DL allows.

A DL can be characterized by the broad purposes it serves or domain in which it operates, such as scholarship, education, e-government, e-commerce (B2B or B2C), entertainment, and more specific purposes, such as providing job-related information, supporting students with homework, supporting the internal work of an organization, supporting clients of an organization, supporting communication among users, etc.

Both user and purpose characteristics can also be used to characterize the types of materials in the collection with respect to their suitability for these users and purposes.

A DL can be characterized by the functions it serves and the services it provides.

3 Functions of Digital Libraries and Beyond

To give the reader a sense of what one should expect from a DL and what is involved in establishing and maintaining a DL, this section gives an overview of functions an ideal DL would provide. An actual DL provides a subset of these functions, each at a given level of sophistication. The list provided here can serve a framework for describing the functionality of a DL.

This section is based on four premises for advanced DLs discussed in Sect. 1:

1. A DL has many functions and should integrate support for information seeking, users' work tasks, information production, and collaboration.
2. A DL links many types of information objects in many formats (including documents and databases) in all media into a complex structure.
3. Users both use and create information, and the processes of using and creating information are closely intertwined. The old distinction between producers of information (the few) and users of information (the many, the people, the masses) is rapidly fading away. Power to the people!
4. Digital libraries must interoperate.

Table 6 gives an illustrative list of DL functions.

Table 6. Illustrative functions of/tools provided by digital libraries and beyond

1 Search and other user-system interaction functions
. KOS (thesaurus or classification or ontology) related tools.
. . KOS use interface.
. . KOS creation and maintenance tool.
. Search and browse.
Search starts from a search element.
A search criterion specifies how the search targets relate to the search element.
The search element can be a term, a text passage, a whole document, or a symbol,image, or sound bite (e.g., a note sequence), or a longer sound passage, or a whole musical work, or another entity.
The search criterion specifies the relationship: the targets sought should be about the search element, contain the search element, be similar to search element, ...;
about could be limited (like a definition of a term) or broad.
. . Search at different depths.
. . . Search on catalog or metadata records (including social tags).
. . . Search on the full content of the documents (text, images, sound) or of a database.

Table 6. (continued)

. . Input query.
. . . Invoke search from multiple places: Input search element or click on a search element found by navigating a hierarchy or in a text, or click on a page representing a document, person, or project to bring up a search form pre-filled to search for similar objects.
. . . Search form for the specification of field values and search logic.
. . . Save search form as an information object.
. . . Search or browse for previously used search forms, public or private.
. . Expand a search term or other search element using a thesaurus (possibly from a concept or terminology server on the Web).
. . Search multiple databases.
. . . Map query to several databases.
. . . Map results to local format (based on Z39.50, for example).
. . . Detect duplicates.
. . Browse.
. . Arrange search output in a meaningful way.
. Graph browser for browsing any kind of structure.
. . Hierarchy browser.

2 Reading tools and document creation and editing tools.
. Viewers for many types of information objects: text, images, 3-D objects, sound, multimedia objects, composite information objects. This includes many functions:
. . Handle and exploit many different document models and templates.
. . Assemble documents "on the fly"; for example, insert links and/or annotations stored in multiple separate locations.
. . Handle documents that are structured into different layers (e.g., appearance layer and OCR text layer, multivalent.sourceforge.net).
. . Manipulate objects, e.g., rotate a 3D object or view it in cross-section.
. An object viewer may be integrated with an object editor (see below).
. Reading, annotation, and linking tool.
. Sense-making tool. Assist users in creating structured representations (concept maps, templates) of data extracted from documents (by the user or automatically).
. Data stream processing tool.
. (Collaborative) authoring tool supporting the use of templates, version control, and authentication. (S. also "writing in the large", Table 3).
. Specialized tools used in creating text documents.
. . Bibliography generation tool.
. . Document glossary generation tool, using definitions from thesaurus
. . Document index and concordance generation tool.
. Access status management tool.
. Print tool. The Creation of print documents (and PDF files) from documents in many formats (esp. XML-tagged documents or several subdocuments linked together).

(continued)

Table 6. (continued)

3 Document processing and link generation tools
. Tool for finding a full text document from metadata (wherever the full text may be).
. Document quality assessment tool.
. Document acquisition tool. Acquire documents in any format and convert them to the system format for easy processing by other tools.
. Document segmentation and tagging tool.
. Citation link and citation index tool (extract citations from text).
. Bibliographic citation parser to convert bibliography entries into bibliographic records.
. Metadata generation tool, incl. automatic/computer-assisted categorization and indexing.
. Summarization tool.
4 Collaboration tools.
. email support from within the DL, email documents and annotations.
. Online meeting support in all modalities, joint viewing of objects (e.g., book discussion forum).
. Archive of email, meetings, fora, with links to documents being discussed.
. (Collaborative authoring, see above).
5 DL Management tools.
. Collection manager.
. . Collection analysis tool.
. . Selection and acquisition manager.
. . Weeding manager.
. Policy manager.
. Preservation manager.
. . Overall preservation program analysis.
. . Preservation monitoring of individual objects.
. Digital rights manager.
. External communications manager: Harvesting data and responding to requests from other systems, using protocols such as Z39.50 or OAI-PMH.
. Usage tracking.

4 Knowledge Organization and Knowledge Organization Systems

What is knowledge organization? This entails two questions: What is knowledge? and What is organization? For our purposes, knowledge is any representation of what is or will be or could be or should be or what is believed or asserted by some person or device, whether true or false; knowledge encompasses what some like to distinguish as data, information, and knowledge. Knowledge serves many purposes: planning, decision making, and action; satisfying curiosity; entertainment; healing (as in bibliotherapy). To be used, knowledge must be embodied in a person or device that can actuate it, reason with it, act on it, use it to govern the behavior of devices. To be useful, knowledge must be organized. We organize information – in our minds and in information systems – in order to collect and record it, retrieve it, evaluate and select it, understand it, process and analyze it, apply it, and rearrange and reuse it. Somewhat tautologically, we can define organization as the arrangement of elements into a structure.

In a DL, knowledge organization comes into play in several closely interrelated ways:

1. Organization of information in substantive databases;
2. Organization of information within documents;
3. Organization of information about documents and databases (metadata);
4. Organization of information about any type of subject treated in documents (needed to support finding documents and other digital objects);
5. Information about concepts and terms and their relationships; organization of ontological and lexical information. Knowledge Organization Systems in the core sense.

There are two important principles in applying knowledge organization in digital libraries:

1. Use KOS behind the scenes to assist users and improve search and processing results.
2. When it is beneficial for users to interact with a knowledge organization system, provide user-friendly displays and interaction that guide users in making sense of what they see.

Underlying all systems for the representation and organization of knowledge is entity–relationship (E–R) representation. Table 7 gives an example of different kinds of data stored in a DL organized in an E-R representation; we will refer to this example throughout this section.

A DL contains many kinds of data. Data consist of statements (propositions, assertions), where a statement consists of a relationship binding together two or more entities. (In the Web context, esp. in RDF, entities are called resources and relationships are called properties; in topic maps entities are called topics.) Statements can be conceived as relationship instances. In a statement, one entity can be put in focus, and we can say that the statement is about the entity. For example, we can say that the statement

P15 <*runBy*> Drug-Free Community Coalition (DFCC)

is a statement about the project identified as P15; but is equally a statement about DFCC if we put DFCC in focus. In that case, we may want to write the same statement as

DFCC <*runs*> P15

Many relationships have two arguments (binary relationships, the easiest and most common case), but often relationships with three or more arguments are needed to express reality.

Table 7. Statements in a DL illustrating relationship types

P15	<*isa*>	Project
P15	<*hasTitle*>	Drinking is not cool
P15	<*runBy*>	DFCC (Drug-Free Community Coalition)
P15	<*hasCollaborator*>	ACS (Alay City Schools)
P15	<*fundedBy*>	NIAAA
P15	<*startDate*>	2006
P15	<*endDate*>	2009
P15	<*hasBudget*>	$1,200,000
P15	<*addressesProblem*>	Alcohol abuse
P15	<*hasTargetAudience*>	Adolescent girls
P15	<*usesApproach*>	Prevention through youth AOD education
ACS	<*isa*>	School system
ACS	<*isa*>	City government organization
D40	<*isa*>	Document
D40	<*publishedBy*>	DFCC
D40	<*hasTitle*>	AOD curriculum for teen girls
D40	<*dealsWith*>	prevention through youth AOD education
D40	<*hasComponent*>	D43
D43	<*isa*>	Image
D40	<*hasAnnotation*>	D58
D58	<*authoredBy*>	"Joe Smith"
D40	<*hasAccessRight*>	(Anna Cole, Modify)
D43	<*depicts*>	Girl
Girl	<*depictedNextTo*>	(Boy, D43)
(Alay, Houston, train)	<*hasTravelTime*>	3 hrs
City government organization	<*isSubclassOf*>	Local govt. organization
Local govt. organization	<*isSubclassOf*>	Government organization
Image	<*isSubclassOf*>	Document
prevention through youth AOD education	<*isSubclassOf*>	prevention through education
<*hasAnnotation*>	<*isSubrelationOf*>	<*hasComponent*>

When a user has a simple question, such as *What projects are run by DFCC?*, the system first checks its database for a directly matching answer statement. If none is found, the system tries inference. If that fails, the system tries to find a text source (or an image) that contains the answer and gives the user that source or, even better, extracts the answer from it. An answer to the following question can be found through a chain of inference combining several statements from the database:

What projects does NIAAA support that target adolescent girls in school?

We are now ready to discuss the different ways of knowledge organization in a DL.

4.1 Organization of Information in Substantive Databases

Database organization is fundamental for DLs, since DLs can be seen as a special form of database. But more specifically, as we saw above, a DL can and often should include access to one or more substantive databases that can be queried in simple and in complex ways to provide immediate answers to users. Conceptually, all database structures are based on entity-relationship representation. The sample data from Table 7 could be stored as relational tables or as objects. The entity types and relationship types in an E-R data model provide the basis for defining tables or object classes.

Ideally, databases in similar domains would use a common E-R schema as the conceptual basis and similar schemas of tables or object classes. Of course, this does not happen, so interoperability requires schema mapping or schema integration – thorny problems in the database field.

4.2 Organization of Information in Documents

It is helpful to the reader if documents belonging to a given genre, such as project reports or descriptions of visual works or recipes, follow a common structure laid out in a *document template.* This idea can be implemented, for example, by using XML schema. The relationship types in Table 7 provide guidance for the project description template shown in Table 8.

A DL or an organization that produces multiple types of documents must create and maintain a hierarchical system of document templates and the tags they use. Again, templates should be standardized, at least within communities of practice, to provide interoperability. A document model (see Sect. 2) is a highly abstract and general document template.

Table 8. Document template for a project report (derived from Table 7, not complete)

<title>
<organizations involved>
<funder>
<time period>
<description>
    <problem>
    <targetAudience>
    <approach>
<budget>

Some widely used document templates (document schemas) are

- TEI (Text Encoding Initiative, tei-c.org).
- MPEG (Moving Picture Experts Group) standards, especially MPEG-7, a schema for encoding both the structure of and metadata about multimedia documents.
- SCORM 2004 (Sharable Content Object Reference Model) for learning objects.

For a long list of specialized markup languages, see Wikipedia, List of XML markup languages, and the references to document models in Sect. 2.

A closely related concept is markup of text to identify specific types of information, such as people or standard names or dates; see, for example, the Orlando project (http://orlando.cambridge.org/).

4.3 Organization of Information About Documents. Data About Data (Metadata)

A piece of data is *used as* metadata if it is used for the purpose of discovering and using information objects which then give the ultimate data wanted; metadata are used to manage, find, interpret, and/or use other data or a source of such data. Note we said *used as* metadata. The "metadata-hood" of an information object does not reside in the information object, but in its relationship to another information object and, more specifically, in its use. The same piece of data may fill the ultimate need of one user and be used as metadata by another: A dean may use a bibliographic database to count the number of publications by a faculty member; she uses authorship data for her ultimate purpose, not as metadata. But we use authorship data as metadata if we use them to find a book from which we then learn what we need to know or to assess the authority of a book. In common usage today, data in a library catalog are considered metadata because they are most often used that way. By extension, similar data in other databases, such as a product catalog, are called metadata, even though they do not lead to other data. Metadata can be analyzed along a number of dimensions, as shown in Table 9.

Metadata schemas are usually represented as a set of tags that form a schema or template for a metadata record (a simple version of an object class). Each tag corresponds to a relationship type in an explicit or implied E-R schema. Metadata schemas are usually adapted to the type of information object and the user requirements. We list a few examples

- *Bibliographic metadata.* A widely used, but for many purposes overly simplistic, schema is the unqualified Dublin Core (DC, Table 10), but DC has many extensions (dublincore.org). The MARC format (loc.gov/marc) is a much more complete and fine-grained schema that covers many types of documents. RFC 1807 defines a bibliographic format for technical reports (ukoln.ac.uk/metadata/desire/overview/rev_19.htm). These three formats

Table 9. Dimensions for the analysis of metadata

Metadata can be analyzed along the following dimensions:

1. The purpose for which the metadata are used and
2. The kind of information given about a resource.

Some kinds of metadata are used for only one purpose, others for several purposes.

Dimension 1. The purpose for which the metadata are used

1.1 Resource (information) seeking and use, by stage in the information-seeking process
  1.1.1 Resource discovery: retrieval and selection of resources, specifically information objects, that are useful for a given purpose (are about a topic, illuminate an abstract theme, assist in performing a task, etc.).
  1.1.2 Dealing with a known resource: use and interpretation
1.2 Manage a resource (*administrative metadata*), in particular
  1.2.1 Manage the preservation of a resource (*preservation metadata*).

Dimension 2. The kind of information given about a resource.
(Categories overlap.)

2.1 Information about the intrinsic nature and the context of the resource.
  2.1.1 Information about identity and formal characteristics, including physical description(*descriptive metadata*).
  2.1.2 Information concerning what the resource is about and what it is relevant for (*subject metadata*).
  2.1.3 Information about the history, future disposition, and other features of the context of the resource (*contextual metadata*). Includes *provenance* (which in turn includes authorship) (also considered part of 2.1.1), *use history* and *relation to other resources*.
2.2 Information about how one can use the resource.
  2.2.1 Information on how to gain legal access to the resource (*access and use rights metadata*).
  2.2.2 Information on how to gain technical access to the resource (what machinery and software is needed to access the resource for a given purpose, such as assimilation by a person or processing by a computer program)(related to 2.1.1 physical description)(*technical metadata*).
2.3 Information about the status of a resource (past, present, and future), in particular
  2.3.1 Information about the preservation status of a resource.

Table 10. A few of the 15 Dublin Core elements

Relationship type		**Dublin core element**
Document <*hasTitle*>	Text	<*dc:title* >
Document <*hasCreator*>	Person	<*dc:creator* >
Document <*dealsWith*>	Subject	<*dc:subject* >
Document <*publishedBy*>	LegalEntity	<*dc:publisher* >
Document <*publishedIn*>	Date	<*dc:date* >

are specified in the Open Archives Initiative Protocol for Metadata Harvesting (OAI-PMH) (openarchives.org). FRBR/CRM, the relatively new approach of dealing with bibliographic data, has its conceptual basis in E-R modeling (loc.gov/cds/FRBR.html, cidoc.ics.forth.gr/scope.html).

- *Archival metadata.* Encoded Archival Description (EAD) (loc.gov/ead).
- *Metadata for learning objects.* (instructional materials) has several standards

  The Gateway to Educational Materials (GEM) (thegateway.org/about/documentation/metadataElements)

  The Learning Technology Standards Committee of the IEEE (ltsc.ieee.org/wg12/files/LOM_1484_12_1_v1_Final_Draft.pdf)

  IMS learning resource metadata information model (imsproject.org/metadata)

  The DCMI Education Working Group. dublincore.org/groups/education

  The CRP Henri Tudor-CITI: Training Exchange Definition: TED. (xml.org/xml/schema/8dbca03a/trainingExchangeDefinition.pdf)
- *Metadata for geospatial data sets.*
  ISO 19115:2003 Geographic information – Metadata iso.ch/iso/en
  fgdc.gov/metadata/geospatial-metadata-standards

4.4 Organization of Information About any Type of Subject Treated in Documents (Needed to Support Finding Documents)

Section 4.1 dealt with access to substantive databases to obtain immediate answers. The nature of the data referred to here is the same, but the use is different: People often look for documents (texts, images, music) based on their content or the circumstances under which they were created. Such queries require a database that can deal with any type of content. To find portraits of physicists, we need a biographic database where we can find physicists so we can then find their portraits; to find descriptions of medieval houses, we need a database of buildings from which we can find medieval houses (each identified by a building identifier) so we can then find texts that describe any of these buildings. In the same way we could find descriptions of buildings designed by the famous architect Pei. The richer this database of content, the richer the possibilities for the user to make connections in finding documents. This is the basic idea behind Topic Maps, a standard for specifying relational databases that are optimized for this retrieval support function. Examples of objects, concepts, ideas of particular importance in this context include

People	Concepts, ideas
Organizations	Problems and proposed solutions
Events	Computer programs
Places	Mathematical theorems
Dates	

Examples of tools that fall under here are *gazetteers*, databases about places and place names, and biographic databases. The tools discussed in

Sects. 4.5–4.9 are a subset: databases of concepts, ideas, and their names (terms), or, put differently, systems that organize ontological and lexical information (information about concepts and terms and their relationships); such systems are called *Knowledge Organization Systems (KOS).*

4.5 What is a Knowledge Organization System (KOS)? A First Look

People often search for subjects, concepts, or ideas, and these are the most difficult searches. Often the user just wants to type in some words, but those words do not always express what the user has in mind. Other times, the user is at a loss for words. DLs must support the user in this quest for meaning . This is one of the chief roles of Knowledge Organization Systems. In some information systems such searches are supported by manual, computer-assisted, or automatic subject cataloging or indexing, using a controlled vocabulary of terms or other concept designations stipulated in the KOS. For an example of hierarchy that epitomizes what a KOS is, see Table 2. There are many types of KOS, some of them are listed in Table 11. Table 12 gives pointers to illustrative KOS.

A dictionary is a listing of words and phrases, giving information such as spelling, morphology and part of speech, senses, definitions, usage, origin, and often equivalents in other languages.

A thesaurus manages the complex relationships between terms and concepts and provides conceptual relationships, ideally through an embedded classification. A thesaurus may specify descriptors authorized for indexing and searching. These descriptors form a controlled vocabulary (authority list, index language). A monolingual thesaurus has terms from one language, a multilingual thesaurus from two or more languages.

A classification is a structure that organizes concepts into a hierarchy, possibly in a scheme of facets. The term taxonomy was originally used for the classification of living organisms, then expanded to any kind of classification. The term typology is used for small classifications, often in the context of research studies. The term ontology is often used for a shallow classification of basic categories or a classification used in linguistics, data element definition, or knowledge management or (increasingly) for any classification. In AI-related contexts, an ontology is a classification with a rich set of semantic relationships that support reasoning.

Table 11. The many forms of Knowledge Organization System

Dictionaries, glossaries	Concept maps
Thesauri, subject heading lists	Classification schemes, taxonomies
Topic maps	Ontologies with rich semantic relationships

Table 12. Examples of Knowledge Organization Systems

AOD	Alcohol and Other Drug Thesaurus. Universal, semi-faceted etoh.niaaa.nih.gov/AODVol1/Aodthome.htm
MeSH	Medical Subject Headings hierarchical, available in many languages nlm.nih.gov/mesh/meshhome.html nlm.nih.gov/mesh/MBrowser.html
UMLS	Unified Medical Language System over 100 biomedical KOS in one database nlm.nih.gov/research/umls/umlsmain.html, umlsinfo.nlm.nih.gov
NCI	National Cancer Institute Thesaurus nciterms.nci.nih.gov/NCIBrowser/Dictionary.do
AAT	Art and Architecture Thesaurus getty.edu/research/tools/vocabulary/aat/index.html
AGROVOC	AGROVOC (agriculture. fisheries, forestry), in many languages fao.org/agrovoc
ERIC	Education Resources Information Center Thesaurus. searcheric.org
LCSH	Library of Congress Subject Headings for alphabetic subject access loc.gov/cds/lcsh.html Search http://authorities.loc.gov/
LCC	Library of Congress Classification for shelving/directory loc.gov/catdir/cpso/lcco/
DDC	Dewey Decimal Classification. Semi-faceted, intended for shelving or directory oclc.org/dewey/about/default.htm
Yahoo	Yahoo classification. Semi-faceted, Web subject directory yahoo.com
ASL	Atlas of Science Literacy project2061.org/publications/atlas/default.htm
CYC	CYC Ontology cyc.com/cycdoc/vocab/merged-ontology-vocab.html
GO	Gene Ontology geneontology.org
WN	WordNet A rich dictionary database with a built-in classification cogsci.princeton.edu/~wn, search notredame.ac.jp/cgi-bin/wn

4.6 The Many Functions of Knowledge Organization Systems

A KOS can serve many functions (see Table 13). Understanding this simple truth is of paramount importance if one wants to maximize the return on the large investment required to construct a good KOS.

One of the most important, but often ignored, functions of an index language that supports retrieval is to make sure that documents are indexed or tagged with concepts that reflect user interests so users can actually formulate queries that express their interest and find what they are looking for. The principles of this request-oriented (user-centered) approach to indexing are summarized in Table 15, with some examples given in Table 16.

Table 13. Functions of a KOS

Semantic road map to individual fields and the relationships among fields.

- Map out a concept space, relate concepts to terms, and provide definitions.
- Clarify concepts by putting them in the context of a classification.
- Relate concepts and terms across disciplines, languages, and cultures.
- Many specific functions build on this foundation.

Improve communication. Support learning & assimilating information.

- Conceptual frameworks for learners. Help learners ask the right questions.
- Conceptual frameworks for the development of instructional materials.
- Assist readers in understanding text by giving the meaning of terms.
- Assist writers in producing understandable text by suggesting good terms.
- Support foreign language learning.

Conceptual basis for the design of good research and implementation.

- Assist researchers and practitioners with problem clarification.
- Consistent data collection, compilation of (comparative) statistics.

Classification for action. Classification for social and political purposes.

- Classification of diseases for diagnosis; of medical procedures for billing; of commodities for customs.

Support information retrieval and analysis. Retrieval of goods and services for e-commerce.

- Support searching, esp. knowledge-based support for end-user searching:
  - assistance in clarifying the search topic;
  - (automatic) synonym expansion and hierarchic expansion (see Table 14)
- Support indexing, especially request-oriented (user-centered) indexing.
- Facilitate the combination of or unified access to multiple databases.
- Support meaningful, well-structured display of information.
- Support document processing after retrieval.

Ontology for data element definition. Data element dictionary.

Conceptual basis for knowledge-based systems. Example:

	inference	
Reading instruction <*hasDomain*> Reading AND Reading ability <*hasDomain*> Reading AND Reading ability <*supportedBy*> Perception	$\Longrightarrow$	Reading instruction <*shouldConsider*> Perception

Do all this across multiple languages

Mono-, bi-, or multilingual dictionary for human use.

Lexical knowledge base for natural language processing (NLP).

Table 14. Query term expansion. Example

A search for Drug use by teenagers formulated as *teenage AND drug* will find
Drug Use Rises for Teenagers but miss Adolescent Drug Abuse Treatment Outcome, KCEOC Substance abuse/youth program, and Smoking still increasing among teens
To find these, use automatic manual query term expansion: OR synoyms and narrower terms and their synonyms, as follows (illustrative only):
(teenage OR teen OR youth OR adolescent OR "high school") AND (drug OR substance OR nicotine OR smoking OR cigarette OR cocaine OR crack)

Table 15. User-centered indexing / request-oriented indexing principles

Construct a classification/ontology from actual and anticipated user queries and interests.
Thus provide a conceptual framework that organizes user interests into a meaningful arrangement and communicates them to indexers.
Index materials from users' perspectives: Add need-based retrieval clues beyond those present in the document. Increase probability that retrieval clues helpful to users are available.
Index language as checklist. Indexing = judging relevance against user concepts. Judging relevance goes beyond just determining aboutness.
Implementation: Knowledgeable indexers. Expert system using syntactic & semantic analysis & inference. Social tagging: tags based on user's own interests.

Table 16. Request-oriented indexing. Examples

Document	User concept
The drug was injected into the aorta	*Systemic administration*
Children of blue-collar workers going to college	*Intergenerational social mobility*
CSF studies on alcoholism and related behaviors	*Biochemical basis of behavior*
Drug use among teenagers (read methods section)	Longitudinal study
Image	Good scientific illustration
Image	Useful for fundraising brochure
Image	*Appealing to children*
Image	*Cover page quality*

4.7 The Structure of KOS

The structure of a comprehensive KOS consists of two levels:

Level 1: Concept-term relationships (Sect. 4.7.1)
Level 2: Conceptual structure (Sect. 4.7.2)
- 2.1 Semantic analysis and facets
- 2.2 Hierarchy
- 2.3 Interaction of hierarchy and facets
- 2.4 Differentiated (refined) concept relationships

Some KOS focus on only one of these two levels. For example, many KOS that are labeled ontologies focus on the concept level and do not worry about terms.

Concept-term Relationships

Table 17 gives some examples of concept-term relationships, making clear the need for vocabulary control either at the point of indexing (controlled vocabulary) or at the point of searching (query term expansion), especially in searching based on free text and user-assigned (social) tags.

Conceptual Structure

The key to a KOS that fulfills the functions listed in Table 13 is the conceptual organization. There are two interacting principles of conceptual structure: facet analysis (componential analysis, feature analysis, aspect analysis, semantic factoring) and hierarchy.

Table 17. Concept-term relationships (Terminological structure)

Controlling synonyms (one concept – many terms)		Disambiguating homonyms (One term – many concepts)
Term	*Preferred term*	administration 1 (management) administration 2 (drugs)
Teenager	Adolescent	
Teen	Adolescent	Discharge 1 (from hospital or program)
Youth (person)	Adolescent	Discharge 2 (from organization or job)
Pubescent	Adolescent	Preferred synonym: Dismissal Discharge 3 (medical symptom)
Alcoholism	Alcohol dependence	Discharge 4 (into a river)
Drug abuse	substance abuse	Discharge 5 (electrical)

Table 18. A facet frame for prevention projects (derived from Table 7)

Relationship	Facet	Sample facet value
<addressesProblem>	*Problem, disorder, disease*	Alcohol abuse
<hasTarget Audience>	*Target audience, population*	Adolescent girls
<usesApproach>	*Approach*	Prevention through youth AOD education

Table 19. More facet examples. Facet frame for disorders

Alcohol abuse		Alcoholic liver cirrhosis	
Pathologic process:	substance abuse	*Pathologic process*:	inflammation
Body system:	not specified	*Body system*:	not specified
Cause:	not specified	*Cause*:	chem.induced
Substance/organism:	alcohol	*Substance/organism*:	alcohol
Hereditary alcohol abuse		Hepatitis A	
Pathologic process:	substance abuse	*Pathologic process*:	inflammation
Body system:	liver	*Body system*:	liver
Cause:	genetic	*Cause*:	infection
Substance/organism:	alcohol	*Substance/organism*:	hepatitis A virus

Semantic Analysis and Facets

Facet analysis is best understood through examples. From the entity-relationship schema in Table 7, we can see three of the facets needed to analyze and describe a prevention project, repeated in the *facet frame* in Table 18.

Each facet describes one aspect of the project. Facet analysis is a great way to conceptualize a search, hence the increasing popularity of facet-based search [1, 86]. Each facet (or slot in the facet frame) has an associated set of values (slot fillers); Table 2 gives a hierarchy of values of the *Approach* facet.

For *disorders,* carrying facet analysis further leads to atomic (or elemental) concepts, see Table 19. Table 20 gives general facet principles and Table 21 gives more examples.

Hierarchy

Table 2 gives an example of a concept hierarchy. For information retrieval and user orientation the main purposes of hierarchy are

1. Hierarchic query term expansion and
2. Organizing concepts into a structure that can be easily understood.

For (1) we can define broader concept (usually called Broader Term, abbreviation BT) pragmatically as Concept B falls under broader concept A if any search for A should find everything on B as well (B BT A or conversely, A has narrower concept B, A NT B). For (2) create suitable headings to structure the hierarchy. Table 22 shows another example of a pragmatic hierarchy.

Table 20. General facet principles

A facet groups concepts that fill the same role:

- Concepts that fall under the same aspect or feature in the definition of more complex concepts;
- Concepts that can be answers to a given question;
- Concepts that can serve as fillers in one frame slot;
- Concepts that combine in similar patterns with other concepts.

Elemental concepts as building blocks for constructing compound concepts:

- Reduces the number of concepts in the KOS, leading to conceptual economy.
- Facilitates the search for general concepts, such as searching for the concept *dependence* (in medicine, psychology, or social relations).

  Facets can be defined at high or low levels in the hierarchy; see Table 21.

Table 21. More facet examples

Top-level facets	Low-level facets
Pathologic process	Route of administration
Organism	. By scope of drug action (Local/topical or systemic)
Body part	. By body site
Chemical substances by function	. By method of application (Injection, rubbing on, etc.)
Chemical substances by structure	

A Area of ability		combines with	B Degree of ability
A1	psychomotor ability	B1	low degree of ability, disabled
A2	senses	B2	average degree of ability
A2.1	. vision	B3	above average degree of ability
A2.1.1	. . night vision	B3.1	. very high degree of ability
A2.2	. hearing		
A3	intelligence		
A4	artistic ability		
Examples		A2.1B1 visually impaired A2.2B1 hearing impaired A3B1 mentally handicapped A3B3 intellectually gifted	

Reasoning requires a more formal definition: B <*isa*> A, which means that instances of concept B have all the characteristics of concept A and at least one more.

Table 22. Hierarchy example

Groups at highrisk of drug use
. *At high risk of drug use due to family background*
. . Persons from unstable or low-cohesion families
. . Children of alcoholic or other drug-abusing parents
. . Children of single teenage mothers
. *At high risk of drug use due to abuse or neglect*
. . Persons subjected to abuse/neglect by parents
. . . Latchkey children
. . Persons subjected to abuse/neglect by spouse
. *At high risk of drug use due to internal factors*
. . Suicidal or physically or mentally disabled
. . Gateway drug users
. . Persons engaged in violent or delinquent acts
. *At high risk of drug use due to external circumstances*
. . Single teenage mothers
. . School dropouts or those at risk of dropping out
. . Unemployed or in danger of being unemployed
. . Economically disadvantaged
. . Homeless
. . . Runaway youth

Interaction of Hierarchy and Facets

Table 21 illustrates how concepts from two facets can be combined to form compound concepts. Combination of concepts may be done just in searching (postcombination) or ahead of search in indexing (precombination):

1. Postcombination (usually, but poorly, called postcoordination).
   Assign elemental (atomic) concepts as descriptors and combine descriptors in searching. In the example this would not work well, since a person could have below average vision and above average hearing.
2. Precombination (usually, but poorly, called precoordination).
   Assign compound concepts as precombined descriptors. These precombined descriptors can be enumerated in the classification schedule ready for use by the indexer, or the indexer must construct precombined descriptors as needed.

The compound concepts form a hierarchy. To find all people who are *above average in vision*, we must also find people who are *above average in night vision* or who are *very high in vision.* Table 23 shows a small hierarchy that results from combining the concepts from two facets (not the facet heads) and shows it both in a graphical representation and as a linear arrangement with cross-references. Many concepts have two broader concepts (polyhierarchy) as shown through the cross-references. As a more efficient alternative to cross-references, one can set up a system that finds compound descriptors in terms of their elemental components (descriptor-find index).

Table 23. Hierarchy from combining two facets

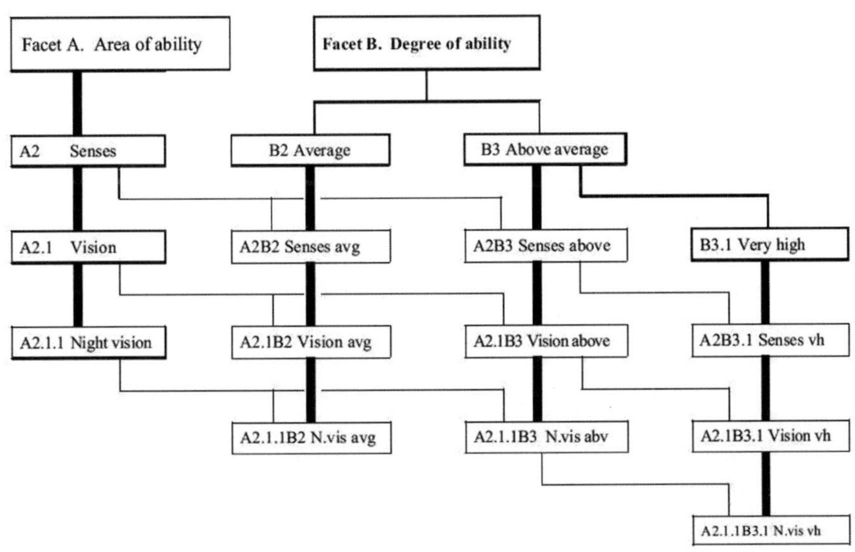

Linear arrangement 1: Facet A primary

A Facet A. Area of ability
. A2 Senses
. . A2B2 Senses average NT A2.1B2; BT B2
. . A2B3 Senses above average NT A2.1B3; BT B3
. . . A2B3.1 Senses very high NT A2.1B3.1; BT B3.1
. . A2.1 Vision
. . . A2.1B2 Vision average NT A2.1.1B2; BT A2B2
. . . A2.1B3 Vision above average NT A2.1.1B3; BT A2B3
. . . . A2.1B3.1 Vision very high NT A2.1.1B3.1;BT A2B3.1
. . . A2.1.1 Night vision
. . . . A2.1.1B2 Night vision average BT A2.1B2
. . . . A2.1.1B3 Night vision above average BT A2.1B3
. . . . . A2.1.1B3.1 Night vision v. high BT A2.1B3.1

B Facet B. Degree of ability
. B2 Average ability NT A2B2
. B3 Above average ability NT A2B3
. . B3.1 Very high ability NT A2B3.1

Linear arrangement 2: Facet B primary not shown

Table 24. Refined relationships for more precise query expansion:
ERIC Thesaurus - A sample of the RT relationships under Reading

ERIC Thesaurus	Refined Ontology
READING	
RT Advance organizers	<*facilitatedBy*> Advance organizers
Bibliotherapy	<*usedIn*> Bibliotherapy
Context clues	<*facilitatedBy*> Context clues
Readability	<*facilitatedBy*> Readability
Reading ability	<*supported/hinderedBy*> Reading ability
Reading assignments	<*isAppliedTo*> Reading assignments
Reading attitudes	<*supported/hinderedBy*> Reading attitudes
Reading games	<*isAppliedTo*> Reading games
Reading materials	<*isAppliedTo*> Reading materials
Reading motivation	<*supported/hinderedBy*> Reading motivation
Reading readiness	<*supported/hinderedBy*> Reading readiness
Reading skills	<*supported/hinderedBy*> Reading skills

Differentiated (refined) Conceptual Relationships

Precise query term expansion and reasoning to find answers require more precise concept relationships than provided in a traditional thesaurus, as illustrated in Tables 24–26 (Tables 25 and 26 adapted from [106]).

The example in Table 24 illustrates the use of refined relationships for more precise query expansion. Assume a user is interested in finding documents on *reading and reading materials*. In the ERIC Thesaurus she could either search for just *Reading* or use all RTs for query term expansion, i.e., *Reading OR all RTs of Reading* – a very imprecise search. Using the refined ontology, the user could instead specify a much more precise selection of search terms:

Reading OR all concepts X for which Reading <*isAppliedTo*> Concept X.

Tables 25 and 26 give examples of inferences that rely on the detailed semantic relationships given in an ontology. But the ERIC thesaurus gives us only some poorly defined broader term (BT) and related term (RT) relationships. These relationships are not differentiated enough to support inference.

For another example, consider the ontological relationships and rules we could formulate with these relationships in an example taken from the AGROVOC thesaurus in Table 26. From the statements and rules given in the ontology, a system could infer that *Cheddar cheese* <*containsSubstance*> *milk fat* and, if cows on a given farm are fed mercury-contaminated feed, that *Cheddar cheese* made from milk from these cows <*mayContainSubstance*> *mercury*. But the present AGROVOC Thesaurus gives only NT/BT relationships without differentiation.

In both examples, many of the relationships are based on statements "about the world" rather than just conceptual definitions or terminology,

Table 25. Refining relationships for inference: ERIC thesaurus

Eric Thesaurus	Refined ontology: Statement and rules
Reading instruction	Reading instruction
BT instruction	<*isSubclassOf*> instruction
RT reading	<*hasDomain*> reading
RT learning standards	< *governedBy*> learning standards
Reading ability	Reading ability
BT ability	<*isSubclassOf*> ability
RT reading	<*hasDomain*> reading
RT perception	<*supportedBy*> perception
	Rule 1: Instruction in a domain should consider ability in that domain:
	X *shouldConsider* Y
	IF X <*isSubclassOf*> instruction AND X <*hasDomain*> W AND Y <*isSubclassOf*> ability AND Y <*hasDomain*> W
	yields: (The designer of) *reading instruction* should consider *reading ability*.
	Rule 2
	X *shouldConsider* Z
	IF X <*shouldConsider*> Y AND Y <*supportedBy*> Z
	yields: (The designer of) *reading instruction* should consider *perception*.

Table 26. Refining relationships for inference: AGROVOC Thesaurus

AGROVOC	Refined Ontology
Milk	Milk
NT cow milk	<*includesSpecific*> cow milk
NT milk fat	<*containsSubstance*> milk fat
Cow	Cow
NT cow milk	<*hasComponent*> cow milk
Cheddar cheese	Cheddar cheese
BT cow milk	<*madeFrom*> cow milk
	Rule 1
	Part X <*mayContainSubstance*> Substance Y
	IF Animal W <*hasComponent*> Part X
	AND Animal W <*ingests*> Substance Y
	Rule 2
	Food Z <*containsSubstance*> Substance Y
	IF Food Z <*madeFrom*> Part X
	AND Part X <*containsSubstance*> Substance Y

blurring the distinction between KOS and the systems discussed in Sects. 4.1 and 4.4.

4.8 Interoperability. KOS Standards

Syntactic interoperability requires that system A know how to read system B data and recognize a character string as a tag or relationship or term. *Semantic interoperability* requires that system A know also the *meaning* of the tag, relationship, or term in system B. Semantic interoperability is much harder. Searching or combining data across languages, cultures, disciplines, or time can be seen as an interoperability problem. There are two ways to approach interoperability: Standards, so system A and B use the same syntax and even the same semantics, and mapping (or cross-walks). In practice, both are used. Standards are easier on the syntactic level than on the semantic level. KOS standards are predominantly syntactic, unless one wants to consider widely used KOS, such as Dewey Decimal Classification as (de facto) standards, at least in a limited domain (such as public libraries in the US).

KOS standards serve three main functions:

- Input of KOS data into programs and transfer of data between programs.
- Querying KOS by people and programs and viewing results.
- Identifying specific terms/concepts in specific KOS, e.g., a unique URI (Universal Resource Identifier) for every concept and term to enable cross-KOS concept relationships and use of such URIs in metadata.

A KOS standard must specify the types of information to be included about each concept and term (relationship types, data fields, and standard symbols for them), as well as, for example, information needed to render a hierarchical display in outline form (with meaningful arrangement of concepts at the same level) or a graphical display, such as a concept map.

Unfortunately, there is no unifying standard for all types of KOS but rather a bewildering array of standards for different types of KOS (see Table 27). As a consequence, KOS management software is also splintered, making it almost impossible for an organization to develop and maintain the type of integrated multi-functional KOS that would be most cost-effective.

4.9 Unification: Ontologies

The relationships between document components in a document model, the tags in a document template or a metadata schema, the table structures in a relational database (or the object structures in an object-oriented database), and the relationships between concepts can all be traced back to (or defined in terms of) an entity-relationship model (possibly with added features to increase expressiveness). Such a model is an ontology, so all structures in a digital library can (and should) be conceived as subsets of an overarching ontology. This ontology can be used to make sure that all structures within the DL are consistent and that new structures, such as a template for a new type of document, can be developed easily and consistently. Ideally, the design of a new DL would start with an ontology.

Table 7 gives some examples of statements using entity types and relationship types that would be defined in an ontology; subsequently, the project description template in Table 8 was defined guided by some of these relationships. Likewise, the facet frame for prevention projects in Table 18 was

Table 27. KOS Standards

Dictionaries, glossaries good ISO standards:
ISO 12200:1999, Computer applications in terminology–Machine Readable Terminology Interchange Format (MARTIF)–Negotiated Interchange
ISO 12620:1999, Computer applications in terminology–Data Categories
Many ISO terminology standards
Thesauri
ISO 2788-1986(E)/ANSI/NISO Z39.19-2005 (*niso.org) Poor and backwards
BS8723, Structured vocabularies for information retrieval. Good
Simple Knowledge Organisation Systems (SKOS) RDF name space see w3.org/2004/02/skos/Restricted in expressiveness but widely used
ISO 5964-1985(E) (multilingual)
USMARC format for authority data (lcweb.loc.gov/marc/authority/ecadhome.html)
Topic maps (reference works, encyclopedias) (topicmaps.org/about.html)
ISO/IEC 13250:2000 Topic Maps
XML Topic Maps (XTM) 1.0 (topicmaps.org/xtm/1.0/)
Concept maps
Classification schemes
MARC for classification data lcweb.loc.gov/marc/classification/eccdhome.html
Ontologies
OWL Web Ontology Language, an extension of RDF (w3.org/TR/owl-ref)
Knowledge Interchange Format (KIF) (meta2.stanford.edu/kif/dpans.html)
Generic standards for knowledge structures, entity-relationship models Resource Description Framework (RDF) (w3.org/RDF/)
The Topic Map standard belongs here as well.

derived from the ontology illustrated in Table 7. Concepts and statements about concepts are conventionally considered to be part of the ontology.

The ontological basis also supports interoperability: Mapping between the ontologies of two DLs, though by no means easy, allows one to derive mappings between the templates, schemas, and KOS used by the two DLs.

Good starting points for finding information about ontologies are the Web sites of Ontolog (`http://ontolog.cim3.net`) and Barry Smith Web site (`http://ontology.buffalo.edu/smith/`).

5 Conclusion

Digital libraries with powerful semantic support (1) for complex searches for documents and immediate answers across system, language, cultural, and disciplinary boundaries and (2) for document creation and collaboration have the potential to transform how work is done by individuals and by groups and to evolve into a true "information commons".

Acknowledgments

The discussions in the DELOS Digital Library Reference Model Working Group (delos.info) were very helpful in preparing this chapter.

Semantic Web and Ontologies

Marcin Synak, Maciej Dabrowski, and Sebastian Ryszard Kruk

This chapter presents ontologies and their role in the creation of the Semantic Web. Ontologies hold special interest, because they are very closely related to the way we understand the world. They provide common understanding, the very first step to successful communication. In following sections, we will present ontologies, how they are created and used. We will describe available tools for specifying and working with ontologies.

1 What is an Ontology?

The shortest possible answer is: An ontology is a specification of a conceptualization.[1]

Basically, it means that an ontology formally describes concepts and relationships which can exist between them in some community. In other words – an ontology describes a part of the world.

A concept in an ontology can represent a variety of things. A concept can be an object of any sort: person, car, building, can describe an activity or state: swimming, being busy or available, abroad. Can represent abstract concepts like time or value. There is no strict restriction what can express as a concept in our ontology. The only restriction is the real world which our ontology tries to reflect.

A relationship in an ontology represents a way in which two concepts, two things, can be connected to each other. The connection may represent some allegiance: *Dog is best friend of Man, Train needs Rails, characteristics of objects: Children are Young, Apples are Juicy, activity: Policemen chase Criminals*, etc.

The whole idea of ontology may sound similar to the concept of RDF [151]. In fact, every ontology is an RDF graph, but the difference is that the ontology sets rules, establishes facts concerning not single objects but classes of

[1] The Semantic Web Community Portal: `http://semanticweb.org`

objects. For example: *Policemen chase Criminals* could be a part of ontology – because chasing criminals is policemen's job in general. It is an established fact. *Inspector Smith chases Johnny-Sticky Fingers* could be an RDF statement compatible with this ontology. We can recognize that *Inspector Smith* represents class *Policemen* (is an individual of this class) and *Johnny-Sticky Fingers* looks like a *Thief*, who is obviously a *Criminal.* To be more specific, we could say that *Thieves* are a subclass of *Criminals.*

Ontologies have different domains and scopes. Some try to describe more general concepts, some are very specific. Hundreds of ontologies are already listed in on-line ontology libraries [53, 188].

2 Ontology Terms

There are some terms established in the field of ontologies. So far, some of these terms were used without their formal definition. Most of them are pretty straightforward and a reader can subconsciously devise what we mean when we say, for example, that "something belongs to class X". Nevertheless, it is a good idea to clearly state the meaning of words we use:

- A *Class*, sometimes called a *Concept* in the ontology is a way to represent general qualities and properties of a group of objects. If a group of objects have the same traits, that fact should be recognized and a class representing these traits should be created. A good idea is to first recognize the groups of objects and then create classes for them. For example, if height is somehow important for what we do, we could describe that all people whose height is more than 1.80m are grouped in a class called "Tall People".
- A *Subclass*, represents a part of the object group with some traits which are not common for the whole group. For example if we have a class of "Staff Members" which contains all the people working in our company, we could devise a subclass called "Management", grouping those members of our staff which work in a management department.
- An *Individual* , or an object, is a single item in our world, which belongs to some class (or many classes). "Ronald Reagan" could be an individual of "American Presidents" class, as well as "message 2341" could be an individual of "E-mails". Two different individuals represent two different objects. We must keep in mind that our individuals may represent abstract concepts (such as activities) as well as solid objects.
- A *property* is used to describe qualities common to all the individuals of a class. Properties represents relationships in ontologies. When we attach a property to a class it becomes this property's Domain. Class of objects a property points to, is its Range.
- A *property restriction* can be set to further shape properties. Some common property restrictions are cardinality and value restrictions. We may also want to specify that some property is required, etc.

3 Reasoning Over Ontologies

We have already described that an ontology provides a common way of representing knowledge about some domain. An ontology is a way to share a common understanding of information structure. Once we have common understanding, we can try to reason over this information, extract parts which are of our interest and work with them.

Reasoning is a wide term which transgresses the boundaries of the Semantic Web. It is often used in AI terminology as well as psychological works. In the Semantic Web, generally we use the term *reasoning* to describe the process of retrieving information from RDF graph.

There are many types of reasoning in the Semantic Web and one reasoning language will not fit all needs. Some types of reasoning are designed to deal with inconsistencies within the graph, other are used when available information is not complete (fuzzy reasoning). Some reasoning languages are similar in purpose to SQL-type querying languages for retrieval of information from databases.

One type of reasoning is based on using the knowledge about graph structure in form of an ontology. It usually consists of two phases:

- Inferencing phase, when additional information (additional triples) is generated from the RDF graph using a set of inferencing rules. The common example is handling transitive properties, where additional information is explicitly written.
- Querying phase, where a part of graph is retrieved. Query languages for RDF, like RDQL [196] or SPARQL [206] are still in development phase. Querying allows not only to simply match triples to given template. RDF graph can be traversed, so queries like *find me addresses of all friends of John Smith* are possible.

Reasoning/querying languages vary in their capabilities. For example, some languages allow datatype reasoning, other not.

3.1 Existing Reasoning Engines

A short description of several existing tools, implementing different languages, which can be used for reasoning:

- Jena [103] is an open source framework written in Java useful for building Semantic Web applications. It provides tools for manipulating RDF graphs, with help of OWL and RDFS technology. One of Jena's tools is a rule-based inference engine, which can be used for reasoning. Jena also supports RDQL [196], the query language for RDF.
- Sesame [198] is an open source RDF database with support for RDF Schema inferencing and querying. Sesame supports several RDF querying languages like RDQL. The most powerful is SeRQL, the language developed especially for Sesame. Sesame inferencing tools use rule definitions

stored in XML file. There is default inferencing (which takes advantage of constructs like OWL definition of transitive properties, etc.). Users can use their custom inferencer and specify their own rules.
- TRIPLE [148] is an RDF query, inference and transformation language. Its syntax uses constructs from Horn logic1 and F-logic [147]. Existing implementation of TRIPLE is based on extensible Prolog implementation, XSB [231].

4 OWL – Web Ontology Language

In the early days of the Semantic Web research there were many formalisms used to describe ontologies. It made interoperability, excepted from semantic solutions, virtually impossible.

4.1 What is OWL?

OWL, the Web Ontology Language [180, 181], is a W3C recommendation of a language for specifying ontologies. It has been designed to facilitate greater machine interpretability than previous solutions. It provides more extensive vocabulary than plain XML, RDF or RDF Schema[2] and better facilitates expressing semantics than these languages. OWL has its roots in DAML+OIL[3] web ontology language, which concepts, revised and updated, were incorporated into OWL.

Currently, the OWL is the choice for creating ontologies unless there are special reasons to use older languages like DAML+OIL (compatibility, etc.).

The practice with creating OWL ontologies showed that while OWL is very expressive, in some cases it is not convenient to use it. Sometimes we do not use all of OWLs sophisticated concepts. But applications always assume that we could and try to reason over these concepts. Designers of OWL predicted the problem and provided three OWL "species", subsets of OWL with decreasing expressiveness. They will be described later. However, there are initiatives to provide even simpler languages than OWL Lite, the least expressive of the three.

4.2 OWL Concepts and Language Constructs

To fully understand how OWL works and what can it be useful for, we need to formulate few concepts of OWL. Described terms are frequently used in literature dealing with OWL. Definitions are roughly taken from OWL specifications.

---

[2] RDF Schema: `http://www.w3.org/TR/rdf-schema/`

[3] DAML+OIL: `http://www.w3.org/TR/daml+oil-reference`

- *Class.* Classes in OWL represent groups of objects with shared characteristics. We can define a class in six ways:
  1. Using the class identifier (URI) – named classes
  2. Using the *enumeration* of all individuals which are the instances of the class
  3. Using a *property restriction* – all individuals which match the restriction form a class
  4. As an *intersection* of two or more classes – individuals common to these classes form a new class
  5. As an *union* of two or more classes – the sum of all individuals belonging to these classes form a new class
  6. As a *complement* of a class – contains all individuals which do not belong to this class
- *Class extension.* In OWL terminology, the class extension is simply a set of all individuals which form the class.
- *Class axioms.* The "truths" about classes. The simplest (and the least informative) class axiom is the class declaration which states the existence of the class. Other OWL language constructs used to define class axioms are:
  `rdfs:subClassOf` – (inherited from RDFS) means that the extension of the class is a subset of extension of the superclass
  `owl:equivalentClass` – means the equivalent class has exactly the same extension
  `owl:disjointWith` – means that the two disjointed classes have no common members in their extensions
- *Property.* Properties are used to describe classes. OWL distinguishes two types of properties:
  – Object properties (`owl:ObjectProperty`), which link individuals to individuals
  – Datatype properties (`owl:DatatypeProperty`), which link individuals to data values
- *Property extension.* Property extension is a concept similar to the class extension. It is a set of all pairs of individuals (subject and object) which can be connected with the property.
- *Property axioms.* Similarly to classes, OWL defines property axioms:
  `rdfs:subPropertyOf`, `rdfs:domain`, `rdfs:range` (inherited from RDFS) – a subproperty has the extension which is a subset of superproperty extension. Domain states that subjects of the property must belong to the extension of pointed class. Range states the same, but refers to objects.
  `owl:equivalentProperty` and `owl:inverseOf` – two properties are equivalent if they have the same extension. One property is inversion of another if for every pair (X, Y) in its extension there is a pair (Y, X) in the extension of inverted property.
  `owl:FunctionalProperty` and `owl:InverseFunctionalProperty` – global cardinality constraints, functional property can have exactly one object

for a particular subject (e.g. every person has exactly one year of birth). Inverse functional properties can have exactly one subject for a particular object (e.g. there is only one X in "X is a father of John").
`owl:SymmetricProperty` and `owl:TransitiveProperty` – describe logical characteristics of properties. A property is symmetric if for every (X, Y) pair in the property extension there is a pair (Y, X). Transition means that if there are pairs (X, Y) and (Y, Z) in the property extension, then the pair (X, Z) also belongs to this property extension.

- *Individuals.* Individuals are defined using individual axioms. There are two types of axioms (facts, truths):
  Axioms referring to class membership and property values
  Axioms referring to individual identity (`owl:sameAs`, `owl:differentFrom` - OWL can define that two individuals, two URIs, are actually the same thing or explicitly state that this is not the case).
- *Data types.* OWL uses RDF data types (which refer to XML Schema datatypes) and some of its own constructs like enumerated datatype.

4.3 OWL 'Species': OWL Lite, OWL DL and OWL Full

There are three types or 'species', as authors call them, of OWL. That includes:

- OWL Full (or simply OWL, the 'Full' word has been added to distinct it from the other two OWL languages)
- OWL DL (which is an abbreviation of 'Description Logic')
- OWL Lite

All three OWLs use the same syntactic constructions to build ontologies, the differences are in restrictions which are put on OWL DL and OWL Lite. OWL Full takes advantage of all RDF/RDFS constructs. For RDF developers, transition from RDF to OWL Full is natural, since most of RDF data will translate directly into OWL Full ontologies. To be compatible with OWL DL or Lite, RDF data has to be specifically constructed for these ontology languages.

Basically, the main restriction which does not exist in OWL Full (and exists in the other two) is distinction between a class and an individual. In OWL Full classes can be individuals at the same time. This gives the flexibility of RDFS and allows to represent complicated real-world constructs but in the same time OWL Full ontologies are very difficult to reason over.

Next is OWL DL. Description Logic [64] is an existing segment of business applications and OWL DL was created to support it by providing desirable computational properties for reasoning systems.

The list of restrictions which are placed upon OWL constructs is:

- Class definitions must be constructed using `owl:Class` or `owl:Restriction`. Other definitions can not be used independently (only together with these two). A class can *never* be an individual at the same time (it is possible in RDFS or OWL Full).

- Datatype subproperties can only be constructed from datatype properties and object subproperties from object properties.
- A datatype property can not be inverse/functional.
- Transitive properties can not have specified cardinality.
- In OWL DL we can use annotation properties (to annotate our ontology) only with classes, properties, individuals and ontology headers. Annotation properties can not be datatype or object properties at the same time (they can be in OWL Full), can not have subproperties, can not have range and domain, etc.

Every OWL DL ontology is a valid OWL Full ontology (but not the other way around).

The last, OWL Lite, is, as its name suggests, the least sophisticated (and the least expressive) dialect of OWL. Of course, similarly as in the OWL DL case, every OWL Lite ontology is a valid OWL DL ontology and by transience is a valid OWL Full ontology. OWL Lite was created with software developers in mind, it is easy to implement and use. However, there is a push to create even simpler language for tool developers who would want to support OWL and want to start with something uncomplicated. It is sometimes called OWL Lite- (OWL Lite minus [57]).

OWL Lite has all the restrictions on OWL language constructs and add a few of its own:

- There are no enumerations as class descriptions in OWL Lite
- `owl:allValuesFrom` and `owl:someValuesFrom` used to define classes by property restrictions must point to a class name
- `owl:hasValue` property restrictions can not be used in OWL Lite
- cardinality constraints on properties in OWL Lite can only be set with "0" or "1" value (no multiple cardinality in OWL Lite)
- unions and complements of classes can not be used as class descriptions, intersection use is restricted to named classes and property restrictions
- class equivalence in OWL Lite can be only applied to classes defined with URI and point either to a named class or property restriction
- class disjointness can not be specified using OWL Lite
- domain and range of a property must point to a class name

Examples of OWL constructs which are or are not legal in OWL DL and/or OWL Lite can be found in OWL language reference document [182].

4.4 OWL vs. RDFS – Advantages, Differences

OWL is a build-up on RDFS. It should be considered as a set of ontology building tools which are not provided by plain RDFS. Language constructs of OWL allow to specify such facts like class disjointness or equivalence, defining classes by setting property restrictions or enumerations. At the same time, user has the "freedom" of RDFS like specifying classes as individuals of other (meta)classes (assuming he uses OWL Full).

We could say that OWL constructs are more defined RDFS constructs, with more "finesse". For example `owl:Class` is defined as a subclass of `rdfs:Class`.

RDFS lets us specify a RDF vocabulary. OWL allows us to *ontologize* this vocabulary.

4.5 DAML+OIL

DAML+OIL [51] grows from earlier DAML [211], the DARPA Agent Markup Language and OIL [178], the Ontology Inference Layer. DAML was developed as an extension to XML and RDF. It allowed more sophisticated class definitions than RDFS. OIL was another initiative for providing more complicated classifications which used constructs from frame-based AI.

These two efforts were merged and DAML+OIL language for specifying ontologies was a result.

DAML+OIL introduced such concepts like class equivalence, property uniqueness (concept later broadened in OWL – functional properties), property restrictions, etc. It also redefined the concept of `rdfs:Class`.

DAML+OIL is worth mentioning because it made a way for OWL. OWL is simply a revised and corrected successor of DAML+OIL which incorporates experiences gathered while working with DAML OIL ontologies.

4.6 Ontology Example

Figure 1 shows an example, simple ontology in OWL.

The example ontology describes a class *MaturePerson* which gathers all people who we considered mature (e.g. age 18 and older). A person may be either *Male* or *Female* which are defined as subclasses of *MaturePerson.* An individual of *Male* class can not be an individual of *Female* class at the same time, so class *Male* is disjoint with *Female.*

The example specifies several properties. Every person has properties *hasAge* and *hasFriend.* A person can only have one age but many friends, so *hasAge* is specified as functional property. But being someone's friend also means that this person is also our friend, so *hasFriend* has been defined as a symmetric property. *hasAge* connects an individual to an integer, so it is specified as datatype property. *hasFriend* connects two individuals, so it is an object property.

There are also specified properties *hasWife* and *hasHusband.* A Male can have a wife and a *Female* can have a husband. If we are interested only in monogamous relationships, these two properties are inverse and functional – *I'm a husband of my wife and there is exactly one person which can be my spouse* (at a certain moment in time).

Some concepts were removed from the example to keep it relatively small.

```
<?xml version="1.0"?>
<rdf:RDF
    xmlns:rdf="http://www.w3.org/1999/02/22-rdf-syntax-ns#"
    xmlns:rdfs="http://www.w3.org/2000/01/rdf-schema#"
    xmlns:owl="http://www.w3.org/2002/07/owl#"
    xmlns="http://www.owl-ontologies.com/unnamed.owl#"
  xml:base="http://www.owl-ontologies.com/unnamed.owl">
  <owl:Ontology rdf:about=""/>
  <owl:Class rdf:ID="MaturePerson"/>
  <owl:Class rdf:about="#Male">
    <owl:disjointWith rdf:resource="#Female"/>
    <rdfs:subClassOf rdf:resource="#MaturePerson"/>
  </owl:Class>
  <owl:Class rdf:about="#Female">
    <owl:disjointWith rdf:resource="#Male"/>
    <rdfs:subClassOf rdf:resource="#MaturePerson"/>
  </owl:Class>
  <owl:SymmetricProperty rdf:ID="hasFriend">
    <rdfs:domain rdf:resource="#MaturePerson"/>
    <rdfs:range rdf:resource="#MaturePerson"/>
    <rdf:type rdf:resource="&owl;#ObjectProperty"/>
  </owl:SymmetricProperty>
  <owl:FunctionalProperty rdf:ID="hasAge">
    <rdfs:domain rdf:resource="#MaturePerson"/>
    <rdfs:range rdf:resource="&xsd;#positiveInteger"/>
    <rdf:type rdf:resource="&owl;#DatatypeProperty"/>
  </owl:FunctionalProperty>
  <owl:InverseFunctionalProperty rdf:about="#hasWife">
    <rdfs:range rdf:resource="#Female"/>
    <rdfs:domain rdf:resource="#Male"/>
    <rdf:type rdf:resource="&owl;#ObjectProperty"/>
    <owl:inverseOf rdf:resource="#hasHusband"/>
  </owl:InverseFunctionalProperty>
  <owl:InverseFunctionalProperty rdf:ID="hasHusband">
    <rdfs:range rdf:resource="#Male"/>
    <rdfs:domain rdf:resource="#Female"/>
    <rdf:type rdf:resource="&owl;#ObjectProperty"/>
    <owl:inverseOf rdf:resource="#hasWife"/>
  </owl:InverseFunctionalProperty>
</rdf:RDF>
```

Fig. 1. Example ontology in OWL

5 Developing Ontologies

Developing an ontology is a job which requires cooperation of both IT specialists and domain experts. The first group has experience in building applications using the technologies of the Semantic Web. The second group knows the field which will be covered with the ontology.

A goal for an ontology is to efficiently and accurately describe a 'part of the world'. This goal can not be achieved without extracting information about this realm first. E.g. if we want to create an ontology to improve postal delivery services, we need to ask people involved what are the parts of their job. For example, we need to know:

- What is the difference between a letter and a parcel?
- How does the fee system work?
- What are responsibilities of a postman? etc.

Some of these things may be obvious but in most cases they are not. For example, most people know what a 'letter' is. But how many know what it means to 'porto' pay for a letter? Specialists on every field have their own dictionary of terms and use them accordingly to their regulations. If such dictionary does not exist, the case is even more challenging, because it must be created first.

When it comes to making two or more groups of people work with different knowledge, experience and a way of seeing things together, there is always a question of tools which could support their interactions. Two IT specialists will probably find their common language quickly, because they understand code, standardized diagrams and so on. It is the same case with two postmen. But how to improve interactions between these two groups? Of course we have traditional ways of communication – letters, telephones or simple face-to-face talk. But more than often we have to make people from different cultures or from different time zones cooperate. A need for a set of tools which could improve that contact is apparent.

The described problem is common when we develop specialized software for specific needs. But it is especially clear when it comes to developing ontologies. An ontology can become 'the ontology' only if a compromise between all the parties interested is achieved. It is not only a problem of developing a specialized piece of software, but of developing a standard.

5.1 Common Steps of an Ontology Development Process

We have decided that an ontology could bring new quality to our project. We have IT specialists, specialists from our example post office, all necessary software and tools. Now, where to start?

Here is some general knowledge about developing ontologies. We know some rules which are always useful, techniques giving good results. However, none of existing techniques of developing an ontology could be described as the best or the easiest. Selection may depend on the domain we create an ontology for and any specific requirements. We may also want to ask developers, what are they most comfortable with.

Nevertheless, we can try to systematize ontology development by dividing the process into phases. Developers of Protegé [212] ontology editor, from Stanford University propose in [160] steps as follows:

1. Determine the ontology domain and scope
   First, as in everything we do, we have to ask ourselves what exactly we want to do. It is no different when creating an ontology. We need to know what we want our ontology to cover, what are we going to use it for, etc. By determining the domain, we restrict our interest to certain field of knowledge. By defining the scope we choose what part of this field is important to us.
   A good practice in determining the ontology domain and scope is creating a set of so called *competency questions*. Competency questions are questions we want our ontology to be able to answer. The example competency questions for postal delivery services could be:
   - Is it possible to send a 50 kg parcel to Zimbabwe till next Friday?
   - Can I insure it?
   - Does the postman in my vicinity deliver letters on Saturday?
   - Does delivering a letter on Saturday cost more?
   - What is the weight/cost ratio for local deliveries?
   - Can I get a return receipt?

   The competency questions are a good starting point of evaluating the ontology after it has been created. They should be considered as a necessary but not sufficient condition.
2. Determine which existing ontologies we will reuse (if any)
   There is a number of existing ontologies and vocabularies covering different fields. Many are free to use, so it is always a good idea to put a bit of work in researching existing solutions and evaluating their usability for our project. It might be possible that our ontology could just refine an existing one instead of defining all the concepts from scratch. We can use some concepts directly or inherit from them. An example could be FOAF (Friend-Of-A-Friend [32]) ontology, which provides a good way to describe human resources in the Web.
   Reusing an existing ontology might also be a requirement. Especially if our system is to interact with other systems based on controlled vocabularies, or are committed to some existing ontologies.
3. Gather important terms
   This step consists of creating a vocabulary of terms from a domain we want to describe with an ontology. Basically, we want to gather words which are being used everyday by people working in our domain. For example, if we wanted to create a bank ontology, we would probably write down things like *bank*, *account*, *client*, *credit*, *balance*, *cash* and so on. In this step we are

not concerned what is the meaning of these words or how concepts they represent are the connected to each other. What is important is to get a comprehensive list of terms which will be a base for further work.

4. Define classes
   This and next step are closely intertwined to each other. It is very hard to define a class structure before defining properties. Typically, we define few classes in the hierarchy and their properties before moving to the next group of classes, etc. Some possible approaches of developing a class hierarchy are:

   - Top-down approach, which starts with creating definition of the most general concepts and then their specialization (creating subclasses); the process is recursive for every class until it we reach the most specific definitions.
   - Bottom-up approach, which goes the other way – first we define the most specific concepts ant then group them into more general concepts by creating common superclass for them.
   - Combination of both when we start with few general (or 'top-level') concepts and few specific (or 'bottom-level') concepts and fill the middle levels consequently.

   Choosing the 'correct' approach may depend on the domain or the way the developer sees it. The combination approach is often the easiest, because middle-level concepts tend to be the most descriptive [160].
   There are two important issues which are often encountered while defining class hierarchy. First is to distinguish between classes and instances. We must decide if some concepts represent a subclass or an instance of a certain class. For example we could muse if a concept of *Letter_to_Denmark* should be described as subclass of *Letter* or its instance. While solving such problems we should decide what level of specification our ontology needs. Are we interested in describing single letters which have an address, sender address, etc. or do we only need to sort them?
   The second problem is to decide which characteristics of concept should be represented in a number of subclasses and which should be put into properties. For example there is a limited number of countries in the world. We could create subclass for every one of them indicating letter destination or simply put *destinationCountry* property in *Letter* class.
5. Define class properties
   Properties (or slots) describe internal structure of concepts. A property may point to simple value such as a string or a date (datatype properties) or a class instance (object properties). We use datatype properties to describe object's physical characteristics (often called 'intrinsic' properties) such as parcel's weight as well as abstract concepts (or 'extrinsic' properties) i.e. *deliveryDate* for letter or name for postman. Object properties are commonly used to represent relationships between individuals. A postman could have the *hasBoss* or *worksAt* object property. Of course we

do not restrict usage of object properties to represent relationships only. For example a postman could have property *workSchedule* pointing to an individual, because schedule is a complex object. Object properties are also often used to represent object's parts, if the object is structured.
Properties are inherited by all subclasses. For example, if *PostWorker* has property *name*, and *Postman* is a subclass of *PostWorker*, it will inherit the *name* property. That is why properties should be attached to the most general class that can have it. But we must keep in mind that 'inheriting' means something different in ontologies that it means, e.g. in object-oriented languages. If a subclass inherits a property from its superclass it only means that this property *can* also be applied to this subclass. It is not a requirement.

6. Define properties restrictions
Property restrictions (or 'slot facets') work together with properties. We use them to further specify usage of the property, its features, allowed values, etc. Types of facets available strongly depend on the ontology language used. Some languages are more expressive than others and have more extensive vocabulary of ready-to-use constructs. The common facets are:
   - *Slot cardinality* specifies how many values a property can have. For example, we can specify that a *PostVan* has exactly one *driver* and can carry no more than 10 *mailBags* (if we treat bags as individuals, i.e. A bag can have *ID*, *destination* etc.). Cardinality is handled differently in different ontology languages. For example, RDFS allows only specifying *single cardinality* (minimum cardinality of 0 or 1). OWL allows specifying *multiple cardinality.* It means that every property can be more precisely described using minimum and maximum cardinality. While describing a fact that every van needs a driver requires system supporting single cardinality only, we need a support for multiple cardinality to represent the number of bags.
   - *Slot value-type* defines what kind of values a property can have. Common value types for datatype properties are *String*, *Number* (or more specific types such as *Integer* or *Float*), *Boolean* and *Enumerated* (a list of specific allowed values such as express or *airMail* for *letterType* property). Object properties have Instance-type value. A list of allowed classes from which instances can come is defined.
   - *Domain and range* are facets of object properties. A list of allowed classes as described above is often called *range* of a slot. A list of classes a property is attached to is called *domain.*[4]
7. Create instances
Creating instances is the last step. We choose a class, create an individual of the chosen class and fill in property values. Instances form the actual semantic description.

[4] A *property domain* should not be confused with *ontology domain*, which should be understood as ontology subject, domain of interest.

5.2 Ontology Development Tools

This subsection describes shortly existing solutions for ontology development. Detailed information could be found at referenced websites.

Ontology Editors

- Protegé [212] originates from Stanford University. It is a free, open source ontology editor, written in Java which allows user create ontologies in RDFS and OWL languages. Protegé allows to manipulate classes using a tree-like structure (creating classes, subclasses, attaching properties, etc.). Protegé itself is a standalone tool and does not support cooperative ontology development. However, Protegé is easily extensible through a plug-in system, so appropriate tools can be added. At the moment, Protegé sets a standard for ontology editors.
- Ontolingua [177] is a distributed collaborative environment for ontology browsing, creation, editing, etc. Ontolingua server is maintained by the Knowledge Systems, AI Laboratory at Stanford University. Part of Ontolingua is the Ontology Editor which allows to create and edit ontologies using the web browser. Access to Ontolingua server is free of charge, but requires registration. Currently there is no way of creating your own server with Ontolingua software. Server maintained by Stanford (and two other at universities in Europe) hosts several ontology development projects.

There are other ontology editors like OILed [171], designed for developing DAML+OIL ontologies or DOE [62] (Differential Ontology Editor), focusing on linguistics-inspired techniques, designed to complement advanced editors like Protegé.

Merging/Mapping Tools

- Chimæra [43] is a part of Ontolingua software package from Stanford University. Chimæra's major function is merging ontologies together and diagnosing individual or multiple ontologies. Chimæra can be used for resolving naming conflicts, reorganizing taxonomies, etc.
- SMART/PROMPT [161] is an algorithm and tool for automated ontology merging and alignment. It may be used to detect conflicts in the ontologies, suggest resolutions and guide a user through the whole process of merging/aligning ontologies. PROMPT (SMART is the former name for PROMPT) is implemented as an extension to Protegé ontology editor.

Acknowledgement

This material is based upon works supported by Enterprise Ireland under Grant No. ILP/05/203 and by Science Foundation Ireland Grant No. SFI/02/CE1/I131.

Social Semantic Information Spaces

John G. Breslin

1 From Web 1.0 to Web 2.0

The structural and syntactic web put in place in the early 90s is still much the same as what we use today: resources (web pages, files, etc.) connected by untyped hyperlinks. By untyped, we mean that there is no easy way for a computer to figure out what a link between two pages means – for example, on the W3C website, there are hundreds of links to the various organisations that are registered members of the association, but there is nothing explicitly saying that the link is to an organisation that is a "member of" the W3C or what type of organisation is represented by the link. On John's work page, he links to many papers he has written, but it does not explicitly say that he is the author of those papers or that he wrote such-and-such when he was working at a particular university.

In fact, the Web was envisaged to be much more, as one can see from the image in Fig. 1 which is taken from Tim Berners–Lee's original outline for the Web in 1989, entitled "Information Management: A Proposal". In this, all the resources are connected by links describing the type of relationships, e.g. "wrote", "describe", "refers to", etc. This is a precursor to the Semantic Web which we will come back to later.

Web 2.0 is a widely used and wide-ranging term (in terms of interpretations) made popular by Tim O'Reilly.[1] But what exactly is it? If you ask ten different people you'll probably come up with at least five answers. One source[2] says that "Web 2.0 ... has ... come to refer to what some people describe as a second phase of architecture and application development for the World Wide Web". You can think of it as a web where "ordinary" users can meet, collaborate, and share [content] using social software applications on the Web – via tagged items, social bookmarking, AJAX functionality, etc.

---

[1] http://www.oreillynet.com/pub/a/oreilly/tim/news/2005/09/30/what-is-web-20.html

[2] http://en.wikipedia.org/wiki/Web_2

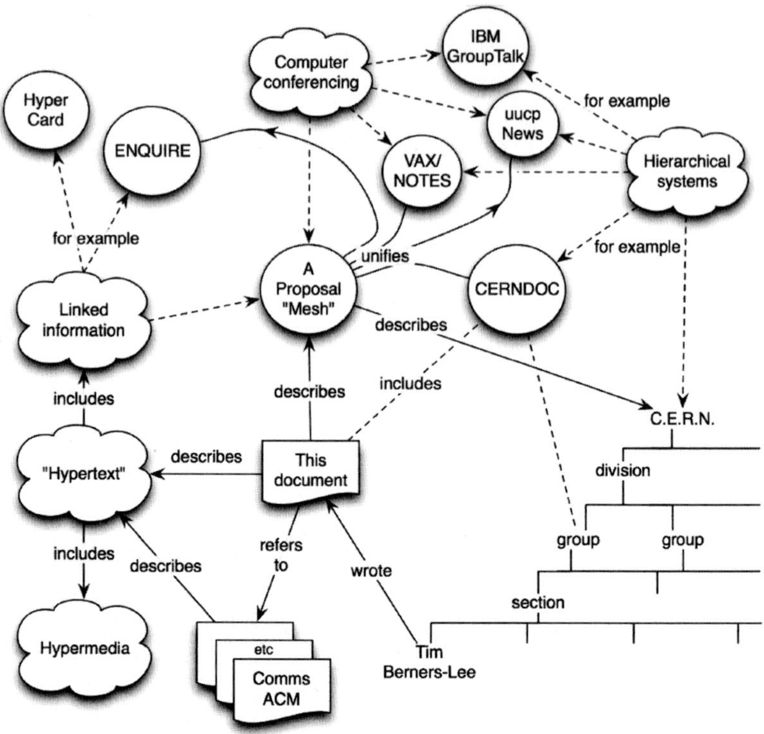

Fig. 1. From Tim Berners–Lee's early proposal for the World Wide Web (http://www.w3.org/History/1989/proposal.html)

There are many popular examples that work along this collaboration and sharing meme: Bebo, del.icio.us, digg, Flickr, UseAMap.com, Technorati, orkut, 43 Things, Wikipedia, etc.

Over the last 13 years, there has been a shift from just 'existing' on the Web to participating on the Web. Web 2.0 is a platform for social and collaborative exchange with reusable community contributions, where anyone can mass-publish using web-based social software and others can subscribe to desired information, news, data flows, or other services. It is "social software" that is being used for this communication and collaboration, software that "lets people rendezvous, connect or collaborate by use of a computer network. It results in the creation of shared, interactive spaces..." Examples include instant messaging, IRC, forums, blogs, wikis, SNS (social network services), social bookmarking, podcasts, and MMOGs or MMORPGs.

O'Reilly wrote on the seven features or principles of Web 2.0, to which some have added an eighth: the long tail phenomenon.[3] But in short, Web 2.0

[3] http://en.wikipedia.org/wiki/Long_tail

Fig. 2. The main aspects of Web 2.0

is all about being more open, more social, and through user-created content, cheaper (see Fig. 2).

2 Tags, Folksonomies, Vocabularies and Web 3.0

A key feature of Web 2.0 sites is community-contributed content that may be tagged and can be commented on by others. That content can be virtually anything: blog entries, board posts, videos, audio, images, wiki pages, user profiles, bookmarks, events, etc. Soon we will see sites with live multiplayer video games appearing in little browser-embedded windows just YouTube does videos, with running commentaries going on about the games in parallel. Tagging is common to many Web 2.0 sites – a tag is a keyword that acts like a subject or category for the associated content. Then we have folksonomies: collaboratively generated, open-ended labeling systems that enable Web 2.0 users to categorise content using the tags system, and to thereby visualise popular tag usages via "tag clouds" (visual depictions of the tags used on a particular website, like a weighted list in visual design).

Folksonomies are one step in the same direction as what some have termed Web 3.0,[4] or the Semantic Web. (The Semantic Web often uses topdown controlled vocabularies to describe various domains, but can also utilise folksonomies and therefore develop more quickly since folksonomies are a great big distributed classification system with low entry costs). As Tim–Berners Lee et al. said in Scientific American in 2001, the Semantic Web is "an extension of the current Web in which information is given well-defined meaning, better enabling computers and people to work in cooperation". The word "semantic" stands for "the meaning of", and therefore the Semantic Web is one that is able to describe things in a way that computers can better understand. Some of the more popular Semantic Web vocabularies include FOAF (Friend-of-a-Friend, for social networks), SIOC (for online communities and content), and Geo (for geographic locations).

[4] http://turing.cs.washington.edu/NYT-KnowItAll.htm

As already mentioned in the previous chapter, the Semantic Web consists of metadata that is associated with web resources, and then there are associated vocabularies or "ontologies" that describe what this metadata is and how it is all related to each other. SEO experts have known that adding metadata to their websites can often improve the percentage of relevant document hits in search engine result lists, but it is hard to persuade web authors to add metadata to their pages in a consistent, reliable manner (either due to perceived high entry costs or because it is too time consuming). For example, few web authors make use of the simple Dublin Core metadata system, even though the use of DC meta tags can increase their pages' prominence in search results.

The main power of the Semantic Web lies in interoperability, and combinations of vocabulary terms:interoperability and increased connectivity is possible through a commonality of expression; vocabularies can be combined and used together: e.g. a description of a book using Dublin Core metadata can be augmented with specifics about the book author using the FOAF vocabulary. Vocabularies can also be easily extended (modules, etc.). Through this, true intelligent search with more granularity and relevance is possible: e.g. a search can be personalised to an individual by making use of their identity profile and relationship information.

The challenge for the Semantic Web is related to the chicken-and-egg problem: it is difficult to produce data without interesting applications, and vice versa. The Semantic Web cannot work all by itself, because if it did it would be called the "Magic Web". For example, it is not very likely that you will be able to sell your car just by putting your a Semantic Web file on the Web. Society-scale applications are required, i.e. consumers and processors of Semantic Web data, Semantic Web agents or services, and more advanced collaborative applications that make real use of shared data and annotations.

The Semantic Web effort is mainly towards producing standards and recommendations that will interlink applications, and the primary Web 2.0 meme as already discussed is about providing user applications. These are not mutually exclusive[5]: with a little effort, many Web 2.0 applications can and do use Semantic Web technologies to great benefit, and the picture in Fig. 3 shows some evolving areas where these two streams have and will come together: semantic blogging, semantic wikis, semantic social networks and the Semantic Desktop all fall in the realm of what he terms the Metaweb, or "social semantic information spaces". Semantic MediaWiki[6], for example, has already been commercially adopted[7] by Centiare (now MyWikiBiz).

There are also great opportunities for mashing together of both Web 2.0 data or applications and Semantic Web technologies, which just require the use of some imagination. Dermod Moore wrote of one such Web 2.0

[5] http://www.oreillynet.com/xml/blog/2005/10/is_web_20_killing_the_semantic.html

[6] http://meta.wikimedia.org/wiki/Semantic_MediaWiki

[7] http://www.sbwire.com/news/view/9912

Web 1.0	*Web 2.0*	*Web 3.0*
Personal Websites	Blogs	**Semantic Blogs:** semiBlog, Haystack, Semblog, Structured Blogging
Content Management Systems, Britannica Online	Wikis, Wikipedia	**Semantic Wikis:** Semantic MediaWiki, SemperWiki, Platypus, dbpedia, Rhizome
Altavista, Google	Google Personalised, DumbFind, Hakia	**Semantic Search:** SWSE, Swoogle, Intellidimension, notitio.us
CiteSeer, Project Gutenberg	Google Scholar, Book Search	**Semantic Digital Libraries:** JeromeDL, BRICKS, FEDORA, Greenstone, SIMILE
Message Boards	Community Portals	**Semantic Forums and Community Portals:** SIOC, OpenLink DataSpaces
Buddy Lists, Address Books	Online Social Networks	**Semantic Social Networks:** FOAF, PeopleAggregator
...	...	**Semantic Social Information Spaces:** Nepomuk, Gnowsis

Fig. 3. From Web 1.0 to Web 3.0

application mashing for a hobby project[8]: a Scuttle[9] + Gregarius[10] + Feedburner[11] + Grazr[12] hybrid that allows one to aggregate ones favourite blogs or other content on a particular topic and then to annotate bookmarks to the most interesting content found. Bringing this a step further, we could have a "semantic social collaborative resource aggregator". In this hypothetical system:

- Social network members specify their favourite content sources
- You and your friends specify any topics of interest
- You specify friends whose topic lists you value
- Metadata aggregator collects content from sites you and friends like (which may be human tagged, or could be auto-tagged)
- Highlights content that may be of interest to you or your friends
- If nothing of interest is currently available, content sources may have semantically-related sources in other communities for secondary content acquisition and highlighting
- You bookmark and tag the interesting content, and share!

We will now discuss three of the most popular Web 2.0 application areas: blogs, wikis and online social networks, and describe how each of these can be enhanced with semantics to not only provide more functionality but also to create an overall interconnected set of social information spaces.

[8] http://bonhom.ie/2006/04/what-weeks-delay-can-produce.html
[9] http://scuttle.org/
[10] http://gregarius.net/
[11] http://www.feedburner.com/
[12] http://grazr.com/

3 Blogging and Semantic Publishing

Blogs are websites which contain periodic time-stamped posts (in reverse chronological order) about a particular genre or touching on a number of topics of interest. They range from individual's online diaries or journals to promotional tools used by companies or political campaigns, and many allow public commenting on their posts. They are also starting to cross the generation gap – teenagers might have a blog via a social networking service, their parents may blog themselves and perhaps grandparents could also be posting, reading or commenting on posts.

The growth and takeup of blogs over the past four years has been dramatic, with a doubling in the size of the blogosphere every six or so months (according to statistics from Technorati[13]). Over 120,000 blogs are created every day, working out at about one a second. Nearly 1.5 million blog posts are being made each day, with over half of bloggers contributing to their sites three months after the blog's creation.

Similar to accidentally wandering onto message boards and web-enabled mailing lists, when searching for something on the Web, one often happen across a relevant entry on someone's blog. RSS feeds are also a useful way of accessing information from your favourite blogs, but they are usually limited to the last 15 entries, and do not provide much information on exactly who wrote or commented on a particular post, or what the post is talking about. Some approaches like SIOC[14] aim to enhance the semantic metadata provided about blogs, forums and posts, but there is also a need for more information about what exactly a person is writing about. When searching for particular information in or across blogs, it is often not that easy to get it because of "splogs" (spam blogs) and also because of the fact that the virtue of blogs so far has been their simplicity – apart from the subject field, everything and anything is stored in one big text field for content. Keyword searches may give some relevant results, but useful questions such as "find me all the restaurants that bloggers reviewed in Dublin with a rating of at least 5 out of 10" cannot be posed, and you cannot easily drag-and-drop events or people or anything (apart from URLs) mentioned in blog posts into your own applications.

There have been some approaches to tackle this issue of adding more information to posts, so that queries can be made and the things that people talk about can be reused in other posts or applications (because not everyone is being served well by the lowest common denominator that we currently have in blogs). One approach is called "structured blogging"[15] and the other "semantic blogging".

Structured blogging is an open source community effort that has created tools to provide microcontent (including microformats[16] like hReview) from

[13] http://technorati.com/weblog/2007/04/328.html
[14] http://sioc-project.org/
[15] http://structuredblogging.org/
[16] http://microformats.org/

popular blogging platforms such as WordPress and Moveable Type. In structured blogging, packages of structured data are becoming post components. Sometimes (not all of the time) a person will have a need for more structure in their posts – if they know a subject deeply, or if their observations or analyses recur in a similar manner throughout their blog – then they may best be served by filling in a form (which has its own metadata and model) during the post creation process. For example, someone may be writing a review of a film they went to see, or reporting on a sports game they attended, or creating a guide to tourist attractions they saw on their travels. Not only do people get to express themselves more clearly, but blogs can start to interoperate with enterprise applications through the microcontent that is being created in the background.

Take the scenario where someone (or a group of people) is reviewing some soccer games that they watched. Their after-game soccer reports will typically include information on which teams played, where the game was held and when, who were the officials, what were the significant game events (who scored, when and how, or who received penalties and why, etc.) – it would be easier for these blog posters if they could use a tool that would understand this structure, presenting an editing form with the relevant fields, and automatically create both HTML and RSS with this structure embedded in it. Then, others reading these posts could choose to reuse this structure in their own posts, and their blog reader or creator could make this structure available when the blogger is ready to write. As well as this, reader applications could begin to answer questions based on the form fields available – "show me all the matches from Germany with more than two goals scored", etc.

At the moment, structured blogging tools (such as those from LouderVoice[17]) provide a fixed set of forms that bloggers can fill in for things like reviews, events, audio, video and people – but there is no reason that people could not create custom structures, and news aggregators or readers could auto-discover an unknown structure, notify a user that a new structure is available, and learn the structure for reuse in the user's future posts.

Semantic Web technologies can also be used to ontologise any available post structures for more linkage and reuse. Blog posts are usually only tagged on the blog itself by the post creator, using free-text keywords such as "scotland", "movies", etc., unless they are bookmarked and tagged by others using social bookmarking services like del.icio.us[18] or personal aggregators like Gregarius.[19] Technorati, the blog search engine, aims to use these keywords to build a "tagged web". Both tags and hierarchial categorisations of blog posts can be further enriched using the SKOS[20] framework. However, there is often much more to say about a blog post than simply what category it belongs in.

[17] http://www.loudervoice.com/
[18] http://del.icio.us/
[19] http://gregarius.net/
[20] http://en.wikipedia.org/wiki/SKOS

This is where semantic blogging comes in. Traditional blogging is aimed at what can be called the "eyeball Web" – i.e. text, images or video content that is targeted mainly at people. Semantic blogging aims to enrich traditional blogging with metadata about the structure (what relates to what and how) and the content (what is this post about – a person, event, book, etc.). In this way, metadata-enriched blogging can be better understood by computers as well as people.

In structured blogging, microcontent such as microformats[21] is positioned inline in the HTML (and subsequent syndication feeds) and can be rendered via CSS. Structured blogging and semantic blogging do not compete, but rather offer metadata in slightly different ways (using microcontent like microformats and RDF[22] respectively). There are already mechanisms such as GRDDL[23] which can be used to move from one to the other.

The question remains as to why one would choose to enhance their blogs and posts with semantics. Current blogging offers poor query possibilities (except for searching by keyword or seeing all posts labelled with a particular tag). There is little or no reuse of data offered (apart from copying URLs or text from posts). Some linking of posts is possible via direct HTML links or trackbacks, but again, nothing can be said about the nature of those links (are you agreeing with someone, linking to an interesting post, or are you quoting someone whose blog post is directly in contradiction with your own opinions?). Semantic blogging aims to tackle some of these issues, by facilitating better (i.e. more precise) querying when compared with keyword matching, by providing more reuse possibilities, and by creating "richer" links between blog posts. It is not simply a matter of adding semantics for the sake of creating extra metadata, but rather a case of being able to reuse what data a person already has in their desktop or web space and making the resulting metadata available to others. People are already (sometimes unknowingly) collecting and creating large amounts of structured data on their computers, but this data is often tied into specific applications and locked within a user's desktop (e.g. contacts in a person's addressbook, events in a calendaring application, author and title information in documents, audio metadata in MP3 files). Semantic blogging can be used to "lift" or release this data onto the Web.

For example, looking at the picture in Fig. 4 from the semiBlog documentation by Knud Möller, Aidan writes a blog post which he annotates using content from his desktop calendaring and addressbook applications. He publishes this post onto the Web, and John, reading this post, can reuse the embedded metadata in his own desktop applications. In this picture, the semantic blog post is being created by annotating a part of the post text about a person with an address book entry that has extra metadata describing that person. Once a blog has semantic metadata, it can be used to perform

[21] http://microformats.org/

[22] http://www.w3.org/RDF/

[23] http://www.w3.org/2004/01/rdxh/spec

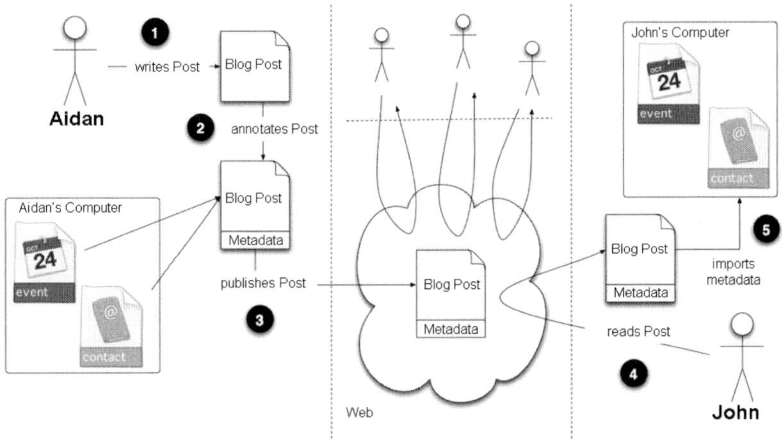

Fig. 4. Lifting semantic data from the desktop to the Web and back again

queries such as "which blog posts talk about papers by Stefan Decker?"; it can be used for browsing not only across blogs but also other kinds of discussion methods; or it can be used by blog readers for importing metadata into desktop applications (or using the Web as a clipboard). As well as semiBlog, other semantic blogging systems have been developed by HP[24], the National Institute of Informatics, Japan[25] and MIT.[26]

4 Using Wikis for Creating Structured Documents

It is not just blog posts that are being enhanced by structured metadata and semantics – this is happening in many other Web 2.0 application areas. Wikis such as the Wikipedia have contained structured metadata in the form of templates for some time now, and at least 20 "semantic wikis" have also appeared to address a growing need for more structure in wikis.

Many people are familiar with the Wikipedia[27], but less know exactly what a wiki is. In short, a wiki is an "information space" (web or desktop application) that allows users to easily add and edit content, and is especially suited for collaborative writing. Wikis rely on cooperation, on checks and balances of the wiki site members, and a belief in the sharing of ideas. The name comes from a Hawaiian phrase, "wiki wiki", which means to hasten or go quickly. Ward Cunningham created the first wiki in 1995, and wikis are now being used for free dictionaries, book repositories, event organisation, and

[24] http://www.hpl.hp.com/personal/Steve_Cayzer/semblog.htm
[25] http://www.semblog.org/
[26] http://theory.csail.mit.edu/dquan/iswc2004-blog.ppt
[27] http://www.wikipedia.org/

software development. They have become increasingly used in enterprise environments for collaborative purposes: research projects, papers and proposals, coordinating meetings, etc. Ross Mayfield's SocialText[28] produced the first commercial open source wiki solution, and many companies now use wikis as one of their main intranet collaboration tools. There are a plethora (hundreds) of wiki software systems now available, ranging from MediaWiki[29], the software used on the Wikimedia family of sites, and Eugene Eric Kim's PurpleWiki[30], where fine grained elements on a wiki page are referenced by purple numbers, to Alex Schröder's OddMuse[31], a single Perl script wiki install, and WikidPad[32], a desktop-based wiki for managing personal information. Many are open source, free, and will often run on multiple operating systems. The differences between wikis are usually quite small but can include the development language used (Java, PHP, Python, Perl, Ruby, etc.), the database required (MySQL, flat files, etc.), whether attachment file uploading is allowed or not, spam prevention mechanisms, page access controls, RSS feeds, etc.

The Wikipedia project consists of 250 different wikis, corresponding to a variety of languages. The English language one is currently the biggest, with over 2 million pages, but there are wikis in languages ranging from Irish to Arabic to Chinese (and even in constructed languages such as Esperanto). A typical wiki page will have two buttons of interest: "Edit" and "History". Normally, anyone can edit an existing wiki article, and if the article does not exist on a particular topic, anyone can create it. If someone messes up an article (either deliberately or erroneously), there is a revision history so that the contents can be reverted or fixed. There is a certain amount of ego-related motivation in contributing to a wiki – people like to show that they know things, to fix mistakes and fill in gaps in underdeveloped articles (stubs), and to have a permanent record of what they have contributed via their registered account. By providing a template structure to input facts about certain things (towns, people, etc.), wikis also facilitate this user drive to populate wikis with information.

For some time on the Wikipedia and in other wikis, templates have been used to provide a consistent look to the content placed within article texts. They can also be used to provide a structure for entering data, so that it is easy to extract metadata about the topic of an article (e.g. from a template field called "population" in an article about London). Semantic wikis[33] bring this to the next level by allowing users to create semantic annotations anywhere within a wiki article text for the purposes of structured access and finer-grained searches, inline querying, and external information reuse. There are

---

28 http://www.socialtext.com/
29 http://www.mediawiki.org
30 http://www.blueoxen.org/tools/purplewiki/
31 http://www.oddmuse.org/
32 http://www.jhorman.org/wikidPad/
33 http://en.wikipedia.org/wiki/Semantic_wiki

already about 20 semantic wikis in existence, and one of the largest ones is Semantic MediaWiki[34], based on the popular MediaWiki system.

Let us take an example of providing structured access to information in wikis. There is a Wikipedia page about JK Rowling that has a link to "Harry Potter and the Philosopher's Stone" (and to other books that she has written), to Edinburgh because she lives there, and to Scholastic Press, her publisher. In a traditional wiki, you cannot perform fine-grained searches on the Wikipedia dataset such as "show me all the books written by JK Rowling", or "show me all authors that live in the UK", or "what authors are signed to Scholastic", because the type of links (i.e. the relationship type) between wiki pages are not defined. In Semantic MediaWiki, you can do this by linking with [[author of::Harry Potter and the Philosopher's Stone]] rather than just the name of the novel. There may also be some attribute such as [[birthdate:=1965-07-31]] which is defined in the JK Rowling article. Such attributes could be used for answering questions like "show me authors over 40" or for sorting articles.

Some semantic wikis also provide what is called inline querying. A question such as "?page dc:creator EyalOren" (or find me all pages where the creator is Eyal Oren) is processed as a query when the page is viewed and the results are shown in the wiki page itself. Also, when defining some relationships and attributes for a particular article (e.g. "foaf:gender Male"), other articles with matching properties can be displayed along with the article. Finally, just as in the semantic blogging scenario, wikis can enable the Web to be used as a clipboard, by allowing readers to drag structured information from wiki pages into other applications for example, geographic allowing readers to drag structured information from wiki pages into other applications (for example, geographic data about locations on a wiki page could be used to annotate information on an event or a person in your calendar application or address book software, respectively).

5 Social Networking Services and Their Features

Social networking services (SNS) allow a user to create and maintain an online network of close friends or business associates for social and professional reasons. There has been an explosion in the number of online social networking services in the past five years, so much so that the terms YASN and YASNS (Yet Another Social Network[ing Service]) have become commonplace. But these sites do not usually work together and therefore require you to re-enter your profile and redefine your connections when you register for each new site.

The "friend-of-a-friend effect" often occurs when someone tells someone something and they then tell you – linked to the theory that anybody is connected to everybody else (on average) by no more than six degrees of separation. This number of six degrees came from a sociologist called Stanley

[34] http://semantic-mediawiki.org/

Milgram who conducted an experiment in the late 1960s. Random people from Nebraska and Kansas were told to send a letter (via intermediaries) to a stock broker in Boston. However, they could only give the letter to someone that they knew on a first-name basis. Amongst the letters that found their target (around 20%), the average number of links was around 5.5 (rounded up to 6). Some argue that this figure should be much lower due to the low percentage of letters that actually arrived. Some other related ideas include the Erdös number (the number of links required to connect scholars to mathematician Paul Erds[35], a prolific writer who co-authored over 1,500 papers with more than 500 authors), and the Kevin Bacon game (the goal is to connect any actor to Kevin Bacon[36], by linking actors who have acted in the same movie). The six degrees idea is nicely summed up by this quote from a film called "Six Degrees of Separation" written by John Guare:

> "I read somewhere that everybody on this planet is separated by only six other people. Six degrees of separation between us and everyone else on this planet. The President of the United States, a gondolier in Venice, just fill in the names. [...] It's not just big names – it's anyone. A native in a rain forest, a Tierra del Fuegan, an Eskimo. I am bound – you are bound – to everyone on this planet by a trail of six people."

It is often found that even though one route is followed to get in contact with a particular person, after talking to them there is another obvious connection that was not previously known about. This is part of the small-world network[37] theory, which says that most nodes in a network exhibiting small-world characteristics (such as a social network) can be reached from every other node by a small number of hops or steps.

There are now many websites acting as a social networking service. The idea behind such services is to make people's real-world relationships explicitly defined online – whether they be close friends, professional colleagues or just people with common interests. Most SNSs allow one to surf from a list of friends to find friends-of-friends, or friends-of-friends-of-friends for various purposes. SNSs have become the new digital public places of Web 2.0 – there has been a huge takeup of sites such as MySpace, LinkedIn, Bebo and Facebook. Most SNSs allow content generation and sharing, and there is also a gradual transformation of SNSs into public e-markets – either through product promotions or targeted ads.

Social networking services usually offer the same basic functionalities: network of friends listings (showing a person's "inner circle"), person surfing, private messaging, discussion forums or communities, events management, blogging, commenting (sometimes as endorsements on people's profiles), and

[35] http://www.oakland.edu/enp/

[36] http://oracleofbacon.org/

[37] http://en.wikipedia.org/wiki/Small-world_network

media uploading. Some motivations for SNSs include building friendships and relationships, arranging offline meetings, curiosity about others, arranging business opportunities, or job hunting. People may want to meet with local professionals, create a network for parents, network for social (dating) purposes, get in touch with a venture capitalist, or find out if they can link to any famous people via their friends.

Before 2002, most people networked using services such as OneList, ICQ or eVite. The first big SNS in 2002 was Friendster; in 2003, LinkedIn (a SNS for professionals) and MySpace (target audience is 20–30 years) appeared; then in 2004, orkut (Google's SNS) and Facebook (by a college student for college students) were founded; these were followed by Bebo (target audience is 10–20 years) in 2005. There has also been a lot of venture capital investment in and sales of social networking services as well. An interesting statistic related to this is that as of November 2006, the ten most popular domains accounted for about 40% of all page views on the Web, and nearly half of these page views were from SNSs (MySpace and Facebook).

Even in a small-sized SNS, there can be a lot of links available for analysis, and this data is usually meaningless when viewed as a whole, so one needs to apply some social network analysis (SNA) techniques. Apart from textbooks[38], there are many academic resources for social networks[39] and SNA.[40] For example, the tool Pajek[41] can be used to drill down into various networks. A common method is to reduce the amount of relevant social network data by clustering. One could choose to cluster people by common friends, by shared interests, by geography, by tags, etc. In social network analysis, people are modelled as nodes or "actors". Relationships (such as acquaintainceship, co-authorship, friendship, etc.) between actors are represented by lines or edges. This model allows analysis using existing tools from mathematical graph theory and mapping, with target domains such as movie actors, scientists and mathematicians (as already mentioned), sexual interaction, phone call patterns or terrorist activity. There are some nice tools for visualing these models, such as Vizster[42] by Heer and Boyd, based on the Prefuse[43] open-source toolkit. Others have combined SNA with Semantic Web technologies[44] to determine social behaviour patterns, and MIT Media Lab are conducting mobile SNA research via their "reality mining"[45] project. On the security front, the NSA are using social network analysis technologies

[38] http://www.amazon.com/Social-Network-Analysis-Applications-Structural/dp/0521387078

[39] http://www.socialnetworks.org/

[40] http://lrs.ed.uiuc.edu/tseportal/analysis/social-network-analysis/

[41] http://vlado.fmf.unilj.si/pub/networks/pajek/

[42] http://jheer.org/vizster/

[43] http://prefuse.org/

[44] http://www.blogninja.com/galway-iswc2005.ppt

[45] http://reality.media.mit.edu/

for homeland security, and there have been reports from the New Scientist of "automated intelligence profiling"[46] from sites like MySpace.

So what does the future hold for SNS sites? It has been theorised[47] that many sites only work where there is some "object-centered sociality" in networks, i.e. users are connected via a common object, e.g. their job,university, hobby, etc. In this way, it is probable that people's SNS methods will move closer towards simulating their real-life social interaction, so that people will meet others through something they have in common, not by randomly approaching each other. In the future, we will no doubt see better interaction methods with friends a'la Second Life.

Another future requirement is for distributed social networks and reusable profiles. There have been a lot of complaints about the walled gardens that are social network sites. Some of the most popular SNSs would not exist without the walled garden approach, but some flexibility would be useful. Users may have many identities on different social networks, where each identity was created from scratch. A reusable profile would allow a user to import their existing identity and connections (from their own homepage or from another site they are registered on), thereby forming a single global identity with different views (e.g. there is Vid項entity[48] which works with OpenID[49] and FOAF[50]).

Acknowledgement

This material is based upon works supported by Science Foundation Ireland Grant No. SFI/02/CE1/I131.

[46] http://www.newscientist.com/article/mg19025556.200?DCMP=NLC-nletter&nsref=samplemg19025556.200
[47] http://www.zengestrom.com/blog/2005/04/why_some_social.html
[48] http://videntity.org/
[49] http://openid.net/
[50] http://foaf-project.org/

Part II

A Vision of Semantic Digital Libraries

Goals of Semantic Digital Libraries

Sebastian Ryszard Kruk and Bill McDaniel

Digital libraries have become commodity in the current world of Internet. More and more information is produced, and more and more non-digital information is being rendered available. The new, more user friendly, community-oriented technologies used throughout the Internet are *raising the bar* of expectations. Digital libraries cannot stand still with their technologies; if not for the sake of handling rapidly growing amount and diversity of information, they must provide for better user experience matching and overgrowing standards set by the industry.

The next generation of digital libraries combine technological solutions, such as P2P, SOA, or Grid, with recent research on semantics and social networks. These solutions are put into practice to answer a variety of requirements imposed on digital libraries.

1 What is a Semantic Digital Library?

Just saying that it is the next generation digital library will not be enough. Following the popular notion of making everything "*2.0*", we can find more and more references to *Library 2.0*. Agosti et al [7] defines seven goals for the Library 2.0; these are:

1. Anyone can use it.
2. All knowledge is accessible there.
3. We can access it anytime.
4. We can access it anywhere.
5. It features a user-friendly, multimodal user interface.
6. It provides efficient and effective ways to access it.
7. It makes use of multiple and interconnected devices.

Blyberg [24] defines five main components of the Library 2.0: open source software, social software, single-sign on, open standards, integrated OPAC.[1] The common key elements in both definitions are openness and user friendliness of *Library 2.0.*

Information access in digital libraries is one of the key functions. Semantic technologies can offer more efficient solutions for accessing content and metadata. Semantic annotations deliver powerful information to build personalized query-answering, similarity-based search, and collaborative filtering systems [153].

Therefore we argue for more involvement of semantic technologies, in order to deliver even more user friendly solutions; semantic and social services can, at least partially, act on behalf of (human) librarians, which we know from our university libraries. We have identified a couple of digital library projects that exploit semantic descriptions and services; to differentiate these solutions from the *Library 2.0*, we call them *Semantic Digital Libraries.*

Digital libraries can be seen from different views (e.g., historical or technological) and perspectives (e.g., library, information science, information retrieval, or human-computer interaction). Due to their interdisciplinary nature (hypertext, multimedia, databases, HCI) they are seen more as a combination of documents, technology, and work [140], than just a collections of resources or enabling technologies for these collections.

Therefore formal models and theories are important to clearly define and understand characteristics, structure, and behavior of digital libraries. This chapter focuses an the architecture model for the semantic digital library. We will also identify some key concepts related to the object model handled in the semantic digital libraries.

The key challenges for the semantic digital libraries are:

- Integrate information based on different metadata sources, e.g., bibliographic descriptions, user profiles, bookmarks, controlled vocabulary; this can be achieved with high quality semantics, i.e., highly and meaningfully connected information.
- Provide interoperability with other systems (not only digital libraries) on either metadata or communication level, or both; using RDF as common denominator between digital libraries and other services can support both metadata and communication interoperability.
- Deliver more robust, user friendly and adaptable search and browsing interfaces empowered by semantics (legacy, formal, and social annotations), community interactions and user profiles, and reasoning and recommendations engines.

Following sections will present in more details how this objectives can be achieved.

[1] OPAC: Online Public Access Catalog

2 Object Model

One of the major requirements imposed on next generation digital libraries is to support a more extensible object model [136]. The object model should make use of connectivity and computability of digital assets [54]. It should support complex types of information objects, e.g., streaming resources (multimedia, sensor data); it should handle diversity of information objects, e.g., spacio-temporal [13, 232], and multiple representations of information objects. The model has to support relationships between objects; these include both structured relationships for constructing complex objects, extensible administrative relationships [136], and references between resources, e.g., citations [69]. It should allow for managing both static and dynamic objects , e.g., flexible, created ad-hoc collections or different representations of the binary data computed on demand [35]. Semantic digital library should allow for reuse of objects [134]; these can be supported with aforementioned references (instead of inclusions) and dynamic resources. The library should also support interactions with the information objects, such as self-actualization [134], e.g., for sensor data or dynamic collections, and augmenting original resources [14], e.g., with community annotations.

3 Indispensable Services

Semantic digital libraries have to implement a number of indispensable services:

3.1 Search, Browsing, and Recommendation Services

The key objective of the semantic digital library is to deliver information discovery that out-stands solutions known from current digital libraries. Users should be able to exploit interconnected information about resources while browsing, filtering, or finding similar information objects [123]. Query refinement engines should tailor their results to solutions matching users profiles; the engines should exploit complex semantic relations between results. Finally, semantic digital library should offer various recommendation services, e.g., based on the context and resource(s) annotations or based on collaborative filtering [117]. The search engine should allow for exploiting information about different media types, complex objects, streaming and spacio-temporal resources [7]. In the case of resources with complex annotations it is important to support content-based search together with similarity search algorithms [166]. In the case of heterogeneous, competitive networks of content providers, the semantic digital library should implement query trading algorithms to support the users in their searching [186].

3.2 Services for Augmenting Resources

One of the most distinguishing features of semantic digital libraries are additional annotations augmenting the original information provided during the resource uploading process. It is expected that semantic digital libraries can provide both automated and user-based annotations. The latter should harness the power of social networking, i.e., community annotations, tagging, and ranking. The annotation services should be flexible enough to adapt to various user groups and content being augmented, e.g., time-tagging stream media or annotating regions-of-interest (ROI) in images and geo-spatial resource [8]. User-based annotations are the key technology to actively engage users in the process of sharing knowledge. Semantic digital library services should ensure that users providing annotations benefit from better recommendations and search results.

3.3 Dissemination and Notification Services

Modern digital libraries should help their users to access their metadata in various formats allowing, among the others, constructing mash-ups of services and content. These metadata should be provided as a customizable RSS and ATOM feeds [230], SIOC descriptions [30], RDF graphs [151], and in JSON format [217]. Extensible and customizable notification services, especially across distributed or federated digital libraries, have to be delivered as a part of the information retrieval process; this integration can enhance user experience related to the digital library system [37, 88].

3.4 Security and Policy Assurance Services

Library should adapt to various policy enforcements; it should provide flexible authentication and access control mechanisms [134].

3.5 Services Providing Interoperability

These include both backward and forward compatibility of content, metadata, services, and protocol standards. Literature [39,71,84,111,123,169,185] identifies technical, information, and social levels of interoperability. Interoperability services can be greatly supported by appropriate object model and metadata annotations. Semantic digital library should provide services compatible with both legacy standards, e.g., Dienst [135], Z39.50 [145], and OAI-PMH [87], and modern protocols, e.g., SPARQL [187], or OAI-ORE [144].

3.6 Preservation Services

Digital library should ensure versioning, archiving (backup and recovery) as well as, provenance tracking (especially in the context of open world approach of semantic and social technologies), and keeping track of history of events related to information objects. It has to be ensured that both inter-object relations and augmented information is supported by the preservation services [134].

3.7 Quality Assurance Services

Special attention should be addressed to the quality of metadata-based services; semantic digital library have to ensure efficiency, security and semantics of maintained metadata. The efficiency can be achieved, e.g., by hard-coding parts of the metadata; restricting on actions that can be performed on given metadata can improve security. Semantics of the metadata can be determining through meaning of new concepts [38, 39].

3.8 Integrated Documentation

Semantic digital libraries, and the services they provide, are in many cases too complex to be easily understood by non-technical users [14]. It is a vital requirement from the perspective of the library usability to deliver documentation integrated within the digital library system; an example can be a set of short screencast videos attached directly to certain features of semantic digital library. Semantic digital library can also make use of the interactions within the community of users, and engage in helping one another, e.g., through collaborative filtering or browsing [117, 121].

4 Software Requirements

Semantic digital libraries should support a number of features in order to answer growing demands from both librarians and users and to handle ever growing number and diversity of resources.

It is important that the implementation of the semantic DLMS (digital library management system) is modular and expandable, e.g., supports plugin or service oriented architecture, or both. The system should support a number of customization levels; these should range from easy, out-of-box sets to complete customization, including delivering own services and features [14].

The Semantic DLMS should provide integrated management of all resources, e.g., metadata, content, and services [134]; it should adapt to various set ups, including distributed, heterogeneous, or autonomous [7].

The software should provide an open framework for assuring distributed access, indexing, and management. Some projects [84, 152] stress the importance of minimizing barriers to entry and providing for gradual engagement from content and service providers and consumers. To achieve that, federations of semantic digital libraries should operate without a central repository [7,74, 112]. The distributed repositories should ensure adequate change notification protocols; in case of the support for mobile client applications, semantic DLMS should provide robust transaction models and data replications [31,158].

Services and metadata delivered by Semantic Digital Libraries are no longer for just service-to-client interaction, but can be (and should be) accessible by other services. Also, the libraries should allow for using external services; it might be beneficial for the library to model business processes and support composing, managing, and executing workflows. Support for workflows and external services, including those offered by grid infrastructures, is key when indexing, processing, and managing continuous datastreams, e.g., multimedia or sensors data, or performing other heavy duty tasks [7,58,77,108].

Through the flexibility of their object model, semantic digital libraries can greatly improve building of specific types of digital libraries, such as: e-Science library and virtual digital libraries. The former requires infrastructure to support visualization, simulations, and data mining [74]. The latter can provide support for temporary activities small, distributed, and dynamic groups of users; these activities can range from course, exhibitions, to projects [40]. Lightweight, easy to deploy solutions can serve for examples as personal libraries. These libraries will become a part of, so called, *ephemeral web* [73].

Important aspect of the semantic digital libraries is their approach towards the end-user. The semantic annotations of resources should be used to support personalization. User should be presented with search results, set of services, etc., depending on the current context; the context can be the user profile, his/her interests, communities, content of the data base, current view, or event location of the user. The semantic DLMS infrastructure should support delivering such a personalization services [7,74,77,113,154].

Above all, semantic DLMS has to provide solutions which will ensure high degree of availability, scalability, dependability, and reliability [7,74].

Acknowledgement

This material is based upon works supported by Enterprise Ireland under Grant No. ILP/05/203 and by Science Foundation Ireland Grant No. SFI/02/ CE1/I131.

Architecture of Semantic Digital Libraries

Sebastian Ryszard Kruk, Adam Westerki, and Ewelina Kruk

The main motivation of this chapter was to gather existing requirements and solutions, and to present a generic architectural design of semantic digital libraries. This design is meant to answer a number of requirements, such as interoperability or ability to exchange resources and solutions, and set up the foundations for the best practices in the new domain of semantic digital libraries.

We start by presenting the library from different high-level perspectives, i.e., user (see Sect. 2) and metadata (see Sect. 1) perspective; this overview narrows the scope and puts emphasis on certain aspects related to the system perspective, i.e., the architecture of the actual digital library management system. We conclude by presenting the system architecture from three perspectives: top-down layered architecture (see Sect. 3), vertical architecture of core services (see Sect. 4), and stack of enabling infrastructures (see Sect. 5); based upon the observations and evaluation of the contemporary state of the art presented in the previous sections, these last three subsections will describe an in-depth model of the digital library management system.

From a high level perspective a semantic digital library is the same as the usual digital library [75]. Its purpose is to deliver particular *content* to a specific *user* using a given *IT infrastructure* system (see Fig. 1). We use the same concepts as presented by Fuhr et al. [75] to describe high level concepts of semantic digital libraries; the difference, however, is in the realization, behavior, and relations between particular components.[1]

Contemporary libraries have to face new, more dynamic and more heterogeneous content; they also have to adapt to the requirements of new generations of users, especially the Generation Y (so called Internet Generation). The contemporary user, a person approaching the library, requires more from the library and has more expectations towards it; one of the reasons is that the users do not want to work in isolation, but rather a part of a

[1] Analyses presented in this chapter are based, among others, on the research results of DELOS project [39].

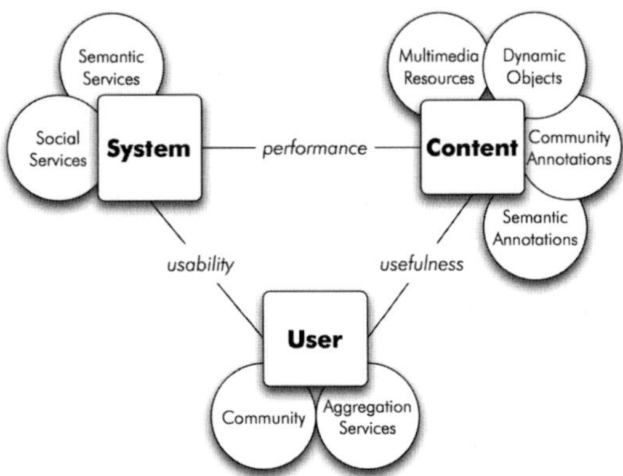

Fig. 1. High level components

community visiting a particular library. To meet these demands, the system (and also the content) component must be extended with services based on the Semantic Web and Social Networking solutions. Since all three components of the high level architecture have developed and became more complex, the relations between these components must be adjusted as well.

In order to maintain the same level of *usability* the system has to offer new means of interactions, including adaptive hypermedia user interfaces, or collaborative filtering and recommendation services. Adding semantic web and social networking technologies should not overwhelm the user or decrease the overall user experience in other ways. New types of resources, abundance of various kinds of metadata, should also remain *useful* to the user. Last, but not least, it is important to ensure the performance of the core digital library management service, which now has to deal with new and more demanding types of content and users.

1 Metadata Perspective

The core difference of semantic digital libraries is the emphases put on the metadata to become more *open*, *unstructured*, and what is most important, highly interlinked. The architecture of the semantic digital library takes into account not only the legacy metadata descriptions of the resources but also annotations provided by the community of users and the information about the users themselves. Services offered by semantic digital libraries should now assist users in efficient discovery techniques in the new, interconnected information space. The solutions range from new recommendation-type solutions to applying research in human computer interaction to filtering and browsing features to involving communities of users in joined experience of knowledge discovery and sharing.

Ontologies are one of key enabling technologies introduced to semantic digital libraries; they are not mere specification of metadata schemata. Ontologies do not put constraints on the metadata but rather enable reasoning over interconnected concepts; they provide the meaning to the information objects and to the relations between them. Hence in semantic digital libraries, the metadata become a network of meaningful, interlinked concepts; these can be used by the digital library management services to leverage the usefulness of the content from the perspective of the end users.

2 User Perspective

The benefits of possessing well annotated library resources with a flexible metadata schema create the opportunity to introduce many innovative library features. Introducing highly interconnected, open, and pretty unstructured metadata to digital libraries posed requirements for new information discovery and management technologies; highly extensible faceted navigation [121], natural language-based interaction [127], or community-driven collaborative filtering [117] are examples of such solutions introduced to support users of the semantic digital libraries.

Nevertheless, it should be noted that when a user approaches a library he/she cannot be flooded with a variety of new features. Regardless of the benefits that the metadata-rich content provides, a semantic digital library needs to fulfill the same basic user requirements as the conventional digital library. Furthermore the contemporary user interaction models, e.g., Web 2.0 or instant messaging, have to be taken into account. Benefits that users can derive from SemDL have to be delivered as enriched services of what users already have in contemporary solutions.

One of possible solutions to accomplish the aforementioned smooth introduction of enhanced solutions is to provide a different view on the library to different types of users and users with different experience (see Fig. 2). The system could recognize users, e.g., based on their social links to certain user groups; depending on the user context, some features will become visible, while other remain hidden, unless explicitly enabled by the user him/herself. User groups can reflect privileges within the library; they can also adhere to certain levels of expectations and needs. For instance, in the university library, researchers might access a complex interface to enable faceted navigation; at the same time the freshmen are provided with the basic search interface, which will be extended over time, e.g., when they become sophomores, or when they choose to.

In the semantic digital library the variety of content views and user perspectives should be reflected in the metadata layer in the library. User profiles can be captured with a special ontology that describes characteristics, groups they belong to, and relationships with other users. Semantic DLMS can select

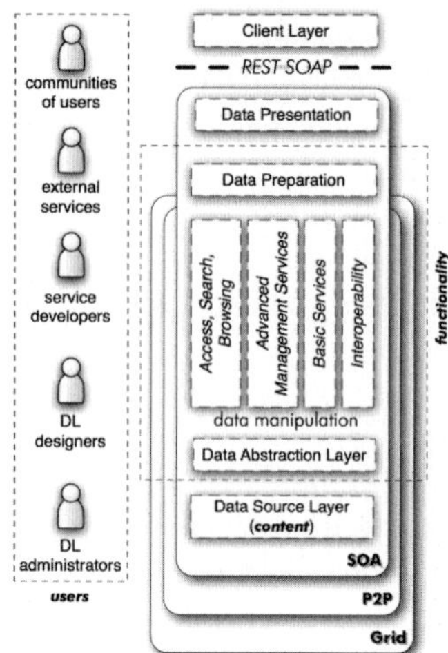

Fig. 2. High level concepts of semantic DL architecture

only the desired part information and process it to deliver a given functionality for a specific user; it became especially feasible with the underlying unstructured metadata and ontologies (see Fig. 2).

Semantic digital libraries should also support interoperability with other systems, not only digital libraries. This requirement allows construction of the on-demand mash-ups with services, such as Google Maps. Therefore one of the potential *user* that are supported by the semantic DLMS are *external services*.

3 Layered Architecture

The previous two sections presented the semantic digital library environment architecture from the perspective of metadata and users. We will now focus on the digital library management system (DLMS) itself. In this section we will describe the multi-tier architecture of semantic digital libraries (see Fig. 3). In the next section we will focus on the business logic services, followed by analysis of the stack of underlying infrastructures.

The semantic digital library architecture has been decomposed in six layers; the lower tiers are more data-oriented, while the upper layers answer the requirements of the end-users and external services. We propose the Service Oriented Architecture to specify, organize, and execute services delivered by each abstraction layer. We will analyze the architecture top-down, starting with the *Client Layer*.

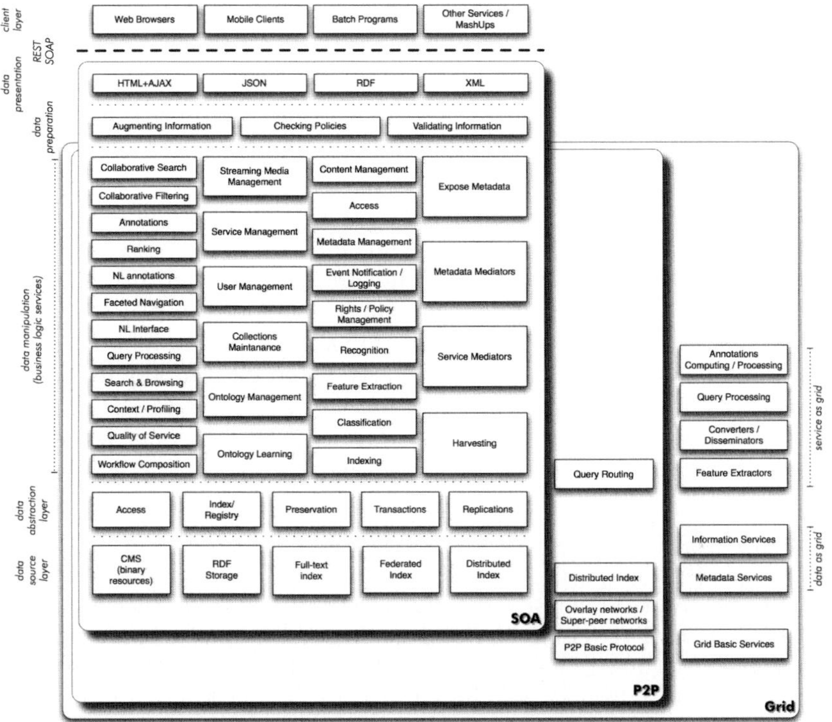

Fig. 3. The architecture of semantic digital libraries

3.1 Client Layer

The client layer represents applications used to access library content. This includes human operated systems with graphical user interface that renders library content, as well as other systems that process library information and use it for their own purpose. The variety of end-user clients and services can be served with different endpoints delivered by the data presentation layer.

3.2 Data Presentation

The data presentation layer is responsible for encapsulating raw data in a format readable by particular clients. Data encoded according to different standards have a different level of expression. Some of the formats require more information and processing while other can be directly sent over from the underlying the RDF storage. This layer shows the benefit of using RDF object model and ontologies to define meaning of concepts and relations. In most cases we do not need to know the particular schema in advance; if necessary the specification required for transformation can be derived from these ontologies. In some cases it is just a matter of "reformatting" the information to other standards like JSON. Hence this layer assures that information modeled using concepts of one ontology can be translated and tailored to fit understanding of other users and client services.

3.3 Data Preparation

We must differentiate services delivered by this layer from those implemented in the layer below. The rationale for defining this layer was that there are a number of services in semantic digital libraries which do not exactly manipulate the data or deliver new presentation of the data. An example of such services can be checking access policies to ensure that the information can be presented to a particular user; this layer is the last outpost for checking it. Another important service implemented in this layer is validating incoming information; it should ensure the consistency of data and, if necessary, augment with additional information from this library or other services.

3.4 Data Manipulation

The data manipulation level is the most developed layer of the semantic digital library model. It retains the core mechanisms responsible for delivering particular library functionality to the end user (see Sec. 4). The layers above process the data to fit the appropriate client needs, while the layers below provide means to perform operations needed to fulfill a given service goal.

3.5 Data Abstraction Layer

The data abstraction layer provides atomic data operations for the data manipulation layer. This is the last level before accessing the actual databases. It is responsible for data consistency, its proper preservation, and access. The presence of the data abstraction layer enables to split data manipulation (the layer above) and low level database operations (layer below). This layer enables clear distinction between business logic implementation and multiple different data repository access. It delivers an abstract object model, which allows to seamlessly access and manage various data models, e.g., RDF, full-text index, distributed index.

3.6 Data Source Layer

The data source layer represents a variety of data repositories used for the semantic digital library. This includes RDF storage for metadata retention and conventional storages for binary resources. This level also delivers full-text index storage, and separate services for managing distributed and local data. We have identified a federated index as a separate type of distributed data source; federations of digital libraries allow to manage the resources on the lower levels of the hierarchy, e.g., department digital libraries, and aggregate them on the higher levels, e.g., faculty and university-wide digital libraries. The data source level is simply responsible for providing data repositories while the layer above adds a consistent and unified way to access them.

4 Vertical Architecture of Business Logic Services

We have identified four classes of data manipulation services (see Fig. 2). These services deliver the business logic operations for the semantic digital libraries. They can be represented as four *columns* (vertical layers), based on the role they play in the everyday interaction of the end-users with the semantic digital library:

- *Information discovery (access, search, browsing) services* are the services the end-users interacts with most often. The services implemented in this column range from enhanced search and browsing, natural language interfaces, faceted navigation to community services, such as annotations, ranking, collaborative filtering and collaborative search. Additional services support context based operations, user profiling, and overall quality of service. End-users can also interact with the DLMS to compose workflows to support their business needs.
- *Advanced management services* are mostly accessible by the librarians and library administrators. They deliver service, user, collection, and streaming media management. Librarians can also manage the set of ontologies deployed in the semantic digital library; they can also invoke ontology learning processes on the corpus of recently added resources.
- *Basic services* support core operations of the semantic digital library, such as content and metadata management, ensuring access and policy management. A set of basic services support librarians in the classification process by indexing, feature extraction and recognition operations.
- *Interoperability services* are furthest from the end-user, but close to the external services. To support interoperability, semantic digital libraries can offer different solutions; they range from simple exposing metadata and SPARQL endpoints to metadata harvesting solutions (e.g., OAI-PMH) to service and metadata mediation services [128, 129].

Depending on the goals of the given semantic digital library, some of the *columns* of services might not be delivered; if the library does not provide interaction with the end users, the *information discovery services* are not necessary. However, a number the *basic services* is indispensable for proper operation of the semantic digital library.

5 Stack of Core Technologies Architecture

Previous sections presented the semantic digital library architecture from the perspective of metadata, users, and services. In this section we will present three enabling technology architectures within which the business logic and other semantic digital library services operate.

5.1 Service Oriented Architecture

We have presented the layered architecture and the business model services with the assumption that they operate in the service-oriented architecture style. The success of the FEDORA SOA approach [136], and research done by Suleman [208], argues for applying service oriented architecture to infrastructure of services provided by semantic digital libraries. We need to ensure, however, that SOA is not understand as only SOAP web services. The research done by Wozniak [227] argues for using REST-ful architecture in the context of semantic web service. In our understanding, especially in the higher level of the architecture it is beneficial to support REST API instead of SOAP web services; the main rationale is the effortlessness of integration (mash-up) with other online services.

5.2 Peer-to-Peer

The Peer-to-peer and Grid layers are network infrastructures that support the digital library from the system efficiency perspective. Both of those technologies can be used for data and processing distribution. However, it is most common to use Peer-to-peer network to create a distributed index for data stored on different machines. Referring to the presented data-oriented library architecture, peer-to-peer networks support the lower levels of library architecture. The rich semantic annotations of resources maintained by the semantic digital libraries can empower the P2P infrastructure with the Semantic Overlay Networks; they can be used to improve peet-to-peer network efficiency based on the semantic information about the resources [6].

5.3 Grid

The Grid networks are mostly employed to cope with heavy-weight data processing tasks. Most of the important services delivered by the semantic digital libraries is implemented in the business logic layer (see Fig. 3). In order to ensure continues improvement of the quality of the aforementioned performance and usability of services, the grid infrastructure can support digital library in execution of the most heavy-weight operations. Some of them, like query processing, must be executed at the runtime. Other services for converting resources, processing annotations, and indexing, can be executed behind the scene; hence these services can fully exploit the grid infrastructure. The indexing operations can be very demanding as they might involve natural language processing, reasoning, and feature extraction of multimedia content. The semantic digital library should not deliver new features at the cost of lowered system efficiency; therefore, grid networks can support processing annotations and Semantic Web languages query processing to maintain overall system performance.

6 Conclusions

Semantic digital libraries are the next step in the evolution of current digital library management systems. They offer services which exploit the notion of semantics and cater to online communities of library users to keep up with growing demand on the quality of provided services.

In this chapter we analyzed research in the architectural solutions for the digital libraries. We highlighted a few existing semantic digital libraries, i.e., FEDORA, BRICKS, Greenstone, and JeromeDL. We synthesized the most important architectural aspects of semantic DLMS and proposed an abstract architecture for the semantic digital libraries. We hope that this research will allow others to pick up the most important concepts which should be implemented in the semantic digital libraries.

Acknowledgement

This material is based upon works supported by Enterprise Ireland under Grant No. ILP/05/203 and by Science Foundation Ireland Grant No. SFI/02/CE1/I131.

Long-time Preservation

Markus Reis

1 Introduction

Our society produces more and more information every day and also tends to be increasingly dependent on it. Although some information is less/more costly to create or less/more relevant to our environment, some of it is definitely worth saving and may be of great value for next generations. Libraries (as well as similar institutions like archives) have the legal responsibility to safeguard long-term access to our scientific, social, and cultural heritage. The need for long-term preservation however is not necessarily limited to libraries and similar institutions, but is also relevant for governments, businesses, and even for individuals, e.g. in order to keep a photo album or important documents accessible for a longer period of time.

Information artifacts can be both of analogue (e.g.: documents/photos/etc. on paper or microfilm) or digital (digital data stored on appropriate media) form with a clear increase of the latter and a decrease of the former. Over the last decades digitization of analogue assets started to play an increasingly important role over analogue preservation (paper, microfilm, etc.), among other reasons due to miniaturization and improved storage. Libraries have thus invested billions[1] of Euros over the last decade(s) in the digitization of their assets.

This chapter would not exist if digitization were be the final answer to all our preservation problems. One general drawback of digital long-term preservation is the fact that humans cannot directly understand bit-streams, whereas cave paintings – although thousands of years old – are still perceivable in the same manner (i.e. with the same sense organs). This can lead to a significantly different perception of the same digital asset in the future if rendered with a future application running on a future operating system with a future output device (that may possibly completely differ from today's

[1] This number is based on the work of Bergman [19] and Lyman and Varian [143].

monitors). Emulation is an approach to address the application and operating system part of this problem and will be explained in detail in the next section – hardware in the sense of I/O devices or computers cannot be 'emulated' and could in principle be preserved in some kind of hardware museum (which may be a viable approach due to the limited number of computer architectures and device categories compared to software applications). Another problem is related to storage media failure. This problem is of secondary importance though, since it can be solved (or at least suitably addressed) by regular backup copies. As a consequence of technical progress a further problem arises from outdated (proprietary) data formats unsupported by future applications. In the next section we will take a closer look at data migration being a solution that addresses this problem category. Apart from the above technical threats, natural disasters, external or internal attacks as well as economic and organizational failures remain of course also undiminished dangers.

Although digitization and creation of 'born digital' information is an integral part of our every day lives, it took at least 10 years to clearly articulate the digital preservation challenge [173]. If it takes comparably long to create first industry-proof methods and tools, our offspring will find a 'black hole' in our cultural record of at least 10–15 years. This assumption is based on Jeff Rothenberg's plausible statement that "Digital documents last forever – or 5 years, whichever comes first" [194].

The scope of this chapter is strictly limited to digital long-term preservation and presents information in a technically-oriented manner from a research background. We particularly want to create awareness of higher-level document-related preservation strategies, rather than on lower-level storage-related preservation strategies (such as data replication and refreshing), because the latter is in comparison to the former already the subject of many research and commercial projects and is far more mature. In the next section we will introduce, describe and evaluate migration and emulation as the most important and dominant strategies in the field of digital long-term preservation. This will be followed by an overview of some selected representative projects, each of them being a cornerstone in every preservation system. We close the chapter with a discussion about the role and importance of semantics – as semantics is a central focus of this book – in digital long-term preservation.

2 Preservation Strategies

In this section we will introduce, describe and evaluate preservation strategies, starting with migration, following with emulation, and concluding with a hybrid approach that combines the best of both strategies.

2.1 Migration

"Migration is the periodic transfer of digital materials from one hardware/software configuration to another or from one generation of computer technology to a subsequent generation. The purpose of migration is to preserve the integrity of digital objects and to retain the ability for clients to retrieve, display, and otherwise use them in the face of constantly changing technology" [173].

In this context, one should distinguish between content migration, which transforms data from a source format in to a target format, and media migration from one digital medium to another (either digital or non-digital) medium.

Content Migration describes the transformation of data from one logical structure (i.e. format) in to another logical structure.

In our daily life we are confronted with a diverse spectrum of different software applications and document formats. Both the number of software applications that are used for rendering and manipulation and the number of data formats is already huge (ten thousands) and continues to grow constantly (especially as a result of versioning). Standardization of formats seems to be an appropriate solution to this problem, but is diametrically opposed to rapid innovation and strategic economic ambitions (e.g. market leadership) of software vendors. Therefore the number of proprietary formats is by far higher than the number of standardized formats. In order to illustrate this diversity we present here some selected formats in the image domain.[2]

Although the above table only lists some selected formats (without distinguishing different versions) in a very specific domain, the number of formats listed is 19. The ratio between proprietary and open specifications is approximately 3:1. Interoperability problems are further significantly boosted by constant versioning of formats. The TIFF format for example has ten different instantiations and/or versions (Tagged Image File Format v1–v6, Tagged Image File Format for Electronic Still Picture Imaging, Tagged Image File Format for Image Technology, Tagged Image File Format for Internet Fax).

Given the rapid changes in document formats, the need for constant migration is unavoidable, if one wishes to secure the ability to manipulate the information contained with future software applications. Possible content migration variants range from upgrades within a product family (e.g. from MS Word for Windows 6.0/95 to MS Word for Windows 2003) to import/export filters to/from (preferably, but not necessarily) standardized formats.

Content migration is likely to be lossy. If the target format's logical model is not a supermodel of the source format's logical model[3], transformation cannot be lossless.

[2] From the Technical Advisory Service for Images in the UK, which can be downloaded from `http://www.tasi.ac.uk/resources/formats.xls`

[3] If source and target format belong to the same product family this would be called backwards compatibility.

Table 1. List of selected image document formats

Format Name	Ext	P/S[a]	Description
Windows Bitmap	BMP	PS	Native raster format for Microsoft Windows and supported on many other platforms. There is also an OS/2 version that is virtually identical
DjVu	DJVU	POV	Proprietary document imaging format developed by AT&T and now owned by LizardTech
FlashPix	FPX	OS	Originally a proprietary Kodak format, but turned in to an open I3A format. Now largely superseded.
Graphics Interchange Format 89a	GIF	PS	There are two versions of GIF – 87a and 89a (introduced in 1987 and 1989). 89a added background transparency and better animation support
JPEG 2000	JP2, JPC, J2K, J2C	OOS	Upcoming standard format using the JPEG 2000 compression. JP2 is the open standard with JPX including proprietary extensions. J2C and J2K contain raw code streams capable of being incorporated in to other file formats
JFIF – JPEG (Joint Photographic Experts Group) File Interchange Format	JPG, JPEG, JIF, JFIF	OOS	De facto standard using the JPEG compression
Portable Network Graphics	PNG	OS	Sponsored by W3C, expected to become the official ISO standard. Intended to replace the GIF format
MrSID	SID	P	Proprietary format for displaying large images
Tagged Image File Format 6.0	TIFF, TIF	PS	De facto standard owned and developed by Aldus and now Adobe
Computer Graphics Metafile	CGM	OOS	Standard format for storing and transferring (mainly) vector images
Enhanced Metafile Format – Windows	EMF	P	Windows metafile
Encapsulated PostScript	EPS	PS	De facto standard page description language developed by Adobe
Adobe Portable Document Format	PDF	PS	De facto standard developed by Adobe, based on Postscript
Macintosh PICT	PCT	P	Native graphic format for Macintosh
Scalable Vector Graphics	SVG	OS	SVG is an open standard for 2-D graphics. It is expressed in human-readable XML, and can contain vector, raster and text.

Table 1. (Continued)

Format Name	Ext	P/S[a]	Description
Macromedia's Flash/Shockwave format	SWF	POV	SWF is a proprietary format, but has open versions. It can contain vector, raster and text.
Windows Metafile format	WMF	P	Microsoft format used (mainly) for the interchange of vector images within Windows applications
Fractal Image Format	STN, FIF	P	Native formats of Genuine Fractals software
Verctor Format for Zooming	VFZ, PFZ	P	Owned and developed by Celartum. VFZ is the general format; PFZ is a password protected VFZ file

[a]P/S = proprietary/standardized; PS = proprietary, de facto standard; OOS = open, official standard; OS = open standard; POV = proprietary, but open versions

Media Migration describes the transfer of data from one storage medium to another storage medium. Similar to content migration, media migration can hardly be avoided.

Bilateral digital media migration (i.e. from a digital storage to a new digital storage) is primarily motivated by the following:

- Information loss due to physical effects like de-magnetization of tapes
- Digital media storage constantly becomes cheaper, smaller, and faster
- New hardware platforms no longer support certain media storage systems (e.g. 5,25" floppy drives simply disappeared)

Due to the limited lifetime of digital media and the fact that migration is lossy, it might even be necessary to transfer digital media (back) in to analogue media. Although paper may be an option as well, microfilm is the media of choice for retro-digitization. Current developments like the ARRILASER[4] even allow institutions to save binary coded information on microfilm.[5]

2.2 Emulation

Emulation is "a means of overcoming technological obsolescence of hardware and software by developing techniques for imitating obsolete systems on future generations of computers."[6]

[4] Was co-developed by ARRI (`http://www.arri.com`) and Fraunhofer IPM (`http://www.ipm.fraunhofer.de/`)

[5] microfilm has an expected lifetime of about 500 years, if stored under optimal conditions.

[6] Taken from Digital Preservation Coalition's Definitions and Concepts, `http://www.dpconline.org/graphics/intro/definitions.html`

Emulation does to software what content migration does to logical data structures – it migrates (i.e. ports) software from one computer generation to the next. An emulation environment may address one or more layers that make up a computer system, ranging from the hardware itself, to the hardware bundled with an operating system (including appropriate device driver software), to a complete rendition environment, including all of the previously named components as well as the necessary software applications. For redundancy purposes, emulating only the hardware (rather than storing a complete rendition environment with every digital asset in the library) has proven to be a best practice. Information about how to render a certain digital asset must be administered in some sort of registry. For example, if you would like to render a MS Word for Windows 6.0/95 document in 30 years, you would query the metadata registry for an application that could render the file, an operating system that could run this application, a set of required device drivers, and an emulator that emulates the necessary host environment on your current hardware/software platform.

Although it has been determined that it is only necessary to emulate the computer hardware, there are still various configuration options to choose. These options range from multilayered emulation to emulation using virtual machines.

Multilayered emulation describes a scenario in which an application is run on a stack of emulators, i.e. emulators running on emulators. From the technical point of redundancy, multilayered emulation seems to be a good approach – it may however be critical with respect to performance, because emulation is very resource intensive and requires a host environment that is significantly more powerful than the emulated environment. For this reason, it may eventually become necessary to replace multilayered emulation by a new single emulator that emulates the original environment directly on the current host system.

Emulation based on a virtual machine is based on the principle that emulators are not directly tied to a host environment but rather run in a virtual machine that itself runs on the host system. With virtual machines the number of 'emulators' in the chain can be drastically reduced in comparison to the multilayered approach. Only one virtual machine for every host system and one emulation software application (that runs on the virtual machine) for each emulated system are required (which means an order of $m+n$), whereas with layered emulation one would need an emulator for every possible combination of host and emulation environment (that is, on the order of $m*n$). Virtual machine based emulation is therefore in general the favoured approach.

2.3 Evaluation and Conclusion

In this section we attempt to evaluate the pros and cons of (content) migration and emulation, and finally recommend a hybrid approach that combines the best of both methodologies.

The most convincing argument for migration is based on the fact that migrated documents can instantly be rendered and manipulated in future computer environments within future application software. There is no need to run and configure emulators or rebuild the old computer system (e.g. from a hardware museum), neither is it necessary to train people how to use the 'old' software. The strongest argument against migration is related to authenticity – transformation leads to unequal successors. Experience however shows that migration is a widely accepted approach for reasons mainly due to its simplicity compared to emulation.

The main argument for emulation is authenticity, because the original digital documents are never changed. Furthermore, emulation works equally well for all document types, whereas migration may be problematic with interactive documents. The integrated effort required to enable emulation is relatively low compared to migration, where documents whose formats are at risk must be transformed regularly – with emulation only the emulation software and the virtual machines need to be created and stored. Emulation is however a very complex method and depends on various components – consider the vast number of different software device drivers or the changing landscape of hardware devices – who knows which input and output devices will be used 100 years from now. It is therefore legitimate to be sceptical about whether emulation is really an appropriate preservation solution or not.

The conclusion is that neither emulation nor migration provide a fully satisfactory solution; still, both have their advantages and they are quite complementary. A hybrid or combined approach thus appears to be a desirable option. A library should both preserve the original document (probably on very durable media like microfilm) together with an appropriate emulation environment for future rendering, and migrate the document for instant access as well. This approach provides the opportunity to authentically render the original document using emulation if necessary and also provides an easy-to-use and instantly accessible migrated working copy. In order to minimize migration and emulation efforts, it will also be of greatest importance to establish standardized formats and to restrict the uncontrolled growth of proprietary formats.

3 Selected Examples of Building Blocks

A fully functional preservation process, as described within the OAIS[7] reference model, requires various building blocks throughout all of its phases, including data ingest, management, storage, administration, and access as well as preservation planning. Following the rather technical focus of this chapter, we will now describe some selected examples for important components in a preservation environment.

[7] The Open Archival Information System (OAIS) is an ISO standard on the long-term preservation of digital documents, ISO/IEC 9075-9:2003.

3.1 PRONOM

PRONOM is a web-enabled technical registry for persons "requiring impartial and definitive information about the file formats, software products and other technical components required to support long-term access to electronic records and other digital objects of cultural, historical or business value."[8] The system is developed by The National Archives[9] in UK since March 2002.

PRONOM currently allows users to search for file formats (by name and extension), software products (by name, vendor name, and file format), and software vendors (by name) (see Fig. 1). Similar initiatives in the same field are the Global Digital Format Registry (GDFR)[10] and VersionTracker.[11]

PRONOM manages comprehensive metadata associated with each registry entry (either file format, software product or vendor). File formats are for example described by name, description, version number, compression types (characterized by name, description, lossiness, rights, etc.), byte order, internal (name, description, byte sequences) and external (file extensions) signatures, rights, orientation (e.g. textual or binary), related file formats, classification (e.g. raster image or text), and so on.

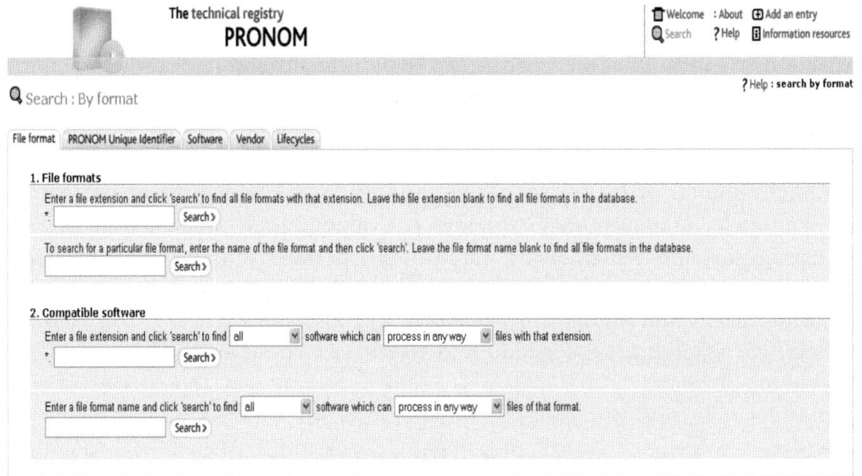

Fig. 1. PRONOM search

---

[8] Taken from `http://www.nationalarchives.gov.uk/pronom/`

[9] The National Archives is the official archive for England, Wales and the central UK government, `http://www.nationalarchives.gov.uk/`

[10] Global Digital Format Registry (GDFR), `http://hul.harvard.edu/formatregistry`

[11] VersionTracker, `http://www.versiontracker.com/`

PRONOM and similar registries provide a valuable basis for many preservation actions and crucial support in the preservation planning process. In the emulation section we discussed setting up an emulation environment for a certain digital document. The person (or software agent) in charge of configuring an appropriate emulation environment could query PRONOM to find appropriate rendering applications specifying the file extension or format name of the digital document and then consequently build up the complete chain of operating system(s) and emulator(s) in order to render the archived document.

3.2 JHOVE

JHOVE[12] stands for JSTOR/Harvard Object Validation Environment and has been under development by JSTOR[13] (Journal Storage – The Scholarly Journal Archive) and Harvard University Library[14] since 2003. JHOVE provides the following three functions:

- Identification of the format of a given digital object
- Validation of the format of a given digital object. JHOVE thereby not only checks the well-formedness (i.e. the syntactic correctness according to the format specification), but also the validity in order to verify whether all additional semantic-level requirements are met.
- Characterization of the format of a given digital object. JHOVE reports format, MIME type, byte size, format version and profiles, file path, last modification date, and optionally, MD5, SHA-1 and CRC32 checksums.

Identification, validation, and characterization are especially important during the ingestion phase of digital document in to an archive in order to (automatically) create metadata about the ingested documents. Tools like JHOVE are also necessary in a migration workflow both to verify that input data conforms to the migration tool's requirements and to verify the well-formedness and validity of the migrated document at the end of the migration process.

JHOVE is implemented in Java and offers both a graphical (Swing-based) and command-line interface. It is extensible through a configurable plug-in architecture, in which modules for different formats can be dynamically loaded at runtime. The basic JHOVE bundle already includes modules for arbitrary byte streams, ASCII and UTF-8 encoded text, GIF, JPEG2000, JPEG, and TIFF images, AIFF and WAVE audio, PDF, HTML, and XML.

---

12 `http://hul.harvard.edu/jhove/`

13 `http://www.jstor.org/`

14 `http://hul.harvard.edu/`

3.3 Universal Virtual Computer

The Universal Virtual Computer (UVC) was developed by Raymond Lorie at IBM in the Netherlands [142]. It uses both emulation and migration concepts in order to preserve documents in the long-term. The UVC consists of four building blocks:

- The UVC itself is a virtual representation of a simplified computer. Detailed instructions on how to (re)build a UVC are documented and must be kept safely in an archive (e.g. on microfilm); given these instructions it is assumed that a UVC can be rebuilt without significant problems at any time in the future.
- The format decoder is a program that runs on a UVC and translates a document in to a logical data view (LDV). A raster image would for example be represented by its pixels in an XML dialect.
- The logical data scheme (LDS) holds metadata that allows for a correct interpretation of the logical data view for a future rendering application. A LDS for raster images would define that a valid LDV must define pixels that themselves specify RGB values.
- The viewer renders a document through its logical data view with the information present in the logical data scheme

The UVC approach distinguishes between the actions to be taken at archiving time (i.e. in the present) and the actions to be taken at restoration time (i.e. in the future). At archiving time a format decoder and a logical data scheme must be created for all file formats of the documents that should be preserved. At restoration time the format decoder is then executed on the UVC and builds a logical data view from the original document (this is actually a migration step). A future viewer can then – by interpreting the additional semantic information specified in the LDS – render the LDV and present the result to the user.

At this time there are UVC programs that translate JPEG and GIF documents in to their corresponding LDV. A project at the Royal Library of the Netherlands attempted to implement a UVC program for PDF, but this could not be realized due to limited resources and the complexity of the PDF format (instead they created JPEGs for every single PDF page and used the existing JPEG UVC program).

4 Role and Importance of Semantics

With the rapidly growing volume of digital documents, the need for automation in digital long-term preservation is constantly increasing. Until now many libraries, archives, museums and similar institutions managed their collections manually, in particular with regard to digital obsolescence of items, through experts with deep knowledge of the stored document types. In a few years this task will no longer be controllable if they are based on processes that require constant human interaction. Experts should instead be notified by a computer system that permanently observes all digital collections and is connected to various types of technical registries (like PRONOM, GDFR, or VersionTracker), as to whether certain documents are in danger of obsolescence.

In the previous section we discussed some interesting components of an environment for digital long-term preservation. Libraries often interlink such components with proprietary technologies, making it difficult to share them with other institutions. A solid and standardized method of integrating these building blocks would guarantee cost-effectiveness and synergies. One should keep in mind however that there is no single best solution to digital preservation and an appropriate technical foundation would have to be extensible and open. Within this section we will introduce the PANIC system, which addresses exactly these issues.

Metadata is the basis of semantic reasoning within a computer system. Library services such as administration or retrieval are heavily dependent on metadata. Therefore a large number of different metadata schemas, both proprietary and standardized, have been developed and used in this domain. In this section we describe METS, as one of the most popular metadata standards used within the library community.

4.1 METS

The "Metadata Encoding and Transmission Standard (METS)[15] is a conceptual framework for describing complex object structures and for linking content with administrative and descriptive metadata [214]". METS is widely used within the library community due to its close relation to the OAIS reference model.[16] METS is rather a metadata container that holds structural, descriptive, and administrative metadata that itself can conform to other metadata schemas (like DC[17], MARC[18], or a proprietary schema). This characteristic is especially important in the library domain, if one considers for example a book digitized as one JPEG image per page, structural metadata must be created in order to keep the images in the correct order according to the pages in the book. A METS document consists of the following sections:

- The METS header contains general document information about the authors, creation date, and so on.

[15] `http://www.loc.gov/standards/mets/`

[16] METS can be used for the description of OAIS submission information packages (during the ingestion phase), archival information packages (during the archival phase), and dissemination information packages (during the retrieval phase).

[17] Dublin Core Metadata Initiative, `http://dublincore.org/`

[18] `http://www.loc.gov/marc/`

- The Descriptive Metadata Section holds or references (from an external location) descriptive metadata for all or selected documents bundled together within the METS description (refer to the book example described above). Metadata in this section could conform to various internal or external metadata schemas (MARC, DC, etc.).
- The Administrative Section documents technical metadata (like compression technique and format type), intellectual property rights metadata, source metadata (i.e. relations to other files), and digital provenance metadata.
- The File Section lists all files that make use of the (composite) digital item; Files may be organized in File Groups.
- The Structural Map defines the logical structure of the (composite) digital item (described by the METS document).
- Structural Links record the existence of hyperlinks between nodes in the hierarchy outlined in the Structural Map, which is particularly useful when archiving websites.
- The Behaviour Section describes executable behaviour of components within the METS item.

4.2 PANIC

The PANIC (Preservation webservices Architecture for Newmedia and Interactive Collections)[19] project is concerned with semi-automated digital preservation based on a Service-oriented Architecture.[20] The project is developed at the Distributed Systems Technology Center in Australia [100], [101].

The motivation for the project was to support librarians in preservation planning and management through:

- Automatic notification services indicating when a preservation action is required (e.g. when digital documents are at risk of obsolescence due to new applications that do not support a certain format any longer)
- Agent-based discovery, recommendation, and invocation of appropriate preservation services
- Choreography (i.e. composition) of preservation services

The main goal of the project is to develop an integrated preservation framework based on Web Services.[21] There is therefore a special focus on machine-interpretability and automation, which was addressed through the use of Semantic Web Services.

[19] Preservation webservice Architecture for Newmedia and Interactive Collections (PANIC), `http://metadata.net/panic/`

[20] `http://en.wikipedia.org/wiki/Service-oriented_architecture`

[21] The W3C defines a Web service as 'a software system designed to support interoperable Machine to Machine interaction over a network'. `http://en.wikipedia.org/wiki/Web_service`

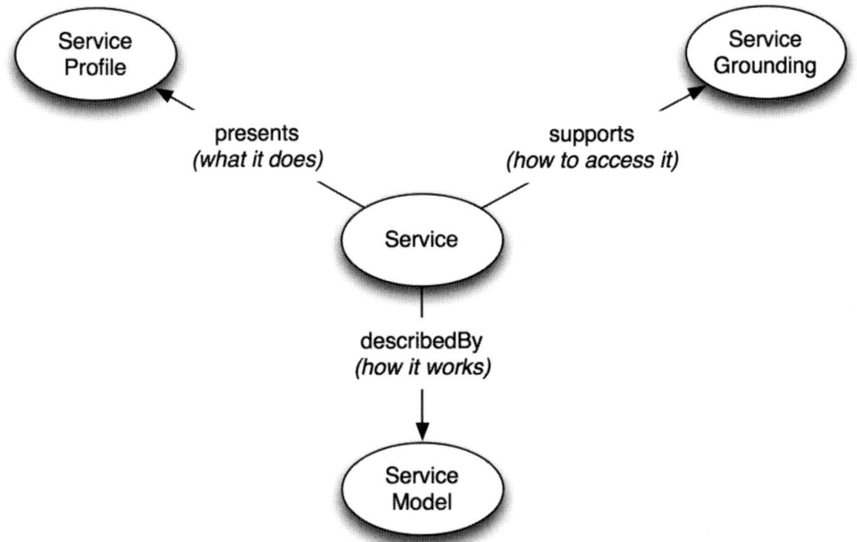

Fig. 2. OWL-S: Top-level view of the Service ontology

The system uses OWL-S [47] ontologies to provide machine-interpretable descriptions of the registered Web Services, allowing software agents to act autonomously without human interaction.

The basic OWL-classes, illustrated in Fig. 2, do not contain any properties relevant for preservation services. Therefore those classes were subclassed (i.e. extended) by preservation-specific OWL-classes. For example: A Migration class with properties for OrginalObjectFormat (i.e. the source/input format for the migration task), OriginalObjectVersion (i.e. the version of the source/input format), TargetObjectFormat (i.e. the target/output format), TargetObjcetVersion (i.e. the version of the target/output format), and Lossiness (i.e. lossy or lossless).

The PANIC system consists of four major components, the first of which is the invocation component. The invocation component includes an obsolescence detector, a service discovery module, a service selection module, a service invocation module, and a requester agent (i.e. a software agent that acts on behalf of the collection manager) and provides a user interface to the collection manager (i.e. a responsible person in the library). The second component is the notification component, which consists of a notification service that closely interacts with various technical registries. The notification service is either invoked by the requester agent or directly by the collection manager. The third component of the PANIC system, the discovery component, includes a discovery agent and a preservation service registry based on OWL-S. The discovery agent (i.e. a software agent) is implemented through an existing service called Semantic Matchmaker,[22] which is able to interpret OWL-S, and is again invoked by the requester agent (or collection manager). Finally, the fourth component, the provider component, registers preservation Web Services through a preservation service provider agent with the OWL-S enabled preservation service registry and executes web services invoked by the service invocation module.

A similar large-scale project called PLANETS (Preserving Long-term Access through NETworked Services),[23] funded by the European Commission, has started in June 2006. It will develop:

- Planning services that empower organisations to define, evaluate, and execute preservation plans
- Methodologies, tools and services for characterization of digital objects
- Innovative solutions for preservation actions (including but not limited to migration and emulation)
- An interoperability framework to seamlessly integrate tools and services in a distributed network
- A testbed to provide a consistent and coherent evidence-base for the objective evaluation of different protocols, tools, service, and complete preservation plans

[22] The OWL-S Matchmaker `http://www.cs.cmu.edu/~softagents/daml_Mmaker/daml-s_matchmaker.htm`

[23] Preserving Long-term Access through NETworked Services (PLANETS), `http://www.planets-project.eu/`

Part III

Ontologies for Semantic Digital Libraries

Bibliographic Ontology

Maciej Dabrowski, Macin Synak, and Sebastian Ryszard Kruk

1 Introduction

The idea of bibliographic ontology comes from actual needs rather than today's common push to use the technology simply because it exists. The librarian community has always been enthusiastic to technical novelties to improve their work and make it more efficient. It is no different today. Managing bibliographic resources such as books was always a serious task. The goals are simple: to allow those who need access to the information quickly and surely. Unfortunately, these simple goals become more and more difficult to accomplish in the environment of dynamically growing number of resources and users.

The problem of information overload has become one of the major concerns in the Internet era. The publishing model of the Internet allows anyone, anywhere and anytime to publish their work and to make it publicly available. It is in both the author's and the reader's interest to make access to such resources as straightforward as possible. What could be accomplished by paper cards in nineteenth century libraries is not enough today. The most common bibliographic resource – a book – may seem simple to manage. We may state the author, title and perhaps a short summary and hope someone will notice it. But what about finding other books from the same field of knowledge? What about checking author's professional background? Or technical article reviews? What about finding aerial photos of San Francisco Bay showing Golden Gate Bridge construction?

That is where ontologies can help. The main point is that well constructed ontology may represent a part of the world. The world which does not end on dry, often not very meaningful text description, which encompassed more than several keywords that can be used today. A semantic description applied to an object can provide information about it in the way people tend to think. We use free associations, group objects by their similarities, allow many types of contexts. We differentiate importance of factors according to the situation. An aerial photo will mean something different to a tourist than to a military.

Building the bibliographic ontology which will stay true to already existing standards and community habits while giving superior capabilities of semantic technology is the first step. In future, it will bring real value to digital libraries and change the way we search, access and use resources today.

MarcOnt ontology, the product of MarcOnt Initiative [130], is an answer to the need for a true bibliographic ontology. In this chapter, MarcOnt's idea, structure and place will be described.

2 Bibliographic Description Formats

2.1 What is a Bibliographic Description Format?

A bibliographic description format is a formal definition of syntax, meaning and rules of describing resources collected by library or other similar entity. Bibliographic description formats are descendants of sets of rules for describing library resources used back in the nineteenth century and are still used today. Rules could describe basic characteristics of librarian cards, "book ID's", from size of the card to the layout of fields on it and their contents. Simple stating that a card should contain book's title, its author's name and year of publishing is actually defining a primitive bibliographic description format.

Formats currently in use are of course much more sophisticated and allow to store such trivia about books like the fact that some particular book has an annotation made with copy pencil on the third page stating: "property of Jane Doe".

The formats that will be described have spawned from the practice of using cataloguing cards in libraries conforming to a certain standard. Some are direct descendants, some only share the idea and are recent development of the computer and Internet era.

2.2 MARC 21 and MARC-XML

History

Machine Readable Cataloging (MARC) is the idea of developing a common system of describing resources for libraries. It originates from works of Library of Congress back in the 1960s that devised the LC MARC format for its own use while it began to use computers. Back then, institutions who could afford to put large amounts of money in their libraries' budgets, such as universities, developed their own library cataloguing systems. Entities with smaller budgets often could not afford to build their own systems. In fact, practice of buying ready cataloguing data (in form of sets of catalogue cards) instead of acquiring it on your own was popular long before the computer era. Such services were available from Library of Congress for almost a century.

MARC record became an electronic counterpart of paper catalogue card which could be created in Library of Congress and sold to libraries which did not have to spend their resources for creating almost identical set of information which was already offered. Even if a library did not have its own computer system compatible with MARC, it could purchase computer printed catalogue cards which were filled accordingly to appropriate bibliographic records in Library of Congress MARC files.

Later, the possibility of acquiring electronic versions of MARC records over phone lines became tempting. Existing bibliographic organizations such as OCLC,[1] WLN,[2] RLIN[3] or A-G Canada[4] along with universities and colleges adapted (using vast amounts of money) their systems to use MARC. From this moment it became possible to get MARC records directly from the entity which created them for an on-going fee. Records could be used accordingly to library needs, such as printing catalogue cards using an attached printer and blank cards (previously ordered). And creating of MARC records became distributed.

MARC 21 is an evolution from original LC MARC, introduced in 1987 by the Library of Congress. Subsequent editions were published in 1990, 1994 and 2000. Currently, there are two groups responsible for reviewing and revising MARC 21 format: MARBI (Machine-Readable Bibliographic Information) Committee and MARC Advisory Committee. Every year, new MARC 21 edition is officially published on the Internet to accommodate changes in the librarian environment.

MARC21 Basics

There are five MARC 21 Concise Formats used for describing relevant data:

- Bibliographic
- Authority
- Holdings
- Classification
- Community

One should also mention a simplified version of MARC 21 – MARC 21 LITE – used for Bibliographic data. Although, it is in fact the *MARC 21 Concise Format for Bibliographic Data* that is being used to describe resources in libraries. Current edition was introduced in 2004. In the bibliographic format, the *MARC record* consists of *leader*, containing general record information (such as record's length) and a number of *fields*, containing data. Every field

[1] Online Computer Library Center, `http://www.oclc.org/`

[2] Western Library Network, merged with OCLC in 1999, `http://www.oclc.org/western/`

[3] Research Libraries Information Network, managed by Research Libraries Group (RLG), `http://www.rlg.org/`

[4] A-G Canada Ltd., `http://www.ag-canada.com/`

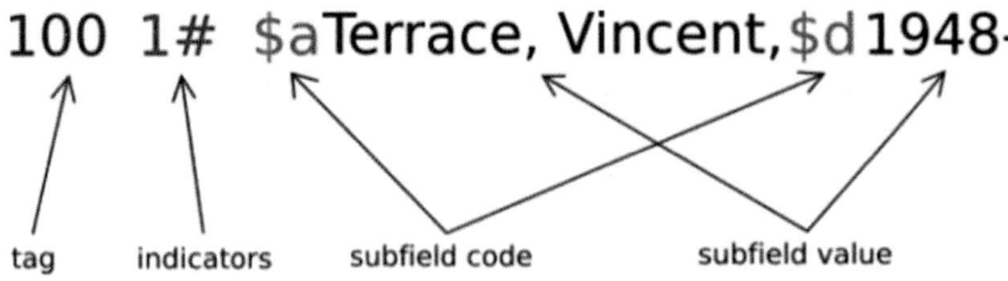

Fig. 1. Example of MARC 21 datafield

is marked by a *tag* which is a number from 001 to 999 (not all numbers are used). Fields with tags 001 to 008 are called *controlfields* while the rest are *datafields*. Furthermore, fields with tag 010 and greater can also be defined with more detail using at most two *indicators*, which are numbers from 0 to 9. Every datafield has *subfields*. Subfields are used to put several related piece of data within one datafield. Subfields are separated with *delimiters* (in MARC 21 a dollar sign: $ is used as a delimiter) and marked with *subfield codes* (a lower-case letter or occasionally a number) (see Fig. 1).

Content of fields with tags 0XX-8XX is classified under 'Authority control', which means that it is defined by the MARC21 standard. Fields with tags 9XX may contain user information (e.g. characteristic to used system, internal library information, local bar codes, etc.) Tags are divided by hundreds, and their content can be shortly described with a follows:

- 0XX Control information, numbers, codes
- 1XX Main entry
- 2XX Titles, edition, imprint (in general, the title, statement of responsibility, edition, and publication information)
- 3XX Physical description, etc.
- 4XX Series statements (as shown in the book)
- 5XX Notes
- 6XX Subject added entries
- 7XX Added entries other than subject or series
- 8XX Series added entries (other authoritative forms)

MARC XML is nothing more than representation of MARC 21 fields and data they contain using the XML syntax (see Fig. 2). Converting between these two format is lossless. According to MARC XML architecture specification, MARC XML should be used for conversions between native binary MARC 21 format and other formats rather than actual format for storing data. For example, it is convenient to parse binary MARC 21 to MARC XML

```
<?xml version="1.0" encoding="UTF-8"?>
<marc:collection xmlns:marc="http://www.loc.gov/MARC21/slim"
   xmlns:marcrdf="http://www.marcont.org/marcrdf#"
   xmlns:jeromedl="http://www.jeromedl.org/"
   xmlns:rdfs="http://www.w3.org/2000/01/rdf-schema#"
   xmlns:rdf="http://www.w3.org/1999/02/22-rdf-syntax-ns#">

<marc:record jeromedl:id="JID24237457333">
   <marc:leader>01450cas 922004331i 4500</marc:leader>
   <marc:controlfield tag="1">
      bb2000159979
   </marc:controlfield>
   <marc:controlfield tag="5">
      20041214021900.0
   </marc:controlfield>
   <marc:controlfield tag="8">
      001019c19329999gw qr|p| ||||0 | 0ger |
   </marc:controlfield>
   <marc:datafield tag="22" ind1=" " ind2=" ">
      <marc:subfield code="a">0044-2992</marc:subfield>
   </marc:datafield>
   <marc:datafield tag="39" ind1=" " ind2="9">
   <marc:subfield code="a">200412140219</marc:subfield>
   <marc:subfield code="b">VLOAD</marc:subfield>
   <marc:subfield code="c">200303101205</marc:subfield>
   <marc:subfield code="d">kopumk</marc:subfield>
...
```

Fig. 2. Example of MARC21 data in XML

and then convert MARC XML entries to HTML for viewing using simple XSL transformation.

MARC 21 and Semantics

There are a number of works describing the problem of semantics and carrying semantic information [5, 215]. This paragraphs shortly presents the problem of lack of semantic information in MARC.

Among other, MARC 21 allows us to describe two specific type of resources: *Language Materials* (which can be roughly described as books, journals, magazines, newspapers, etc.) and *Manuscript Language Materials* (such as valuable, old books, written by hand).

A resource which represents "Language Materials" is identified in MARC 21 by the letter 'a' in field number 06 in leader of MARC 21 record. For "Manuscript Language Materials", the appropriate marking requires the letter 't'. The problem is that there is absolutely no connection between a "Language Material" and "Manuscript Language Material". For people who are not experts in this domain, proper understanding of these terms becomes quite a task. That is also the case when a machine is used to process the data. MARC 21 does not allow us to describe that "Language Materials" and "Manuscript Language Materials" are both suitable to read (have some common characteristics) or that "Manuscript Language Materials" are in fact "Language Materials", too, but have some specific characteristics that make them special. If we wanted to write a search engine which would include manuscripts in searching when there is a lack of ordinary books on the subject, we would have to specify such a connection. An ontology allows to make it automatically.

2.3 Dublin Core

The Dublin Core Metadata Initiative [56] (DCMI) is responsible for The Dublin Core Metadata Element Set, also known as Dublin Core. DC was devised as a standardized way of describing resources (objects) in the Web by adding metadata. Currently, Dublin Core consists of set of 15 main elements (alphabetically):

- *Contributor* – describes entity responsible for contributing contents of the resource
- *Coverage* – describes geographical, temporal or jurisdictional coverage of the content
- *Creator* – indicates who (or what) is responsible for making the content of the resource
- *Date* – indicates some date associated with the resource (i.e. creation date)
- *Description* – may contain abstract, table of contents, short textual description or even point to some other location containing resource's description
- *Format* – some information about representation of the object (like digital document type, physical characteristics, etc.)
- *Identifier* – some ID of the resource (like URI or ISBN)
- *Language* – language of resource's contents
- *Publisher* – describes entity responsible for publishing the resource
- *Relation* – a reference to related resource
- *Rights* – anything related to Rights Management
- *Source* – reference to the source the resource derives from in whole or partially
- *subject* – may contain keywords or other means for identifying subject of the resource
- *Title* – a given title to the resource
- *Type* – describes the genre or nature of the resource

Every resource in the Web, such as file or web page can be described using DC metadata. Dublin Core is very elastic, it does not specify what a certain

```
<dc:creator>John Smith</dc:creator>
```

Fig. 3. Example of dc:creator property as a String

```
<dc:creator rdf:Resource="http://company.com/people#SmithJ"/>
```

Fig. 4. Example of a dc:creator property as a reference

element should contain. DC does not restrict the value of its properties. For example, if the creator element is to be used, should its value contain actual name (see Fig. 3) or an identifier?

This representation is probably the most straightforward, but on the other hand "John Smith" is just a literal. Is the information sufficient? Which John Smith do we have in mind using the label? Therefore it is suggested that instead of using literals in creator element, reference to the object describing a person whose name is "JohnSmith" should be used (see Fig. 4).

Such questions could be applied to many elements in Dublin Core Element Set. DCMI does not restrict what can be encapsulated with a given tag, but suggests using closed vocabularies for some elements The main drawback is that while processing metadata in Dublin Core format, one may encounter some non-standard conventions of expressing information. It can be difficult to deal with. Dublin Core does not restrict users to any particular syntax or representation of DC elements. There are, however, some guidelines for implementing DC in XML or RDF/XML (see Fig. 5).

2.4 BibTeX

BibTeX [184] was designed in 1985 by Oren Patashnik and Leslie Lamport for the LaTeX [137] document preparation system. The BibTeX file format and program can be used to support creating bibliographies in LaTeX documents. Almost any publication, especially of technical nature, contains a bibliography or references. Most of them are put together using some sort of a LaTeX system. This makes BibTeX probably the most common bibliographic format in the Internet. BibTeX records are (like LaTeX files) text-based and expandable (unknown fields are simply ignored). Once created, BibTeX file can be reused in any LaTeX publication referring to resource described in the BibTeX record. In a digital library which contains different technical publications, publishing BibTeX records along with them can be very useful for research community.

Every BibTeX file contains a number of entries. An entry describes single publication, which can be a standalone entity (like a book) or a part of larger

```
<?xml version="1.0"?>
<rdf:RDF
   xmlns:rdf="http://www.w3.org/1999/02/22-rdf-syntax-ns#"
   xmlns:dc="http://purl.org/dc/elements/1.1/">
   <rdf:Description rdf:about="http://www.marcont.org/dc/">
      <dc:title>MarcOnt Initiative</dc:title>
      <dc:description>
         MarcOnt Initiative's goal is to create the ontology
         for librarian purposes and appropriate tools for
         supporting conversion between other ontologies,
         ontology development process, etc.
      </dc:description>
      <dc:creator>Marcin Synak</dc:creator>
      <dc:date>2004-07-31</dc:date>
   </rdf:Description>
</rdf:RDF>
```

Fig. 5. Example of Dublin Core data in XML

container (like a chapter of a book). BibTeX defines a set of standard entries (alphabetically):

- *Article* – article from a journal or magazine
- *Book* – a book
- *Booklet* – a kind of book which does not have named publisher
- *Conference* – same as "inproceedings"
- *Inbook* – part of book, a chapter, section, range of pages, etc.
- *Incollection* – part of book with its own title
- *Inproceedings* – an article in conference proceedings
- *Manual* – technical documentation
- *Mastersthesis* – a Master's thesis document
- *Misc* – miscellaneous (when nothing else fits)
- *Phd thesis* – a PhD thesis document
- *Proceedings* – the proceedings of a conference
- *Techreport* – a report published by a school or other institution
- *Unpublished* – a document never published (but with a title and author)

There are some other entries (e.g. patent), but they are not so commonly used as the ones mentioned above. BibTeX was specifically designed for research and education community which recognizes such documents like thesis' and conference proceedings. It would be difficult to use BibTeX to describe resources from other domains (e.g. musical works of Paganini), but nevertheless possible. One should probably have to describe them with Misc (miscellaneous) category which doesn't say much about the content. An example of the BibTeX record is presented on the Fig. 6.

```
@inproceedings{Huetal2000,
  author = "J. Hu, and H.R. Wu and A. Jennings and X. Wang",
  title = "Fast and robust equalization: A case study",
  booktitle = "Proceedings of the World Multiconference on
  Systemics, Cybernetics and Informatics, (SCI 2000),
     Florida, USA, 23-26 July 2000",
  publisher = "International Institute of Informatics
     and Systemics",
  address = "FL, USA",
  pages = "398--403",
  year = "2000"
}
```

Fig. 6. Example BibTeX record

BibTeXML and BibTeX in OWL

For similar reasons like those who triggered creation of MARC XML, the XML representation of BibTeX was devised. Although there is probably more than one XML format for BibTeX, we use the BibTeXML [216] specification. BibTeXML project supplies DTD and XML Schema for representing BibTeX in XML and tools for conversions. There is also a representation of BibTeX in OWL [110], developed at MIT.

2.5 Other Common Standards

Apart from mentioned bibliographic formats, there are other products of "Library and Information Science" (LIS). LIS studies issues related to libraries like how library resources are accessed and sought for, how people interact with librarian systems (either traditional and computer ones), etc. One of the areas of interest of LIS is resource cataloguing and classification.

Library Classification Systems

Library classification systems help categorize library resources according to domain of interest of their content. Instead of describing a particular book with a word like "Biology", a number of systems were developed to ensure that in every library books with certain subject will be categorized in the same way. At first, classification systems were used to sort books on shelves so they could be easily found (see Chapter "*Digital Libraries and Knowledge Organization*").

- Dewey's Decimal Classification (DDC, also called Dewey's Decimal System) – DDC was invented by a young student assistant in college library, Melvil Dewey, in 1872. Dewey's Decimal System uses decimal numbers to categorize books in a library. It is still the most popular classification system in libraries, mostly because of its simplicity. DDC uses hierarchy of domains of interest. Main domains are divided into hundreds (e.g. 100 – Philosophy & Psychology). The second and third digit further specify the subdomains. For a very specific domains, up to three further digits after the decimal point can be specified.

- Universal Decimal Classification (UDC) – UDC is a descendant of Dewey's system, developed in 1904 and currently maintained by Universal Decimal Classification Consortium. It is an example of faceted classification system (in contrary to DDC or LC which are examples of simple, enumerative systems). It extends the DDC [59] with the idea of classifying resources under a combination of different categories through the use of additional symbols:

  - plus ("+") – 59+636 describes a resource about "Zoology" (code 59) and "Animal Breeding" (code 636)
  - stroke ("/") – 592/599 means everything from 592 to 599 if a book covers many topics
  - colon (":") – relation, e.g. 17:7 describes a book about ethics (17) in art (7)
  - square brackets ("[]") – algebraic subgrouping
  - equality sign ("=") – language specification, e.g. 59=20 covers books about zoology (59) in English (20)

  Different symbols can be used together, e.g. 31:[622+669](485) defines the topic as "statistics of mining and metallurgy in Sweden". UDC constructs worked very well with automatic sorting devices and now with computers. However, the problem is that usage of UDC is not free and appropriate licence fee should be payed.

- Library of Congress Classification (LCC, LC) – Developed by the Library of Congress, used by most research and university libraries in the U.S. (while most public libraries use DDC). Originally developed in 1897, LCC uses letters and numbers to describe categories. The example main categories:

  - A - General works
  - B - Philosophy. Psychology. Religion
  - C - Auxiliary sciences of history
  - D - History: general and old world
  - E - History: America

  Some letters (I,O,W,X,Y) are not used. LCC was designed for specific needs of the Library of Congress and some structures reflect that. Nevertheless, it is one of the most important library classifications, especially in United States.

ISBD – International Standard Bibliographic Description

ISBD is a set of rules produced by the International Federation of Library Associations (IFLA) to describe a wide range of library materials. ISBD rules organize the description of an item in eight areas:

1. Title and statement of responsibility (for example: author, editor, artist).
2. Edition.
3. Material-dependent information (for example, the scale of a map or the duration of a sound recording).
4. Publication and distribution.
5. Physical description (for example: number of pages in a book or number of CDs in the same jewel case).
6. Series.
7. Notes.
8. Standard number (ISBN, ISSN).

ISBD descriptions must contain items described above in supplied order, but some information can be omitted. Figure 25 presents example ISBD description.

Probably the most familiar part of ISBD record is the ISBN (International Standard Book Number)/ISSN (International Standard Serial Number), which can be found on the back cover of every published book or magazine.

3 Main Requirements for a Bibliographic Ontology

The requirements for MarcOnt ontology were specified using the knowledge acquired while researching current state-of-art in librarian domain. Existing standards and legacy formats also have to be taken into account:

- The ontology should provide at least as much description capabilities as MARC 21 bibliographic format. This requirement is easy to explain. MARC 21 is currently the most popular and robust standard of describing library resources. It is very likely that future users of MarcOnt will want to move their storage of MARC 21 records to new format. It would allow them to take advantage of semantics and new services. Smooth conversion, without loss of information, requires MarcOnt to be as extensive, when it comes to describing resources, as MARC 21. MARC 21 is the namesake for MarcOnt which is basically a merge of "MARC" and the word "ontology". Close relation between MarcOnt and MARC 21 does not mean that MarcOnt should be a simple transformation of MARC 21 structures to the ontology language. We would not benefit from that. The aim of ontology is to provide semantic information, which MARC 21 does not provide. Recreating MARC 21 in form of an ontology is not enough.

- The ontology should be written using OWL DL. Web Ontology Language has certain advantages over other, older ontology specification languages. It is the new standard, approved and recommended by W3 Consortium. It is very probable that most, if not all, ontologies in the future will be written using OWL. Out of three "dialects" of OWL, the OWL Description Logic (OWL DL) was selected. OWL DL has sufficient expressiveness and most existing reasoners support it. An ontology written in OWL DL could be extensively used in digital libraries.
- The ontology should reuse (if possible) other existing ontologies or their parts. It should be relatively easy to align the MarcOnt ontology with existing ontologies if required. These requirements are easier to accomplish with OWL. That is why the requirement of OWL was stated first. We can not only import some concepts from other ontologies, but add new properties or facets to them, create subclasses, etc. Such practice is common. For example the Semantic Web Portal Ontology[5] uses the foaf:Agent concept from Friend-of-a-Friend (FOAF) ontology [61] and expands it to reflect specific people/organizations in academic environment.
- It should be easy to translate MarcOnt-compatible semantic descriptions to other formats like MARC 21, Dublin Core or BibTeX. This comes straight from the goals of MarcOnt Initiative. Resolution for the problem of translation lies more in tools which will be developed along with the ontology than the ontology itself. But the requirement of easy translations has to be kept in mind while designing the ontology structure. Lossless conversion between other formats and MarcOnt require MarcOnt to be capable of preserving the information in the first place.

4 MarcOnt Ontology

The first version of MarcOnt ontology[6] [210] was designed to be as flexible as possible, since it will be a subject of many changes when the collaborative development process starts within the community (with tools developed as a part of MarcOnt Initiative).

Semantic Web supports idea of building and sharing knowledge. Ontologies are built to provide description of the given domain of interest. Once a common agreement on a description is reached it becomes a standard (FOAF – Friend of a Friend – ontology is a good example). While building ontologies one should reuse as much knowledge from suitable existing ontologies as possible. This approach is especially important in digital libraries domain, where multiple standards are formulated and widely used, just to mention MARC21, BibTeX or Dublin Core. Having in mind the goals of the bibliographic ontology, authors decided to build the first draft on the base of existing standards

[5] Semantic Web Portal Ontology: `http://sw-portal.deri.org/ontologies/swportal`

[6] MarcOnt Ontology 1.0: `http://www.marcont.org/ontology/1.0/`

for describing bibliographic resources. Following the initial version of the ontology, the authors recently delivered a new, almost completely redesigned MarcOnt Ontology 2.0[7]; the emphases where put on simplifying the ontology (compared to version 1.0) and supporting concepts required to provide bibliographic annotations for scientific publications of work done in a research institute, such as DERI. As a result some ontologies/format specifications were reference or reused:

- FOAF ontology – this ontology is a common standard for describing people, groups or organizations. It is used in many Semantic Web applications. From the perspective of bibliographic ontology, concept foaf:Agent and it subclasses are important. In particular foaf provides concepts:
  - Person – used as a reference to a human, e.g. human creator of a resource
  - Organization – describing an organization, in case of bibliographic ontology – involved in a process of creating or publishing a resource
  - Group – group of people
- BibTeX[8] – specification of the most popular format used for describing bibliographic resources in the WWW.[9]
- Dublin Core[10] – simple but common metadata format, very often used to describe bibliographic resources. The Dublin Core Metadata Initiative (DCMI) is an organization dedicated to promoting the widespread adoption of interoperable metadata standards. Moreover, it develops specialized metadata vocabularies for describing resources that enable more intelligent information discovery systems.
- S3B Tagging ontology[11] – developed at Digital Enterprise Research Institute, Galway. Provides concepts for describing the tagging process; it is based on the TagCommons ontology. It is used in MarcOnt to cover resource tagging aspects.

4.1 The Structure of the MarcOnt Ontology

In this chapter we discuss the structure of the MarcOnt Ontology. We present basic structure of classes used for bibliographic resources' classification. We also provide the overview of crucial properties allowing description of resources.

Structure of Classes

When talking about ontologies, classes are often identified with objects in the real world. Their names often reflect this approach (e.g. `Person` class in the

[7] MarcOnt Ontology 2.0: `http://www.marcont.org/ontology/2.0/`
[8] BibTeX: `http://purl.org/net/nknouf/ns/bibtex/`
[9] BibTeX ontology: `http://zeitkunst.org/bibtex/0.1/bibtex.owl`
[10] DC Elements: `http://purl.org/dc/elements/1.1/`
[11] S3B Tagging Ontology: `http://s3b.corrib.org/tagging/`

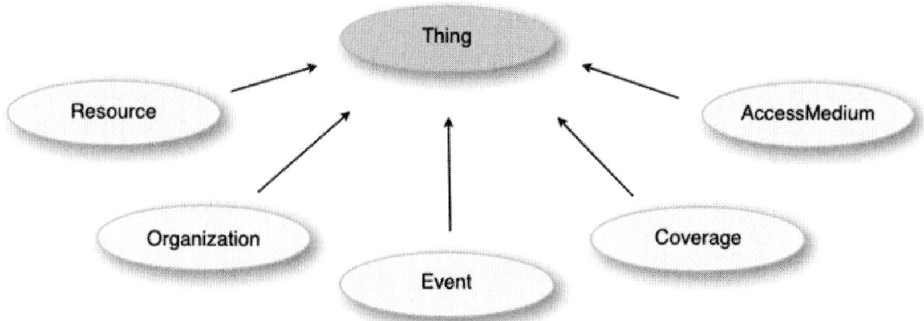

Fig. 7. General (first-level) structurer of classes in MarcOnt ontology

FOAF ontology represents a human being). Because of that creation of list of classes in the ontology and their hierarchy seems to be straightforward. The main problem occurs when one should build a model of particular domain of interest on multiple models existing in this domain. This is a case when building a bibliographic ontology. Such an ontology should be built on the base of existing metadata standards (e.g. BibTeX, DC, etc.). This implies the complicated process of achieving consensus on the ontology. The following crucial classes were defined within MarcOnt Ontology (see Fig. 7):

- Resource – Used as a base to represent all types of material that can be stored in the library, making it one of the most important classes in the ontology. BibTeX specification had a huge impact on the hierarchy of resources. As a widely used format for describing bibliographic resources, it was an intention of the authors to provide BibTeX support. The main subclasses of Resource are (alphabetic order):
  - Article - Represent one of the most common bibliographic resources - article, either from a journal or magazine.
  - Book - means any kind of a book with an explicit publisher. Concept based on book concept in bibtex.
  - Booklet - Following the BibTeX specification this represents a work that is printed and bound, but without a named publisher or sponsoring institution. This class is equivalent to bibtex:Booklet.
  - Collection - This class represents a collection of resources (articles, books, etc). It describes the hierarchy of resources/collections and allows to represent collections of articles, etc. This class is a superclass for Journal (a particular example of a collection) and Proceeding (equivalent to BibTeX:Proceedings).
  - Inbook - a part of a book, which may be a chapter and/or a range of pages. This concept is equivalent of Inbook in bibtex. As an element of structural description it could be moved to JeromeDL ontology defining structure of bibliographic resources.

- Incollection - a part of a book having its own title.
- Inproceedings - represents an article in a conference proceedings.
- Manual - used to describe any piece of a technical documentation.
- Mastersthesis - class equivalent to bibtex:Mastersthesis representing work related to MSc.
- Misc - type used when none of the other types is applicable to the resource.
- Phd thesis - a piece of work related to a PhD.
- Techreport - this type represents a report published by an organization (university, etc.).
- Unpublished - a document having an author and title, but not formally published.

- Organization – used to represent the affiliation of an Agent (*foaf:Agent*) or to represent the organizational structure given digital resource originates from or is owned by. Based on the DERI use case we identified concepts modeling organizational hierarchy in DERI (e.g. *Cluster*, *Project* etc.).[12]
- Event – this class represents all the events important from the perspective of the publication process but also events where given work was published or presented. There are four main types of events captured by the MarcOnt ontology:
  - *Conference* - represents conference event, often used for defining the venue a publication was presented at.
  - *Workshop* - models concept of workshop, where given work was presented
  - *Presentation* - event of presentation of given work. We identified a number of different presentation events, including: *Tutorial*, *Demo Session* or *Poster Session.*
  - *Meeting* - represents concept of a formal or an informal meeting (e.g meeting where the content of a technical report was agreed).
- AccessMedium – Represents different types of media available to access a resource (e.g. particular journal article could be accessible as a printout, or as an electronic version)
- Coverage – provides information about international coverage of a given resource (e.g. International, National).

While classes represent types of objects in the given domain, properties can be understood as their attributes. A simple example of an author of the book explains this approach. An object (a book – "Harry Potter") has an attribute (hasHumanCreator property) linking it with author object ("J.K. Rowling" representing author class – see Fig. 8).

---

[12] For more details see MarcOnt Ontology specification: `http://www.marcont.org/ontology/2.0/`

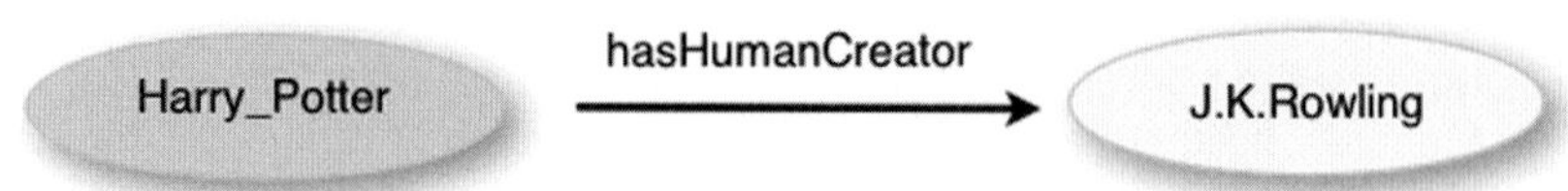

Fig. 8. Example of usage of the *hasHumanCreator* property

Overview of Properties

During the development of MarcOnt ontology a set of the major properties has been developed. Here are some of the most important ones:

- hasPublisher – used to describe a publisher of a given resource
- hasCreator – This property can be used to describe the creator of a given resource or of the given collection of resources. It can be either a person, a group or an organisation.
  - hasHumanCreator - This property can be used to describe the human creator (a person) of a given resource or of the given collection of resources.
- hasCopyright – This property attaches copyrights to a given resource.
- hasSource – Used as citation property to describe a reference source. Allows to create references between resources.
- hasDomain – Describes the domain of interest appropriate for the resource.
- hasTagging – Refers to Tagging concept in ttm ontology and is based on TagCommons. Allows to refer to a tagging performed by a user attaching tags to a resource.

Of course, many other properties were also defined in the ontology. The whole process was targeted at delivering an ontology with full support for BibTeX and DC. Most of the properties and classes from MarcOnt ontology 1.0 used in the Jerome Digital Library are also supported.

General Overview

In the previous sections we presented hierarchy of major classes and properties within MarcOnt Ontology. Following up on this discussion a general overview of the resource description should be presented. In this section an example of description of a resource using MarcOnt ontology is presented.

The Resource class can be identified as a core of MarcOnt Ontology (see Fig. 9). Particular bibliographic resource has been created by its creator. The hasHumanCreator property is used to attach a person (represented with foaf:Person class) to a given resource. Creation of a resource is often related to ownership of the resource in the sense of a set of exclusive rights regulating the use of a particular resource – copyright. Properties hasDomain and hasTagging are also available to provide semantic annotation of a resource. One can

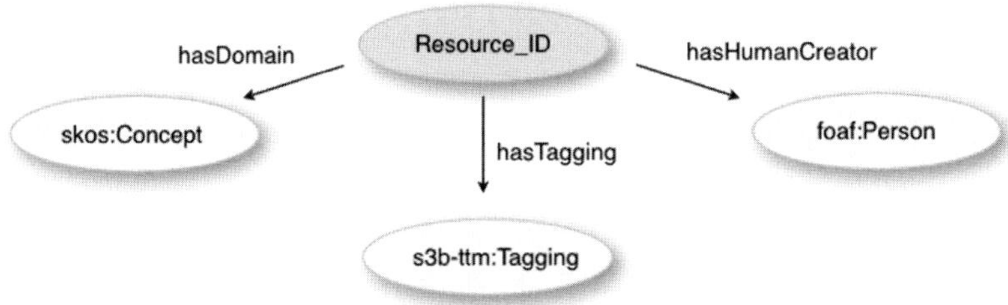

Fig. 9. Simple example of a resource description using MarcOnt ontology

use hasTagging property to attach a Tagging to a resource. Tagging is identified with S3B Tagging ontology (see Chapter "*Community-aware Ontologies*") covering all aspects of the process of tagging (creator of a tag, used tags, time when tagging occurred). On the other hand resource classification is possible with use of hasDomain property. This property represents a domain of interest of a resource and allows to link a resource with a skos:Concept.

5 Yet Another Bibliographic Ontology?

Delivering a bibliographic ontology that would become a respected standard from the point of view of both domain experts and ontology developers is very difficult. Thus, there are not many research initiatives that tackle this problem. In this section we would like to introduce the most well known initiatives targeted on development of a successful bibliographic ontology.

5.1 The Bibliographic Ontology

F. Giasson and Bruce D'Arcus started their initiative[13] based on the "Citation Oriented Bibliographic Vocabuary"[14] developed by Bruce D'Arcus. Five major goal have been identified for the development of the Bibliographic Ontology

- Ontology should be a superset of legacy formats (e.g. BibTeX)
- It must support the most demanding needs in the social sciences, humanities, and law.
- I must be possible to map the class systems to the type system previously designed. They claim that it is not enough to just encode data, it is very important to be able to format it according to the legacy citation styles

[13] The Bibliographic Ontology: `http://wiki.bibliontology.com/index.php/Main_Page`

[14] `http://vocab.org/biblio/schema`

- Should be fairly simple and developer-friendly
- Should be easy to use with the major word processing software (e.g. Open Office[15])

Authors of the Bibliographic Ontology have decided to follow a similar ontology development model to the one used in the Music Ontology.[16] Such a model involves creating many levels of expressiveness for the ontology. This approach allows users to choose the level of expressiveness depending on their scenario (or required level of detail) regarding bibliographic description.

Current version of the ontology defines eight types of concepts:

- Basic bibliographic concepts – category includes basic classes: `Document`, `Collection`, `Part` and general properties: `shortTitle`, `editionName`, `editionNumber`, `presentedAt`, and other.
- Document types – range from `Article` to `WebPage` classes, and a number of individuals, such as `types/booklet` or `types/technicalReport`.
- Collection types – cover concepts like `Series`, `Journal`, or even an `InternetSite`.
- Status – these concepts define basic stages in the document publication process, from `status/draft` to `status/published`.
- Contributions – identify various contribution `Roles`, e.g. `roles/author` or `roles/translator`, and bind the human concepts to resources through `Contribution` information objects.
- Locators – provides concepts to specify location of the reference/citation; these include `issue`, `pages`, and event `physicalLocation`.
- Identifiers – is a set of concepts which allow to identify bibliographic resources using various legacy standards, such as `doi`, `isbn`, or `url`.
- Naming – defines main properties related to naming human concepts (`foaf:Actor`): `familyName`, `givenName`, etc.

Another goal for the developers was to reuse some of the existing standards. The latest version of the Bibliographic Ontology builds on top of the following standards:

- Address Ontology[17]
- Dublin Core Element Refinements and Encoding Schemes[18]
- Friend of a Friend (FOAF) Vocabulary[19]
- The Event ontology[20]
- Geo Ontology[21]

---

15 Open Office: `http://www.openoffice.org`

16 Music Ontology: `http://musicontology.com/`

17 Address ontology: `http://schemas.talis.com/2005/address/schema#`

18 DC Terms: `http://schemas.talis.com/2005/address/schema#`

19 FOAF: `http://xmlns.com/foaf/0.1/`

20 Event Ontology: `http://purl.org/NET/c4dm/event.owl#`

21 Geo Ontology: `http://www.w3.org/2003/01/geo/wgs84_pos#`

5.2 FRBR: Functional Requirements for Bibliographic Records

Functional Requirements for Bibliographic Records (FRBR[22]) [95] is an entity-relationship model developed by International Federation of Library Associations and Institutions[23] (IFLA). This model provides concepts to describe the generalized view of the bibliographic universe. FRBR describes the structure and relationships of bibliographic and authority records; together with more precise vocabulary, FRBR was built to support building catalogs and bibliographic systems.

The general concept of *Book* is precisely defined with four entities: *Item*, *Manifestation*, *Expression*, and *Work*. Moving from *Item* to *Work* the understanding of the *Book* concept becomes more abstract and less tied to the "physical" information object. FRBR organizes defined entities in three groups; the aforementioned four entities are part of *Group 1*. Entities defined in *Group 2*, i.e. *person* and *corporate body*, reflect their role to the entities defined in *Group 1*. *Group 3* defines entities which are *subjects* of the entities defined in *Group 1*; these are: *concepts*, *objects*, *events*, *places*.

FRBR identifies three bibliographic relationships: *inherent* (among entities in *Group 1*), *content*, *whole/part*, and *part to part*. FRBR also defines a number of user tasks: *find*, *identify*, *select*, and *obtain*.

FRBR is becoming more and more popular among digital library projects. Davis and Newman [55] published RDF Schema for FRBR; this work contributes to the efforts of building digital library management systems utilizing semantic web technologies.

5.3 CIDOC CRM

CIDOC [49] is an ISO standard for an ontology that models cultural heritage information. Although it is relevant for digital library community, the coverage of the ontology is much more broad. Originally the reference model was developed independently by the Digital Library community and the museums community; later collaboration between these two communities facilitated merging of both efforts.

The goal of this ontology is to provide means to mediate between heterogeneous database schemas and metadata structures. The central concept of CIDOC is that knowledge is attained by investigating relations between the facts. Therefore, the ontology concentrates on the definition of relationships between items rather then the terminology of a particular domain. The core ontology defines a set of very general classes (e.g. actor, event, period) and supplies a variety of relationship descriptions that can adjust the concepts understanding for a particular environment. Apart from the content preservation and summary, CIDOC provides the concepts related to events, such

[22] FRBR ontology: `http://vocab.org/frbr/core`

[23] IFLA: `http://www.ifla.org/`

as creation, publication, etc. Therefore, with regard to digital libraries, it is possible to utilize CIDOC to talk in detail about items content and their bibliographic description.

6 Conclusions

The digital libraries domain is very specific. In the era of computerization and digitalization digital libraries serve an important function to wide community of users – they provide easy access to enormous number of digital resources. However, this requires digital libraries to come one step forward and transform from simple content providers to highly interoperable, easy accessible pieces in the global knowledge infrastructure's puzzle. This transformation requires a number of efforts to enable interoperability in a heterogeneous environment.

In this chapter we described the idea of a bibliographic ontology. We provided an overview of existing bibliographic standards and explained their importance in the heterogeneous environment of digital libraries. As different digital libraries tend to use different bibliographic description standards, semantic integration becomes a very difficult task. We believe a bibliographic ontology is a solution to this problem. We propose the MarcOnt Ontology as a reference bibliographic ontology, a unique project aiming to provide a semantic solution for librarian community. This chapter also presented how existing bibliographic standards will be covered by MarcOnt ontology.

We strongly believe that MarcOnt will find its place as a semantic bibliographic description in wide variety of applications dealing with bibliographic resources. In order to facilitate this process we provided a number of tools for the community allowing easy development of the standard towards community agreement.[24]

Acknowledgement

This material is based upon works supported by Enterprise Ireland under Grant No. ILP/05/203 and by Science Foundation Ireland Grant No. SFI/02/CE1/I131.

[24] MarcOnt Initiative: `http://www.marcont.org/`

Community-aware Ontologies

Slawomir Grzonkowski, Sebastian Ryszard Kruk, Adam Gzella,
Jakub Demczuk, and Bill McDaniel

1 Introduction to Social Networks

The term "social network" was first mentioned in 1954 by J.A. Barnes [16]. The social network is a structure that consists of nodes; the nodes represent individual people or organizations. Such a structure depicts the ways in which people are connected through diverse social familiarities like acquaintance, friendship or close familiar bonds.

The six degrees of separation theory [109, 165] has initiated the research and development of social networks. The number six derives from an experiment performed in 1967 by a social psychologist Stanley Milgram [156]. He sent several hundred packages to randomly selected people in America with the purpose of getting them delivered to target people. Each recipient was given some details about the target, such as their name and profession, and was asked to send the package to a personal acquaintance whom they believed was more likely to know the target personally. Unexpectedly, the experiment showed that the average length of chain of people was equal to six.

Because Milgram's experiment had been rather small, it was questioned. As a result, some sociologists [223] recruited over 60,000 participants from 166 different countries and they performed tests within an Internet environment, which gave similar results.

The idea of creating on-line social networks and utilizing the concept of the six degrees of separation firstly appeared in 1998. It was possible at a website called *HotLinks*. The website was available for four years. Then, the members were moved to the Friendster [28] network, which was founded in 2002. Since winter 2002, the Friendster network has become more and more popular. As of September 2007, there are more than 21 million members.

Nowadays, there are a few dozen networks that take advantage of the six degrees phenomenon in many ways. For instance, by allowing users to find paths to interesting persons that can be introduced by a network of friends. Hungarian WIW [50] and Orkut[1] require invitations to join the network, which guarantees that at least one relationship with the community exists for new members', this is not necessary in Friendster mentioned above. In addition, we noticed recently a large growth of business oriented networks, e.g. LinkedIn[2] and Ryze[3], that manage professional contacts, enabling users to find an employer or employee.

Social networks are still the main topic of many research projects. *Social networks* [72] is an interdisciplinary international quarterly published journal that publishes both reports of empirical research and formal models. Presented articles consider questions about the structure or patterning in connection with social actors. Furthermore, *Complexity* [201], an on-line journal, published in August 2002 a special issue dedicated to the role of networks and network dynamics. Although, the focus was on showing complexity for different levels of network architecture, a large part of the journal was related to social networks. The mentioned issues were helpful in the comprehension of network-based analyses and explanations.

On-line social networks find more and more practical applications. For instance, this idea was adopted to prevent spam, which has become an ubiquitous problem. Introducing reputation networks and taking advantage of the Semantic Web, TrustMail [104] has applied a standard social network approach. Moreover, various algorithms were considered and a prototype email client was created and tested, which resulted in highly accurate metrics. Valid e-mails from an unknown user can be still received, if there is a link between the sender and the receiver in the social network graph.

2 Using On-line Social Networks to Find and Browse Knowledge

In the previous section we identified that a social network is a set of people or groups of people, with some pattern of interactions or "ties" between them. Moreover, a social network is modeled by a digraph where nodes represent individuals, and a directed edge between nodes indicates direct relationship between two individuals.

From a digital libraries perspective, each person is interested in a couple of topics and has a general idea about the interests of his/her friends, considering some of them having more knowledge on specific topics.

It is possible to construct a sub-graph, on top of a social network, that represents the flow of expertise in a certain domain. This observation is utilised in Social Semantic Collaborative Filtering (SSCF) [117]. Each person in the

[1] http://www.orkut.com

[2] http://www.linkedin.com

[3] http://ryze.com

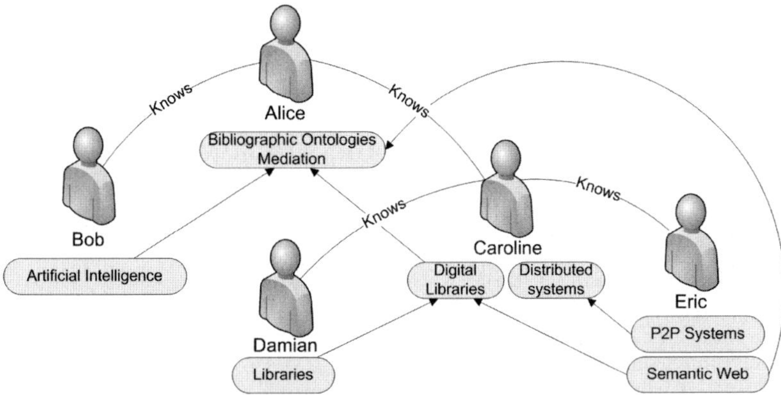

Fig. 1. Social semantic collaborative filtering

social network gathers information such as links to interesting publications in personal collections. Collections maintained by some users can be easily linked into collections created by other users. By linking other peoples' categories users receive bookmarks that are managed and filled in by other people with a level of expertise on particular subjects possibly higher than their own. As we show later the information is easily disseminated through the network of linked collections.

In the given example (see Fig. 1), Alice writes a thesis on "Mediation in Bibliographic Ontologies". She registers with the digital library run by the university and discovers that some of her friends are already registered with the library as well. With features known from on-line communities, she connects her profile to her friends profiles. Later on, Alice starts to gather the information required for her thesis topic. She keeps links to resources she has found in collections managed by the on-line bookmarks system. Soon she discovers that resources which she has bookmarked do not cover the topic of her thesis at a satisfactory level. With the features provided by SSCF, she tries to find other people within her neighborhood with higher expertise on related topics.

Sharing knowledge through social bookmarking services has become very popular; their implementations adapt one of two models: sharing tagged information or sharing folders with bookmarks. The former, such as del.icio.us,[4] digg[5] or connotea,[6] allow users to assign keywords (*tags*) to each resource they find interesting. The latter enables users to collaboratively filter information [68] by transcluding each others' folders. A number of scenarios have been discussed for using online social bookmarking in enterprises [157]. Intriguing

[4] Del.icio.us: http://del.icio.us/
[5] Digg: http://digg.com
[6] Connotea: http://www.connotea.org/

social aspects of sharing knowledge through social bookmarking have initiated research on folksonomies [155] and data mining on social relations between bookmarks and users [207].

3 Community-based User Profile Management

A semantic digital library should take advantage of on-line social networks as well as on-line knowledge provided by its users. In the following sections we show how to use the extra knowledge that is being delivered by web communities.

3.1 Friend-of-a-Friend Standard

The Friend-of-a-Friend (FOAF)[7] standard was created to enable the publication of machine readable user profile descriptions as well describing users' social networks. The FOAF vocabulary consists of semantic web vocabularies such as RDF [93], RDFS,[8] OWL.[9] For example, statements describing that Alice knows Bob can be written in the following way:

```
<foaf:Person>
 <foaf:name>Alice</foaf:name>
 <foaf:mbox_sha1sum>9485f8a93ec9284a541c0581b48d7a193a74ef89
 </foaf:mbox_sha1sum>
 <foaf:homepage rdf:resource="http://very.basic.example/Alice/"/>
 <foaf:depiction rdf:resource="http://very.basic.example/Alice/
 photo.jpeg"/>
 <foaf:knows rdf:resource="mailto:bob@bobsemail.com"/>
</foaf:Person>
```

The FOAF vocabulary is not limited to the aforementioned properties. The standard specifies about 60 properties and divides them into several categories: FOAF Basics, Personal Info, OnlineAccounts/IM, Project and Groups, Documents and Images.

In RDF, statements can occur any number of times. By repeating the *foaf:knows* statement with another attribute, Alice can easily express knows relationships with much more people.

3.2 FOAFRealm

FOAF [2] embodies the idea of using RDF to describe a user's profile and *knows* relationships within the users community, therefore the *foaf:knows*

[7] http://www.foaf-project.org
[8] RDFS: http://www.w3.org/TR/rdf-schema/
[9] http://www.w3.org/TR/owl-guide/

property is crucial. The property enables FOAF to support describing social networks; the usability of the *foaf:knows* information, however, is rather negligible because it does not specify the kind of the relationship. Fortunately, the reference FOAF model might be easily extended with a new vocabulary such as XHTML Friends Network (XFN)[10] to make it suitable for an application's needs.

The *foaf:knows* relationship can be easily adapted to many needs. For example, we can use such a social network graph to control access to resources or give different weights of votes during negotiations. The core consideration is how well we know another person in the network. It would make possible to describe how one can view our photos by specifying the maximum length of the path between us and him or her. Our suggestions in negotiations would gain more points if they were approved by people we know less.

FOAF's idea of describing graphs of persons, where everyone specifies people they know causes some significant security and privacy issues. Firstly, it seems that saying *Alice knows Bob* is not enough and in the physical world we would rather consider this relation in a more precise way like *Alice knows-very-well Bob*; it also seems that the threshold values should be smoothed as much as it is possible. Moreover, the *SHA1* value of email should be provided to keep users' emails confidential. Last but not the least is the trust issue; if the information is distributed, how can we control that no one else can ie. add additional knows relations and in that way violate the security constraints imposed by owner of the resource and gain access to it. To assure users of secure profiles, FOAFRealm [116, 119] proposes extending the FOAF vocabulary with digital signatures and other security enhancements.

How Well do I Know You?

In the real world it is common that some of our friends are closer than others. In most cases we are able to evaluate our friendships on the base of hitherto interactions. Expressing relationships could be done by means of numeric values of predefined values. However, the Orkut on-line community portal, for example, proposes additional properties to express friendship level using concepts such as *very good friend* or *never-met acquaintance.*

Who do I Know Better?

The core idea of the Semantic Web, and hence FOAFRealm, is to model real world situations in the virtual space. In some cases we would rather share some resources with friends of our friends than our own friends. For example, if we have a very good friend it means that his/her very good friends are better known by us, than some of our friends that we barely know or have never met at all. For instance Fig. 2 depicts a situation where Alice knows

[10] XHTML Friends Network: http://www.gmpg.org/xfn/

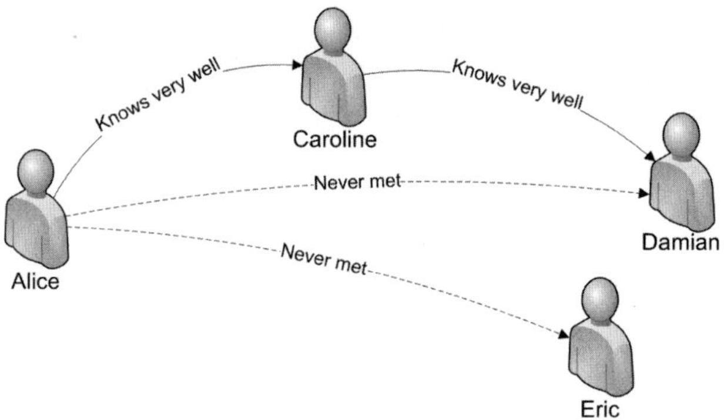

Fig. 2. Who is a closer friend?

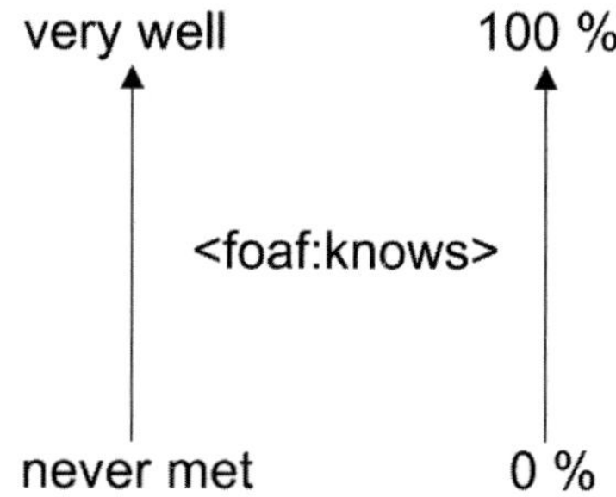

Fig. 3. How much <foaf:knows> is true?

Caroline very well, and Caroline knows Damian also very well, there is also Eric who is not known by anyone. Alice has never met Eric nor Damian, but Damian is a closer friend for her since he knows Caroline who is a very good friend of Alice's.

Expressing the Friendship Value

Let's assume that the *<foaf:knows>* represents an average friendship value. There is, however, a range of friendships from very close (very good friend) to very distant one (person I have never met). Let's now evaluate every friendship from 0% (very distant) to 100% (very close), with 50% representing average friendship (see Fig. 3 – How much *<foaf:knows>* is true?). Now we have to attach this information to the <foaf:knows> statement. The most convenient way is to make use of reifications to make statements about statements. Reified *foaf:knows* statement (see Fig. 4) presents how to evaluate the friendship between two people.

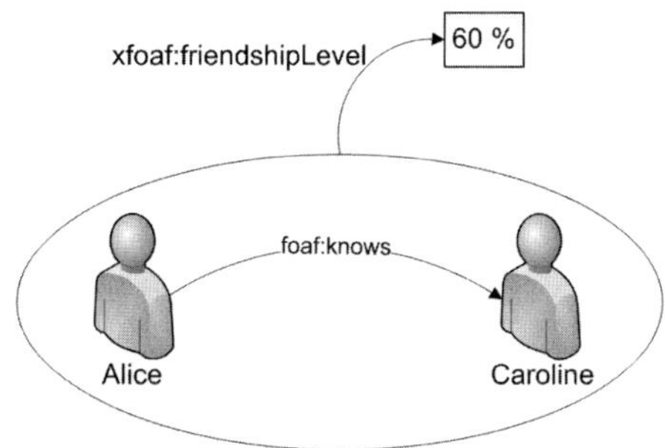

Fig. 4. Reified foaf:knows statement

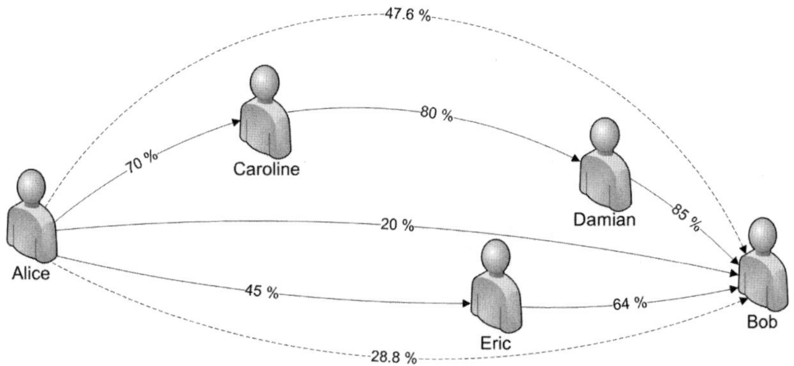

Fig. 5. Evaluating the friendship between Alice and Bob

Evaluating Friendship Between Two People

To find out if a specified person is allowed to access a given resource within defined roles, we have to find the closest distance between the interested people and the highest friendship's level. We can compute it using for example the Dijkstra [60] algorithm.

Figure 5 presents possible solutions depending on a given goal. The shortest path between Alice and Bob is a direct connection, but the connection of the highest overall level of friendship is Alice → Caroline -> Damian -> Bob [47.6%]. If the minimal requirements are 2 connections and level of friendship above 25% the algorithm can end up with path Alice -> Eryk -> Bob [28.8%]. In many real situations, constraints on the distance can significantly speed-up the algorithm.

It is Really Me

Another significant drawback of FOAF is the lack of authentication information. The *<foaf:mbox>* property can be successfully used for login information although in some situations only the *<foaf:mbox_sha1sum>* is stored. The SHA1 sum of *<foaf:mbox>* can be easily generated resulting in the value of *<foaf:mbox_sha1sum>* property. The FOAF vocabulary does not contain any property for storing password-like information. FOAFRealm extends the vocabulary and provides *<xfoaf:passowrd_sha1sum>*. This value can be easily compared with the SHA1 sum generated from the password provided by the user.

4 Social Semantic Collaborative Filtering (SSCF)

A social network maintained by FOAFRealm allows users to develop a new direction in digital libraries; focusing on community aspects and utilising the benefits of social networking, a user would be no longer only a reader of the information, but she/he would become a contributor of content.

Usually, when a user browses a digital library, some articles and materials seem more valuable than others to him/her. Common practice is to bookmark those resources. Recently, collaborative bookmarking such as del.icio.us[11] has become more and more popular. Users want to see the bookmarks of their friends, and use the knowledge collected by them.

Users maintain their private collections of bookmarks to interesting, valuable resources. In other words, each user gathers, filters, and organises a small part of knowledge. Social Semantic Collaborative Filtering (SSCF) [117] allows a user to share this knowledge with others within a social network; one could easily import friends' bookmarks and utilise their expertise and experience in specific domains of knowledge.

In SSCF, users collect the bookmarks and store them in special directories; each directory is semantically annotated using popular taxonomies and thesauri, such as WordNet [70], DMoz,[12] DDC,[13] or other supported by JOnto project.[14] They can be used to determine the content of the directory or to find the correct one. For example, a student is able to easily find the subject or the topic, which he is interested in, related to the course that he attends to.

Another important aspect is the security in the SSCF, the place where FOAFRealm plays an important role. Very often users collect information that should be shared only within specific group of people: closest friends, classmates, students, etc. SSCF allows users to set fine grained access rights for every directory; access control is based on the distance and the friendship level between friends in the social network. For example, a resource can be shared only with friends with distance not greater than two and at least 50% friendship level. *Distance not bigger than two* refers to a maximum two degrees of separation between the owner and the requester.

---

[11] http://del.icio.us/

[12] http://dmoz.org/

[13] DDC: http://www.oclc.org/dewey/

[14] JOnto: `http://jonto.sf.net/`

5 Semantically Interlinked Online Communities

Wikis and blogs [18, 23] have recently become a major means of free publishing; they are used by many people to tell about their everyday life. Blogs are being applied to the commercial and political world [192]; companies use blogs to inform their clients about new product releases; politicians communicate through blogs with their electors. Blogs are also considered as one of the additional sources of e-Learning material [92]. Since blogs can be rich sources of information a number of research activities have been initiated to enrich blogs with semantic technologies. SemiBlog [159] allows users to link other resources related to the blog post, and semantically annotate the blog and the references. Cayzer [42] presents how blogs can be used to create a collective knowledge space. Finally, initiatives, such as the SIOC (Semantically-Interlinked Online Communities) project[15] [30], allow users to export blogging metadata for further processing in semantic applications (see Chapter "*Social Semantic Information Spaces*").

SIOC is an initiative whose goal is to interconnect online communities [29]. SIOC can be used in published or subscribed mechanisms, as it stores community-like metadata such as information about the post's author, enclosed links, the creation time, and connections with other web pages. Thanks to SIOC, each part of a community portal, blog, forum, etc. can be semantically described using one, unified vocabulary. Therefore, the applications that utilise SIOC could easily search, exchange and link the content created by communities. The core of the SIOC framework is the SIOC ontology which consists of a set of classes and properties which link them:

- *Site* – is the location of an online community or set of communities.
- *Forum* – is a discussion area, housed on a site.
- *Post* – can be formed as an article, a message or an audio- or videoclip. A post is written by an author, has a topic, a content, external links, etc.
- *User* – represents an account held by an online community member.
- *Usergroup* – is a set of accounts of users interested in a common subject matter.

After the success of the first version of the ontology, the SIOC community decided to expand the ontology with support for other collaborative services; it is now possible to express data from services, such as wikis, image galleries, event calendars, address books, audio and video channels.

SIOC allows users to exchange community data by importing and exporting information to/from different native vocabularies. SIOC-enabled sites take advantage of exchanging relevant information with other SIOC-enabled services. SIOC allows its users to perform cross-site queries, topic related searches and importing SIOC data from other sites. SIOC can also provide a statistical method to find the most active user. Finally, SIOC metadata can be detected by using crawlers or using browser plugins [26].

[15] SIOC: http://sioc-project.org/

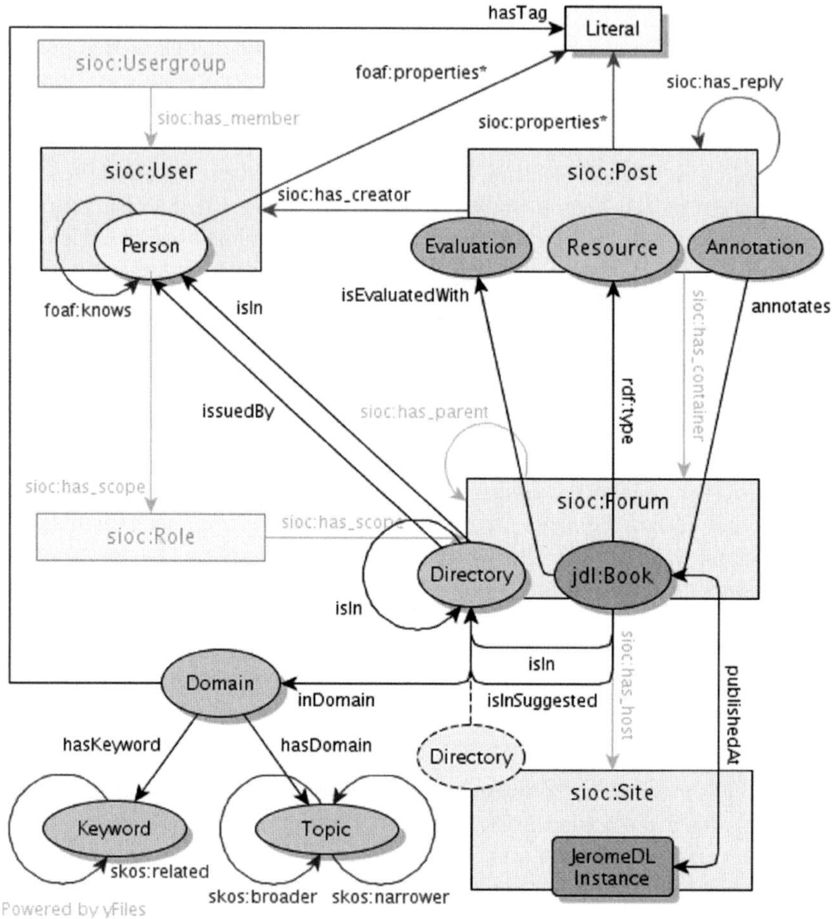

Fig. 6. Alignment of SSCF and SIOC ontology

Digital libraries can no longer be *only* libraries; To serve the next generation of users they need to become isomorphic with other Internet services; they need to adapt both semantic web and social networking technologies, to continue their mission.

6 Towards a Social Digital Library

To create a community-aware digital library we have built a platform that joins three separate applications: digital library, blog and bookmarking applications. In such a model (see Fig. 6) every resource becomes a blog (with SIOC support). SSCF allows us to freely create, share and import bookmarks to the resources. With SSCF and SIOC integration, community based materials can be added and browsed with a SSCF interface (see Chapter "*JeromeDL - the Social Semantic Digital Library*").

7 Further Directions

One of the possible directions of further improvement of the community-aware digital library would be to allow users to manage tagged data they have gathered in various on-line places. With a bookmarking application integrated, our platform would aggregate user's activities from all over the web making it even easier to share knowledge with friends; managing various sources separately would not be needed anymore.

Tagging services deliver, however, a heterogenous APIs; they also use different conceptual models to represent the tagging concepts [83]. This is where TagCommons initiative provides us with help. The goal of TagCommons is to create mechanisms for the sharing and interoperating of tagging data, so that it will render accessible various social tagging sources across applications, sites, etc. The TagCommons working group has already identified use cases and functional requirements for tag data sharing.[16] One of the key concepts is a universal ontology for representing tagging called TagOntology [83], created by Tom Gruber. TagOntology identifies 4 main concepts:

- *Term* – a phrase used to describe Documents that is human and machine readable
- *Document* – a thing (identified by a unique URI) that is being tagged
- *Tagger* – a person or an agent doing the tagging
- *Tagged* – a statement saying that Document has been tagged with Term by a Tagger.

Gruber also proposes two properties.

- *Polarity* – allows communities to filter out bad tags created by spammers by stating that the given tag should not be applied to the given resource.
- *Source* – describes the system where the tagging occurred thus allowing to say something about the collections of tags only related to a specific application they come from.

Therefore, the tagging notion could become a five-place relation [82]:

```
Tagging(document, term, tagger, source, polarity)
```

Of course not all systems would have to agree on the five-place version. Default values should be considered for the missing places. For example, the polarity argument might have "+" as a default value. Hence, different systems could easily exchange data, even with ones that do not offer a full support [82].

[16] http://tagcommons.org/

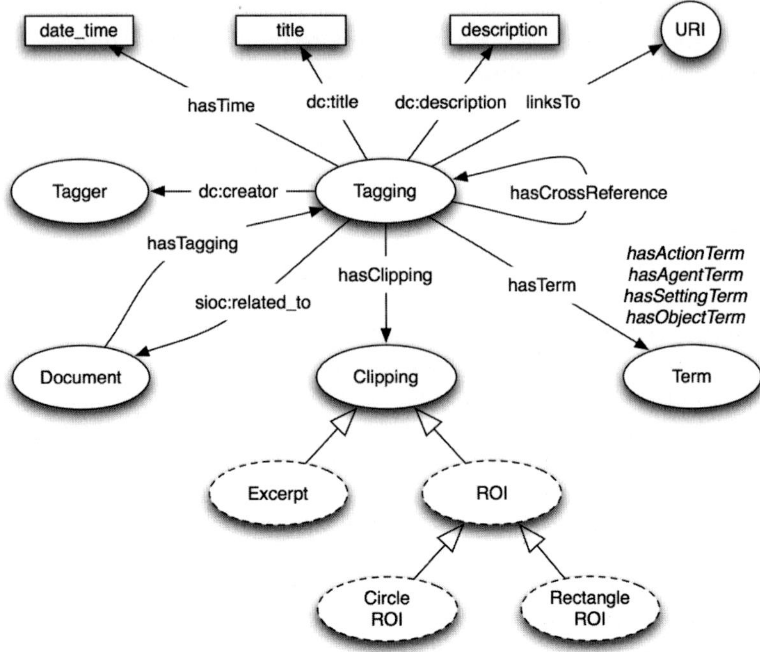

Fig. 7. Extended Gruber's ontology with support for multimedia tagging

Providing support for the TagCommons ontology will allow a digital library to be more isomorphic with other Web 2.0 services. Accessing user data through provided APIs will allow to enrich the data with semantic adding a way-in support in the digital library. The digital library should also support way-out (export) solution to various tagging solutions; and thus provide an easy way of migrating documents between them.

Our solution is a part of JOnto,[17] whose core is based on Gruber's ontology and extends it with support for multimedia tagging[18] (see Fig. 7):

- *Pictures* – Region of Interest (ROI) tagging of circular and rectangular shapes
- *Video* – movie excerpts

It also allows to create cross-references between tagged documents and links to external resources. The library itself is accessible through REST API (XML and JSON calls).

The TagCommons ontology is similar to the aforementioned SIOC ontology. Both projects define minimal concepts that are required to allow heterogenous systems to interchange data. However TagCommons focus only on

[17] JOnto: `http://jonto.sf.net/`

[18] S3B Tagging Ontology: `http://s3b.corrib.org/tagging/`

the process of tagging itself, whereas the SIOC ontology is more abstract, dealing with community-like metadata.

There is yet another solution similar to TagCommons called int.ere.st.[19] It allows aggregation of Social Semantic Cloud of Tags (SCOT)[20] ontologies from tagging sites based on persons, objects or tags. Users can bookmark, tag and share their own SCOT ontologies as well as others. int.ere.st provides mechanisms for tag meta-searches enabling finding similar patterns of tagging or persons based on their tags.

8 Conclusions

In this chapter we have identified a huge potential in the notion of online communities, which can be used to fill in the gap that was created when human librarian was moved out of the scope in digital libraries. We have described benefits of using social semantic filtering and on-line ontologies. We have also presented how to take advantage of other ontologies such as TagCommons.

Our conclusion is that browsing and searching techniques that involve community-aware ontologies, such as FOAF or SIOC, can significantly improve search results and information utilization; therefore these techniques should be considered by every novel semantic digital library.

Acknowledgement

This material is based upon works supported by Enterprise Ireland under Grant No. ILP/05/203 and by Science Foundation Ireland Grant No. SFI/02/CE1/I131.

---

[19] int.ere.st: `http://int.ere.st/`

[20] SCOT Project: `http://scot-project.org/`

Part IV

Prototypes of Semantic Digital Libraries

JeromeDL: The Social Semantic Digital Library

Sebastian Ryszard Kruk, Mariusz Cygan, Adam Gzella, Tomasz Woroniecki, and Maciej Dabrowski

The initial research on semantic digital libraries [115] resulted in the design and implementation of JeromeDL [118]; current research on online social networking and information discovery delivered new sets of features that were implemented in JeromeDL. Eventually, this digital library has been redesigned to follow the architecture of a social semantic digital library (see Chapter "*Architecture of Semantic Digital Libraries*" and Sect. 6).

JeromeDL describes each resource using three types of metadata (see Fig. 2): structure, bibliographic (see Chapter "*Digital Libraries and Knowledge Organization*" and Chapter "*Bibliographic Ontology*") and community (see Chapter "*Community-aware Ontologies*"). It delivers services leveraging each of these information types. Annotations based on the structure and legacy metadata (see Sect. 2), and bibliographic ontology (see Sect. 3) are rendered to the users in one, mixed, representation of library resources (see Fig. 1). Community annotations are managed by separate services, such as social semantic collaborative filtering [117] or blogging component (see Sect. 4.1 and Sect. 4).

1 Architecture of JeromeDL

Our current research focuses on combining ontologies and components presented in [118] into sets of semantic services.

Our research on semantic digital libraries showed how digital library content management might benefit from the Semantic Web [118]. In this chapter we describe how the semantic technologies (we have applied) can be coupled together in sets of usable services. Building upon previous work, we extend a semantic digital library with social services. These features enable a community of users to actively participate in the process of knowledge organization. Delivered social services include collaborative filtering, blogging and tagging (see Sect. 4).

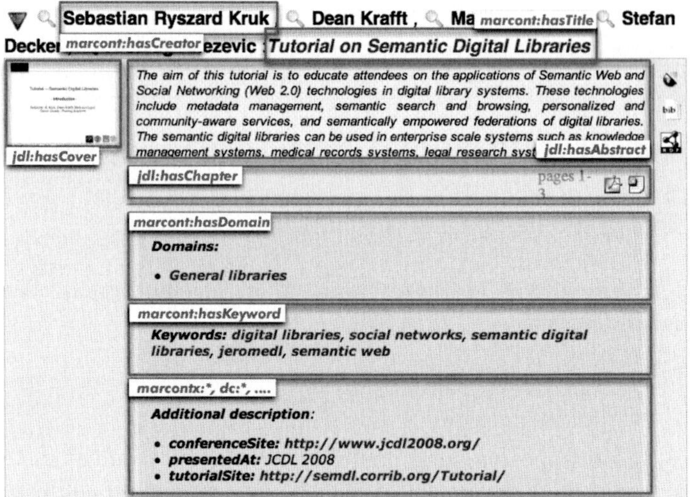

Fig. 1. Structure and Bibliographic Information Rendered by JeromeDL

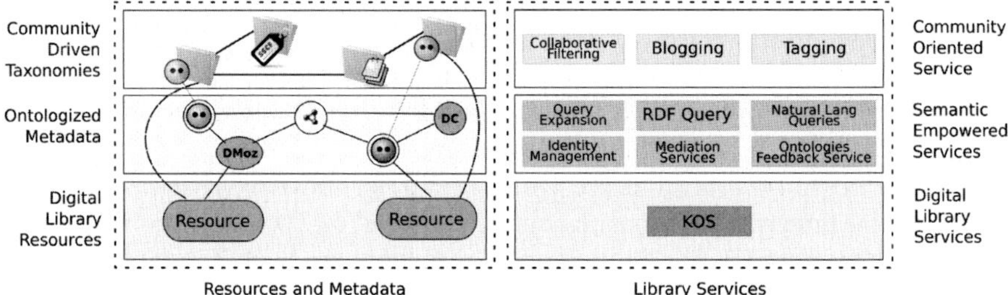

Fig. 2. 3-layered architecture of JeromeDL

We present a three-layered architecture of metadata management on top of a digital library system (see Fig. 2). Each layer enriches basic information gathered in a library with semantic annotations and provides additional capabilities to browsing and searching.

The bottom layer handles typical tasks required from a digital objects repository, that is, keeps track of physical representation of resources, their structure and provenance (see Sect. 2). With an extensive use of a structure ontology (see Fig. 4) the bottom layer provides a service for a flexible and extendable electronic representation of objects; it is especially significant in expressing relations to other resources.

The middle layer lifts up legacy bibliographic descriptions to a semantic level. It utilizes ontologies, to represent concepts defined in legacy metadata formats, such as Dublin Core, MARC21 or BibTEX (see Sect. 3). The main advantage of the semantic layer are the services, which exploit machine-understandable, semantically rich relations between various kinds of resources;

they enhance the usability of information retrieval in the digital library or interoperability between different digital libraries. An example service, a natural language query interface [127], take advantage of a social network of users and creators, specified using FOAF[1] metadata.

For example, the users feedback service iteratively discovers new properties used by librarians to annotate resources and applies them as suggestions for extending the bibliographic ontology; the mediation services allow to translate between a number of bibliographic formats. Furthermore, the middle layer offers information retrieval and identity management services. All the services are supported by semantic technologies; for example, the natural language queries [127] take advantage of a social network specified using FOAFmetadata.

The top layer utilizes benefits from engaging community of users into annotating and filtering resources (see Sect. 4). In today's Internet the influence of user communities cannot be overestimated; collaborative efforts in information sharing and management proved to be the right way to go and led to the success of many of the Web 2.0 sites.

2 Core Digital Library Services

This section presents the core digital library solutions implemented in JeromeDL: knowledge organization systems supported by the JOnto component [105] and the JeromeDL structure ontology, which defines concepts for describing the core structure of information objects.

2.1 Knowledge Organization Systems

There might be many definitions of a digital library system; the most accurate, however, always adhere to knowledge organization systems (see Chapter "*Digital Libraries and Knowledge Organization*"). Digital libraries manage resources; but these are controlled vocabularies, such as authority files or thesauri, that allow efficient resource management. JeromeDL allows librarians to maintain and use the following controlled vocabularies:

- Authority files, with a list of authors, editors and publishers;
- Classification taxonomies, such as DMoz, DDC or other, for annotating resources with topics;
- WordNet thesaurus or OpenThesaurus, for specifying keywords;

An AJAX interface (see Fig. 3) delivered by the JOnto[2] project is used to support librarians in describing resources using controlled vocabularies.

[1] Friend-Of-A-Friend (FOAF): `http://www.foaf-project.org/`
[2] JOnto: `http://jonto.sf.net/`

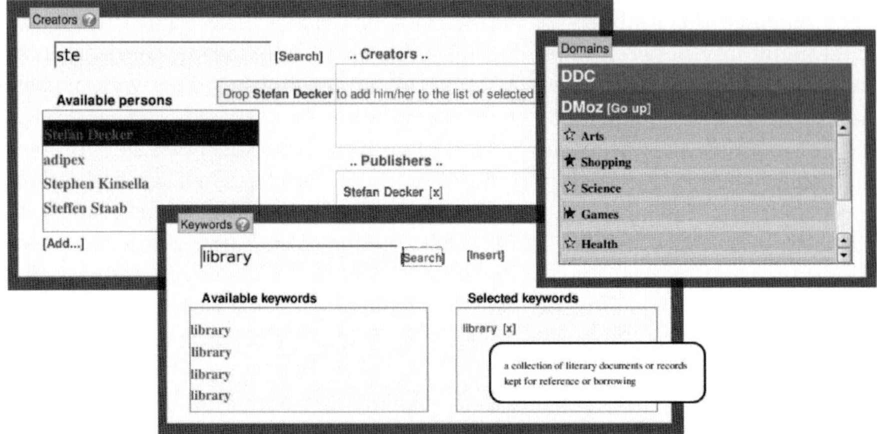

Fig. 3. Annotating JeromeDL resources with KOS

2.2 Structure Ontology

Modern digital library systems not only store bibliographic metadata; they also manage an electronic representation of the content itself. The structure of the content might, however, depend on the type of the resource, e.g.: a book can be decomposed into chapters, a multimedia presentation into media parts. The structure information can be maintained using non-RDF technologies, such as relational or XML databases; it is, however, virtually impossible to easily extend such a structure definition with additional annotations or relations to other resources.

RDF[3] [76], enables to extend the description of a resource with new properties, and to easily mix and interlink annotations from different sources. Since this gives semantic digital libraries a leverage over using non-RDF technologies, such as relational or XML databases, the resource structure information is also modeled in a form of an ontology (see Fig. 4). This ontology provides a universal layer for metadata and content retrieval; it allows us to extend the structure description with new concepts, without violating the integrity of existing data [118].

3 Semantic Services

JeromeDL was designed and built with an extensive use of semantic web technologies. Therefore, even though it now supports a number of social features (see Sect. 4), semantic metadata and services are the key ones; they enrich digital library metadata and services; semantic components are the enabling infrastructure for social features. In this section we present semantic features,

[3] RDF: Resource Description Framework

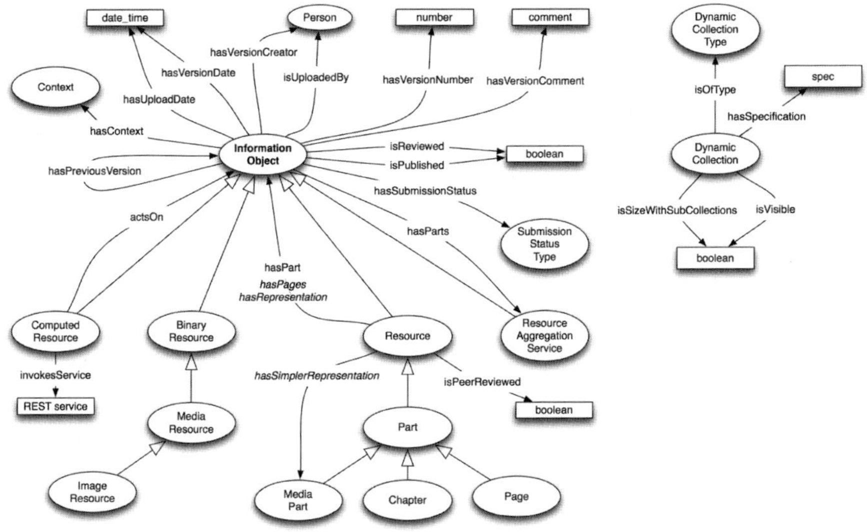

Fig. 4. Structure ontology

which enhance legacy information; finally we describe search and browsing services delivered by JeromeDL.

Semantic descriptions in JeromeDL are based on relations between different types of objects. Bibliographic information is enhanced by referencing entities defined with controlled vocabularies, such as domain (topic) classifications, defined in various taxonomies, (see Fig. 1 – *marcont:hasDomain*) or keywords (see Fig. 1 – *marcont:hasKeyword*), which can be concepts from the WordNet thesauri or tags, introduced by a community of librarians.

The uploading process in JeromeDL adopts research on folksonomies [155]; librarians, who manage resources in JeromeDL, can annotate resources with semantic concepts. Each annotation consists of a name of a property and a value, literal value or URI to another resource. The properties, and other concepts, are defined in the MarcOnt ontology [128] (see Fig. 5); the purpose of this ontology is to capture definitions of concepts from and mediate, using MarcOnt Mediation Services [129], between various legacy metadata standards, such as MARC21, BibTeX or Dublin Core.

The librarian, however, is free to use any properties, he/she finds appropriate, in the annotation process; these can be referenced by the name or by the URI. In the former case, if the name is not defined in the MarcOnt ontology, a concept for a given name is created in the MarcOntX namespace. These properties form an extension to the core MarcOnt ontology, defined by the community of librarians; they are gathered by the MarcOntX agent, a process on the MarcOnt Portal [228], and presented to the domain experts as a feedback from the community of users.

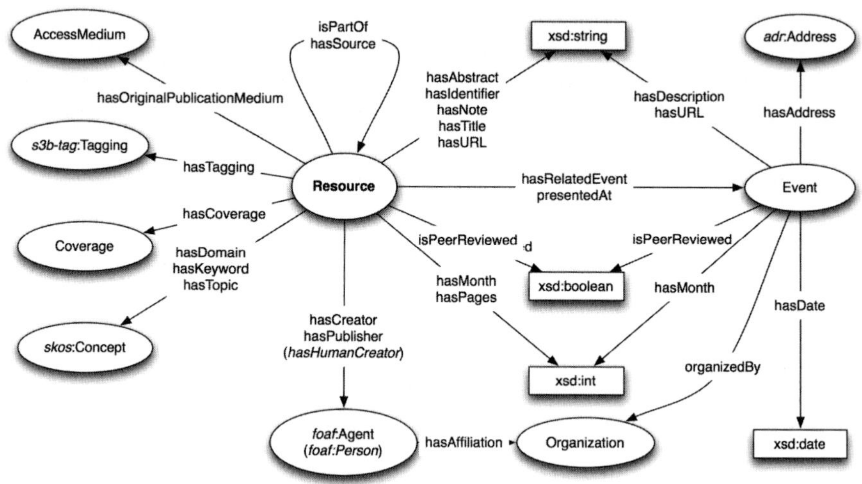

Fig. 5. Bibliographic ontology

3.1 Bibliographic Ontology

There are many approaches to the development of library resource description formats. Heterogeneity becomes one of the most important problems in the digital library domain. There are many, more or less popular, legacy formats being used, e.g., MARC21, BibTEX or Dublin Core; different resources can be described by different metadata. There is a need for the existence of a mediation standard such as MarcOnt Ontology [128] which defines concepts used in JeromeDL for bibliographic description (see Fig. 5).

The MarcOnt Ontology (see Chapter "*Bibliographic Ontology*") defines concepts used in JeromeDL for bibliographic description (see Fig. 5); these are concepts from the most used bibliographic formats such as MARC21, BibTEX, Dublin core. The quality of MarcOnt ontology during still ongoing development is ensured by the community of domain experts using a collaborative ontology development platform - MarcOnt Portal.[4]

3.2 User Feedback – MarcOntX Concept

As mentioned in the previous paragraph – a librarian can use any properties they find appropriate to annotate a resource during the uploading process. In JeromeDL each property is referenced by a URI or a short name. In the latter case, if the property is not recognized as a property from the MarcOnt ontology, a new property is created in the MarcOntX namespace.[5] Any new properties are automatically retrieved from known instances of

[4] MarcOnt Portal: `http://portal.marcont.org/`

[5] MarcOntX namespace: `http://www.marcont.org/xontology#`

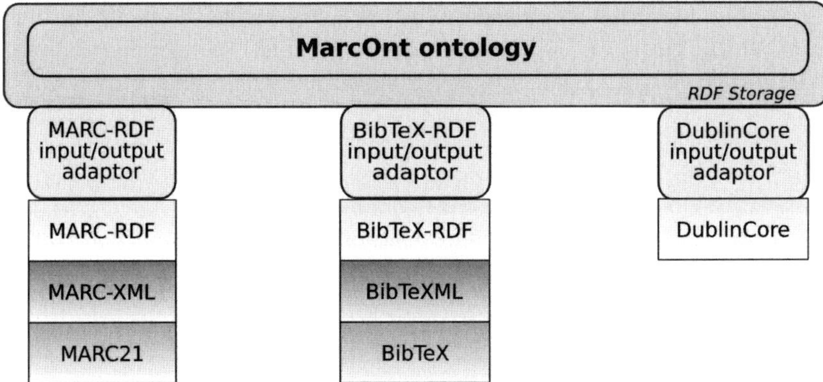

Fig. 6. MarcOnt mediation services diagram

JeromeDL by the MarcOntX agent. They are suggested as proposals for the community involved in the MarcOnt ontology development process; the community decides whether it is necessary to incorporate these concepts into a new version of the MarcOnt ontology.

3.3 MarcOnt Mediation Services

MarcOnt ontology is not only a uniform bibliographic description format; it also serves as a mediation standard for MarcOnt Mediation Services [129,132]. There is number of bibliographic description formats used in librarian systems. The most popular MarcOnt Mediation Services uses mediation rules which are defined during the ontology development process with MarcOnt Portal. It allows users to translate the bibliographic description of the resource in JeromeDL between any of other formats aligned with the MarcOnt ontology (see Fig. 6).

3.4 Information Discovery Services

JeromeDL offers a number of search and retrieval services, such as NLQ [127], MultiBeeBrowse [121], TagsTreeMaps [126] or SSCF [117]; these services improve users' experience in digital library navigation (see Chapter "*Evaluation of Semantic and Social Technologies for Digital Libraries*").

Secure Snapshot Repository

JeromeDL uses RDF as the common data model; it allows users to easily integrate information from different sources, such as structure, legacy and community. Some of the data, however, might be very sensitive for a library user; information like passwords, access control protected bookmarks (see

Sect. 4), etc. should not be revealed to unauthorized users. Filtering out information during query execution time, however, could be inefficient and might not be secure enough. Therefore, in JeromeDL legacy and structure data has been separated from community data; since the latter one contains some sensitive information. Search and retrieval techniques described in this section are performed on a repository created as a secure snapshot of two base repositories; the secure repository does not contain any sensitive information from community repository, while it does contain complete information from the legacy-structure repository.

Semantic Query Expansion

An important part of the full text search is the ability of the search engine to refine the query to reflect a user's expectations. The semantic and social assets of social semantic digital libraries deliver machine processable and community-aware information (see Chapter "*Architecture of Semantic Digital Libraries*"), which can be used during this process. The previous query processing in JeromeDL consisted of 3 steps [115]: full-text search, bibliographic description search and query expansion based on statistical analysis; in further development [118] the first two steps were integrated into one.

During the query expansion step all words provided by the user are mapped to one or more types, e.g., a topic, a keyword, or a person; each type is refined using different types of properties, Each of new concepts is ranked according to the user's interests expressed in the social semantic collaborative filtering (SSCF) profile (see Sect. 4); the ranking values associated with SSCF categories are propagated to the resources bookmarked in those categories, and further to person, thesauri and keyword concepts.

Direct RDF Query Service

Searching for resources in the network of digital libraries became a commodity; protocols like Z39.50 or OAI-PMH are used for the communication purposes. Semantic web service technologies are still on their way to becoming industrial standards; in the meantime, many services are being mashed-up together [22]; standards like SPARQL [187] define means for these and other solutions based on semantic-enabled services [132].

JeromeDL delivers a direct RDF query service to be able to act as one of the mash-up services; it supports various query languages, such as RDQL, SeRQL and SRQL; the query results in RDF can be serialized to XML, N3 or TURTLE format, or presented in HTML. Each query is evaluated by the Sesame engine [3] on a secure snapshot repository.

Navigation Services

JeromeDL users can filter out resources by: publication type, such as *article*, *in-proceedings* or *book*, publication author, keywords tagging publication,

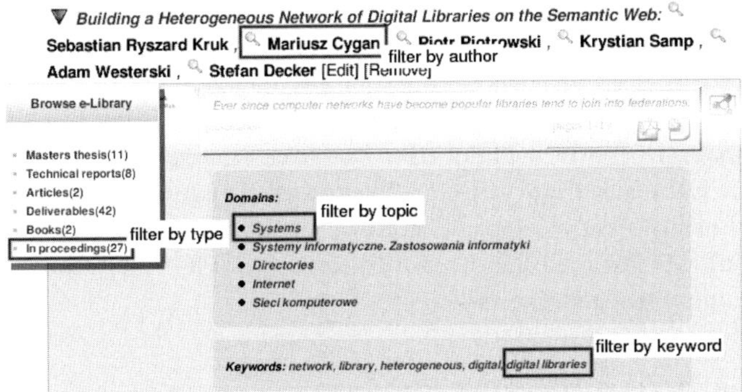

Fig. 7. Navigation filters in JeromeDL

topics annotating publication. Each filter can be executed by selecting part of resource description (see Fig. 7).

Additionally, users can switch from the JeromeDL browsing view to using one of filtering and browsing plugins, such as MultiBeeBrowse [121], TagsTreeMaps [126], or Exhibit [94].

3.5 Identity Management Services

Each library resource has at least one author; together with the library user, they form a part of controlled vocabulary maintained by JeromeDL (see Sect. 2) with FOAF [61] metadata.

FOAFRealm [116] (see Chapter "*Community-aware Ontologies*"), a distributed identity management system based on FOAF allows JeromeDL users to control their profile information; it also manages an authority list (authors, editors, publishers). During registration users construct the FOAF profile (with an easy to use form) or upload an existing one. FOAFRealm also allows the system to keep JeromeDL user preferences. In distributed FOAFRealm (called D-FOAF [120]) instances of the system are connected in a P2P network; this allows users to register only in one instance and sign-in to any other across the network.

4 Social Services

A social network maintained by FOAFRealm allowed JeromeDL to develop in a new direction; focusing on community aspects and utilizing the benefits of social networking. A JeromeDL user is no longer only a reader of the information, she/he becomes a contributor of the content and a creator of the knowledge.

4.1 Social Bookmarking

Usually, when a user browses a digital library, some articles and materials seem to him more valuable than others. Common practice is to bookmark those resources. Recently collaborative bookmarking sites such as del.icio.us[6] have become more and more popular. Users want to see the bookmarks of their friends, and use the knowledge collected by them. These features are provided by the Social Semantic Collaborative Filtering (SSCF) [117] component (see Chapter "*Community-aware Ontologies*").

4.2 JeromeDL as a Blogging Platform

The next generation Internet is a convergence between social communication and semantically-rich information; digital libraries can no longer be *only* libraries; in order to serve the next generations of users they need to become isomorphic with other Internet services, such as blogs or wikis.

Digital libraries boast high quality information; their content, however, remains virtually immune to the knowledge acquired by readers; they are unable to pass the knowledge to other readers in any form other than the "word of mouth". A solution implemented in JeromeDL allows users to extend the information space related to each resource with their own comments and thoughts.

JeromeDL exports users' comments, which are in the form of blog responses to a blog post, a library resources in this case, using SIOC metadata [30]

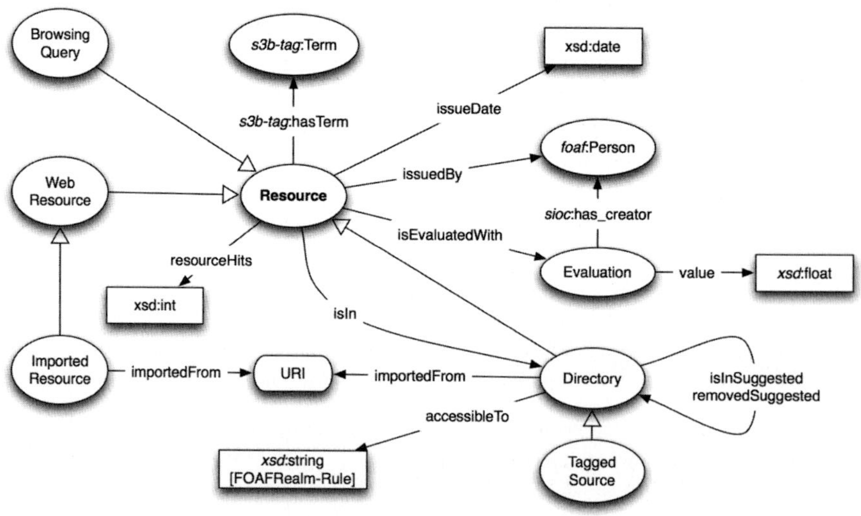

Fig. 8. Community ontology

[6] http://del.icio.us/

(see Fig. 8), an emerging standard for expressing information from blogs and fora; therefore, these comments can be easily integrated with other semantic-aware community information [122] (see Fig. 6 in Sect. 6). As a result, current readers can easily deliver new knowledge for future readers; furthermore, the knowledge created by the users along with the library resource can also be find and used outside the library world. For example, in the SSCF bookmarks interface which supports SIOC information, a user can browse the comments for each library resource.

In order to achieve the interoperability between JeromeDL and other community-based sites, our system needed to ensure compatibility between SIOC and SSCF/JeromeDL ontologies. We achieved that by creating some content using SIOC metadata and a delivery mediation mechanism for other SSCF/JeromeDL content.

A module for annotating and evaluating the content in JeromeDL uses the SIOC:Post class for representing the information in RDF.

The rest of the classes in SSCF and JeromeDL ontologies required mapping to the SIOC ontology. A JeromeDL instance is presented as a site containing the forums; a forum represents the resource in the digital library - JeromeDL's book concept. Directory, the SSCF class, can also be seen as a Forum or as a Site (a root directory). A user (Person) is translated to SIOC:User; the Resource is simply mapped into SIOC:Post concept.

4.3 Social Tagging

Tags are just simple words that describe the given content; they are chosen informally and personally by the Internet users. Tagging is currently a very popular method of categorizing the Web content. Current research in Web 2.0 introduced the notion of *folksonomy*; it is an Internet-based information retrieval methodology consisting of collaboratively generated, open-ended labels that categorize Web content. A folksonomy is contrasted to a taxonomy; both are used for the same purpose, but a folksonomy is created by the community of users.

JeromeDL allows users to use both taxonomies and folksonomies for annotations; therefore, we are able to join the semantic and social description of resources. Generally tagging in JeromeDL uses semantic keywords from thesauri; however a user is also able to tag a resource with some free keyword (a tag), which has not been defined in thesauri. With this approach we are able to benefit both semantic and social tagging.

5 Conclusions and Future Work

This chapter described the JeromeDL architecture and how it provides semantic and social networking power to digital library system. Adding semantic power to the tasks required of instruction designers, educators, presenters, and students improves the efficiency, applicability, and appropriateness of eLearning software platforms and systems. We have shown how this can be done by simplifying the assembling of material, simplifying and adding natural language abilities to the process of query making, and by providing single sign-on access to systems coupled with social networking of friends, classmates, colleagues, and collaborators. Thus, we have shown how digital libraries can regain their position in the eLearning activities; a position their ancestors, brick-and-mortal libraries, held in classic learning process.

JeromeDL has been installed in a number of locations[7]; the two most used, DERI Galway library[8] and WBSS[9] at Gdansk University of Technology, serve their community of users in everyday activities. DERI Galway library is used by researchers as a pre-print server to locate and share publications. WBSS maintains a set of scans of antique books and a number of books written by lecturers at GUT; the latter ones are used as learning material, similar to the eLearning scenario presented in Chapter "*Conclusions: The Future of Semantic Digital Libraries*" (see Sect. 2).

Future work should further investigate augmenting library mechanisms with other technologies available. We envision future digital libraries will become multipurpose knowledge management systems based on technologies like semantic web, social networks or meshing up web services.

Acknowledgement

This material is based upon works supported by Enterprise Ireland under Grant No. ILP/05/203 and by Science Foundation Ireland Grant No. SFI/02/CE1/I131.

---

[7] A list of JeromeDL instances: `http://wiki.jeromedl.org/Instances`

[8] DERI Galway library: `http://library.deri.ie/`

[9] WBSS library: `http://www.wbss.pg.gda.pl/`

The BRICKS Digital Library Infrastructure

Bernhard Haslhofer and Predrag Knežević

Service-oriented architectures, and the wider acceptance of decentralized peer-to-peer architectures enable the transition from integrated, centrally controlled systems to federated and dynamic configurable systems. The benefits for the individual service providers and users are robustness of the system, independence of central authorities and flexibility in the usage of services.

This chapter provides details of the European project BRICKS,[1] which aims at enabling integrated access to distributed resources in the Cultural Heritage domain. The target audience is broad and heterogeneous and involves cultural heritage and educational institutions, the research community, industry, and the general public. The project idea is motivated by the fact that the amount of digital information and digitized content is continuously increasing but still much effort has to be expended to discover and access it. The reasons for such a situation are heterogeneous data formats, restricted access, proprietary access interfaces, etc. Typical usage scenarios are integrated queries among several knowledge resource, e.g. to discover all Italian artifacts from the Renaissance in European museums. Another example is to follow the life cycle of historic documents, whose physical copies are distributed all over Europe.

A standard method for integrated access is to place all available content and metadata in a central place. Unfortunately, such a solution requires a quite powerful and costly infrastructure if the volume of data is large. Considerations of cost optimization are highly important for Cultural Heritage institutions, especially if they are funded from public money. Therefore, better usage of the existing resources, i.e. a decentralized/P2P approach promises to deliver a significantly less costly system,and does not mean sacrificing too much on the performance side.

[1] BRICKS – Building Resources for Integrated Cultural Knowledge Services (IST 507457) `http://www.brickscommunity.org`

1 Requirements

Besides better usage of existing resources, the decentralized and service-oriented approach has an additional advantage: all its functionalities are spread over many locations, ensuring that the system can survive a number of failures while being able to continue to be operable. If a server crashes in the client-server architecture, the whole system stops until the server is repaired. The reliability of servers could be increased by replicating their functionalities in the system, but this would increase the total of system maintenance required.

It is always a good strategy to design a system that is able to handle loads which were not foreseen during the initial design phase. For standard client-server the system load must be carefully estimated, e.g. by guessing the maximum number of users. In open systems like BRICKS such estimation is hardly possible. Due to the simplicity of joining the system the number of nodes can increase rapidly. Thanks to better usage of available resources, loads should be distributed within the system without losing much on performance. Thus, the decentralized approach ensures that the system will perform well even given unpredictable loads.

The lack of central points removes the need for centralized system maintenance. Important infrastructure functionalities are all implemented in a self-organizing way. That is a strong advantage of the decentralized approach because a centralized administration costs additional money and personnel must be dedicated to the tasks. Keeping the cost of the system maintenance at a minimum is one of the major requirements, and the decentralized approach is a way to achieve it.

In order to reduce the costs further, the system should be deployed on top of the regular Internet. With its expansion in the last few years, connectivity can be obtained anywhere at a reasonable low cost. Institutions should be able to reuse their existing Internet connection when joining the BRICKS community.

Figure 1 shows a possible topology of the future BRICKS system. Every node represents a member institution, where the software for accessing BRICKS is installed. Such nodes are called BNodes. BNodes communicate with each other and use available resources for content and metadata management.

To summarize, the BRICKS infrastructure should be fully decentralized, use the Internet as a communication medium and fulfill the following requirements:

- Expandability – the ability to acquire new services, new content, or new users, without any interruption of service.
- Scalability – the ability to maintain excellence in service quality, as the volumes of requests, of content and of users increase.
- Availability – the ability to operate in a reliable way over the longest possible time interval.

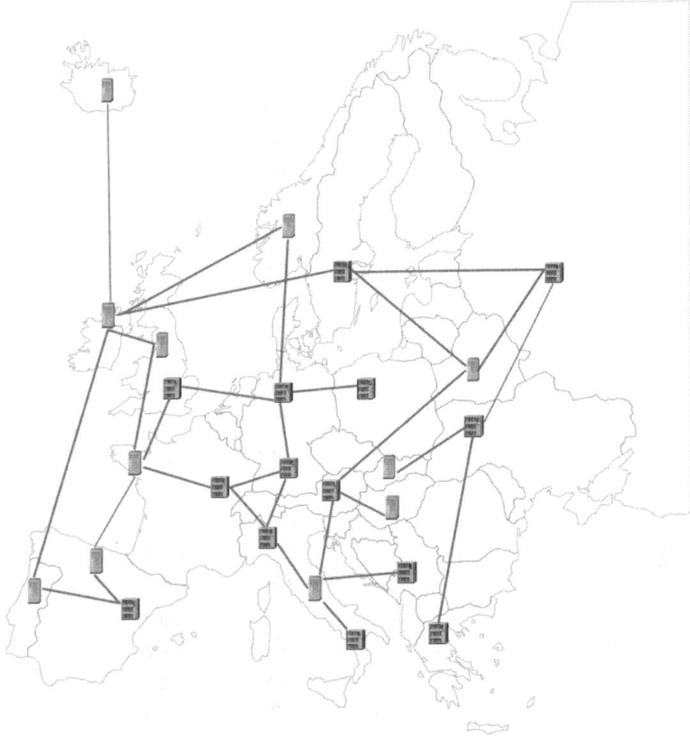

Fig. 1. Decentralized BRICKS topology

- Graduality of Engagement – the ability to offer a wide spectrum of solutions to the content and service providers that want to become members of BRICKS.
- Interoperability – the ability to make available services to and exploit services from other digital libraries.
- Low-cost – an institution can become a BRICKS member with minimal investment. In the ideal case the institution should only get the BRICKS software distribution, which will be available free of charge, install it, connect it to the Internet and become a BRICKS member. To minimize the maintenance cost of the infrastructure any central organization, which maintains, e.g. the service directory, should be avoided. Instead, the infrastructure should be self-organizing so that the scalability and availability of the fundamental services, e.g. service discovery or metadata storage, are guaranteed.
- Flexible Membership – institutions can join or leave the system at any point in time without significant administrative overheads.

2 Approach

The major challenge in designing a fully decentralized system like BRICKS is to fulfill the listed requirements without the help of a central coordination unit. Every BNode knows directly only a subset of other BNodes in the system. However, if a BNode wants to reach another member that is unknown to it, it will forward a request to some of its known neighbors that will deliver the request to the final destination or forward it again. This is depicted in Fig. 2. It shows also that BRICKS users access the system only through a local BNode available at their institution. Hence every user request is first sent to the institution's BNode and then the request is routed between other BNodes to the final destination. Search requests behave like that; the BNode will preselect a list of BNodes where a search request could be fulfilled, and then the BNode will route it there. When the location of the content is known, e.g. as a result of the query, the BNode will directly be contacted.

A BNode could be seen as a set of services that are required to manage an institution's presence in the system, and to provide services for the rest of the community. They run within a Web service framework that provides a standard set of functionalities: service management/invocation, parameter serialization/deserialization. The architecture is layered and shown in Fig. 3.

The BNode consists of three types of components (i.e. in the project terminology they are called bricks): fundamental, core and basic bricks. Most of them are standard Web services, described by WSDL (Web Services Description Language) documents. It allows that applications can be developed any language with a decent Web-service support. By default Java bindings are

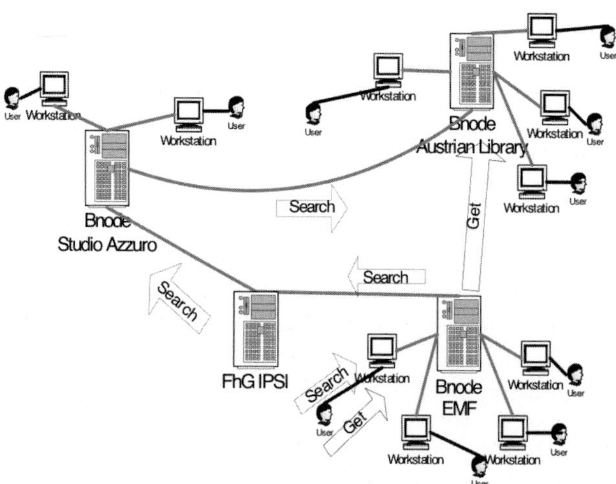

Fig. 2. Request routing in BRICKS

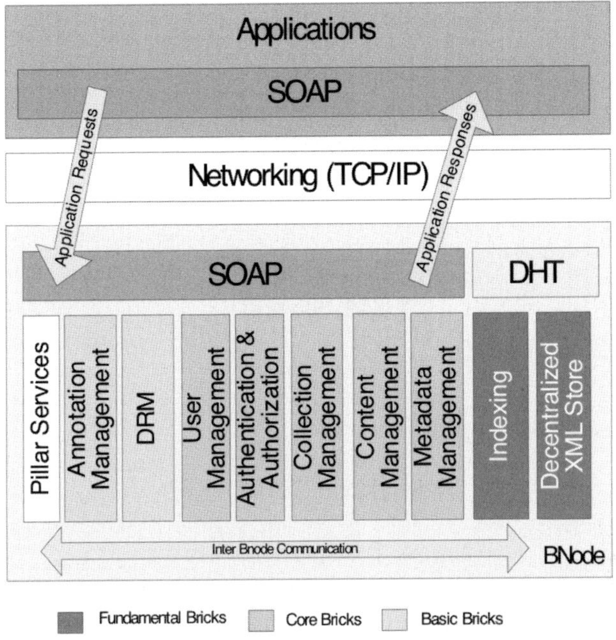

Fig. 3. BNode layered architecture

available, but invoking BNode services is pretty easy as well using C#, C++, Python or PHP.

Since the BNode architecture is service-based, a BNode installation can be spread over more than one machine at the installation site. In such a case, fundamental Bricks (see Fig. 4) are needed on every machine that is part of the local installation, and core and basic bricks could be present only on some machines. The fundamental bricks include components like the Decentralized Storage and Index, a Distributed Hash Table implementation, and Service Registration and Discovery. As their name suggests, core bricks provide core system functionalities to users, i.e. a minimal set of services that enables users to use the system. They include services like Content, Metadata, and Collection manager. On other hand, basic bricks like Translation or Annotation Manager are optional, and they need not be present at every installation site.

Each BNode organizes it own content into collectionsindexcollection which are later exposed to the rest of the community. The information about their existence is published with the help of decentralized storage, i.e. collection metadata are managed there, and are available to all BNodes. The system design distinguishes two types of collections: physical and logical. A physical collection has a role similar to a role of a directory/folder in a filesystem. Every content item managed by a BNode may belong exactly one physical collection and it must exist at the time when an item is inserted into the BNode. On

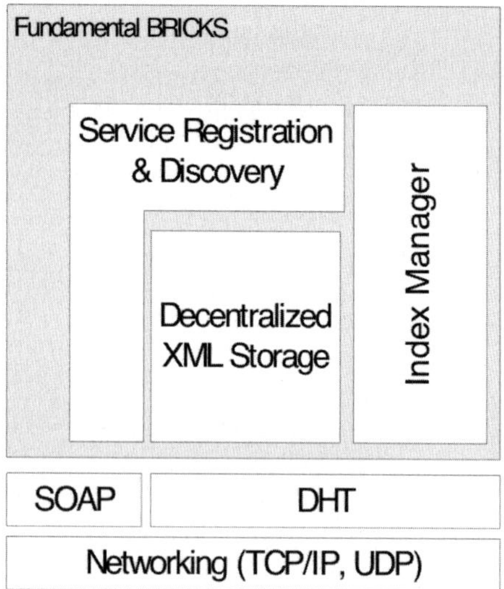

Fig. 4. Fundamental BRICKS

other hand, a logical collection can be seen as a set of links pointing to various content items. Thus, an item can belong to many logical collections at the same time. The main purpose of logical collections is to help grouping content according to some logic, comparable to views in databases.

Although collection metadata are available to all BNodes in the network, content and its metadata never leave BNode without an explicit permission of BNode administrator. Fine and detailed security policies can be specified both for local and remote users. Remote users can be further classified into different access groups according to the trust that the BNode where they are coming from has. The security mechanisms are fully decoupled from the BNode services and the policy can be changed at any time without need to reinsert managed content and metadata.

Content is managed in a JCR 170 compliant backend. JCR can handle binaries of any media type (e.g. images, audio, video, documents, etc.) and is completely configurable with respect to content models. By creating a content model definition (XML file) application developers can freely define how compound media objects are put together, for example, how pages are ordered to form chapters. Therefore, from a content management perspective, the BRICKS network practically fulfils the requirements of any application scenario. Additionally, managed content can be protected by various Digital Rights Management licenses based on MPEG21 standard.

Descriptive metadata, thus metadata describing resources for discovery and identification [163], are stored in semantic-aware repositories that are controlled by the Metadata Manager. Rather than imposing a single, fixed metadata schema (e.g. Dublin Core), BRICKS applies the RDF [219] metadata framework which is technically open to any kind of metadata because of its simple and flexible graph data model. Metadata schemes – which reflect the structure and semantics of metadata descriptions – can be defined by creating ontology models in OWL [221]. Opposed to the traditional way of creating metadata schemes (e.g. database schemes) this approach is a much more decentralized and community-driven process: parties agree on the explicitly declared meaning of ontology concepts and can easily exchange and reuse ontology definitions in other application scenarios [167]. The extensibility of OWL ontologies allows institutions to create application profiles in order to tailor existing metadata standards to their needs. OWL also allows domain experts to define individuals (e.g. authors, places) within ontology models, which is a convenient way to include controlled vocabularies (e.g. list of authors, list of places) in schema definitions.

For retrieving digital objects from the BRICKS network, each BNode exposes a query interface which accepts simple full-text as well as advanced metadata-field based search requests. Inside a BNode, search requests are handled by the Metadata Manager which – in the case of advanced search – translates the requests to SPARQL [220] and executes them against the RDF metadata base. However, since queries must be sent to all relevant BNodes in the network, all schemes definitions must be available to all BNodes. Furthermore, semantic as well structural heterogeneities among metadata schemes must be resolved. This task is performed by the Schema Manager: it uses the decentralised XML storage to manage schema definitions and reformulates search requests according to mapping definitions between specific schemes. This of course implies that the Schema manager must be available on each BNode installation.

Metadata about managed content are indexed and managed within a decentralized index, available to all BNodes in the network. Its existence helps building an efficient query execution plan, i.e. sending queries only to BNodes that might match them. Such a strategy should ensure better scalability of BRICKS network with the increase of content volume and the number of active participants.

3 Building Semantic and Community-based Applications

In this section we give an overview of applications that have been developed within the BRICKS projects and integrate certain semantic concepts or community features. All these applications have in common that they build upon the BRICKS framework described in the previous section. This approach has significantly reduced the effort to implement application scenarios in a distributed setting like BRICKS.

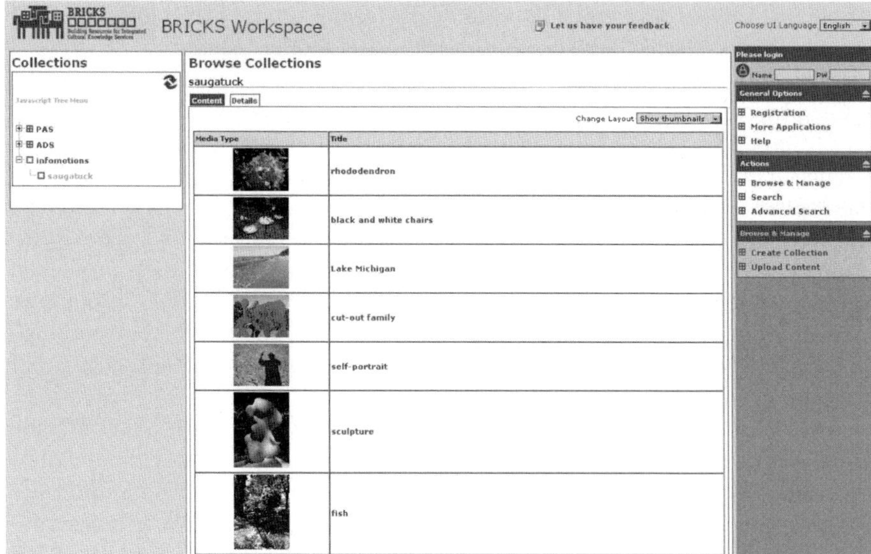

Fig. 5. The BRICKS Workspace

3.1 The BRICKS Workspace – Exploring the Framework Features

The main purpose of the BRICKS Workspace (see Fig. 5) is to serve as blueprint application which implements and demonstrates the features of the BRICKS framework. Application developers can reuse the Workspace as a template for building their own domain specific web applications on top of the BRICKS framework.

With the BRICKS Workspace, cultural end users can browse the content collections available in the BRICKS network, contribute their own contents by creating personalised collections, and create virtual, logical collections that contain references to contents in other physical collections. Through a full text and an advanced, schema-aware search interface they can retrieve contents, view content details, and optionally tag or annotate content objects. The Workspace also comprises user management and access control on the use case (e.g. Create Physical Collection) and the object level (e.g. Physical Collection with a certain identifier).

Technically, the BRICKS Workspace is a Struts web application that can run in any Servlet Container (e.g. Apache Tomcat). It connects to a single BNode instance which transparently handles all the distributed aspects. The communication between BNode and Workspace instances runs via SOAP.

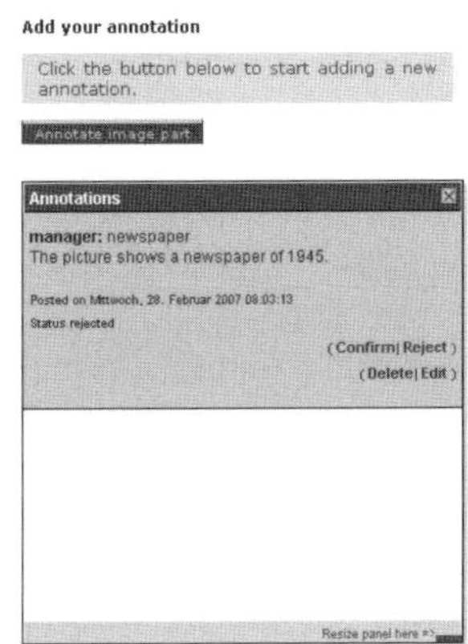

Fig. 6. Annotations in the Living Memory application

3.2 Living Memory – Fostering User Communities

Most applications in the digital libraries domain focus on technologies to manage and provide access to contents and metadata. However, in many cases they do not fully exploit the potential of web technologies to build user communities. The BRICKS Living Memory scenario (see Fig. 6) demonstrates that besides content and metadata, the user and communities play a central role. Annotations, for instance, are a means that encourages end users to actively participate in digital libraries and contribute their knowledge in terms of tags, free text, or any other kind of annotation. The central application in the Living Memory scenario is a web-based annotation tool built upon the BRICKS framework. It allows users to annotate images as well as parts of images.

Annotations can be shared and commented by other users; in that way it is possible to build threads of annotations which is an important requirement for building communities. Although libraries and other memory institutions have discovered the added-value of user involvement and user contributions, they still require appropriate tools to monitor and control user input. In order to address this problem the Living Memory Annotation Tool provides an annotation management component that enables the organisation's staff to control the contents of annotations and access to annotations.

Living Memory utilises AJAX techniques, which allows the user to create annotations in an intuitive and user-friendly manner. Through AJAX, changes are presented to the user without any disturbing page reloads and communication with the back-end is streamlined. The user interface can be adapted to different languages by creating a translated version of the English language resource file.

3.3 Finds Identifier – Managing Archaeological Finds Using CIDOC-CRM

Transparent handling of the structural and semantic heterogeneities is a key requirement in BRICKS. In the Finds Identifier scenario the choice was on the CIDOC Conceptual Reference Model (CIDOC CRM) [46] in order to provide interoperability among the metadata of the archaeological institutions. The CIDOC CRM is a comprehensive standardised ontology tailored to the cultural heritage domain. Interoperability can be achieved by mapping each proprietary metadata schema to this global ontology.

The target user group of this application scenario are archaeologists that want to identify their finds (e.g. coins) by comparing them with already catalogued finds. A web application (see Fig. 7) allows end-users to search for and browse through existing finds through a faceted-style, guided search interface which dynamically narrows the search result set with each user interaction. For some finds – for those that have the finding habitat stored in terms of GIS metadata – it is possible to resolve these metadata via an external GIS server and display the finding location on a map.

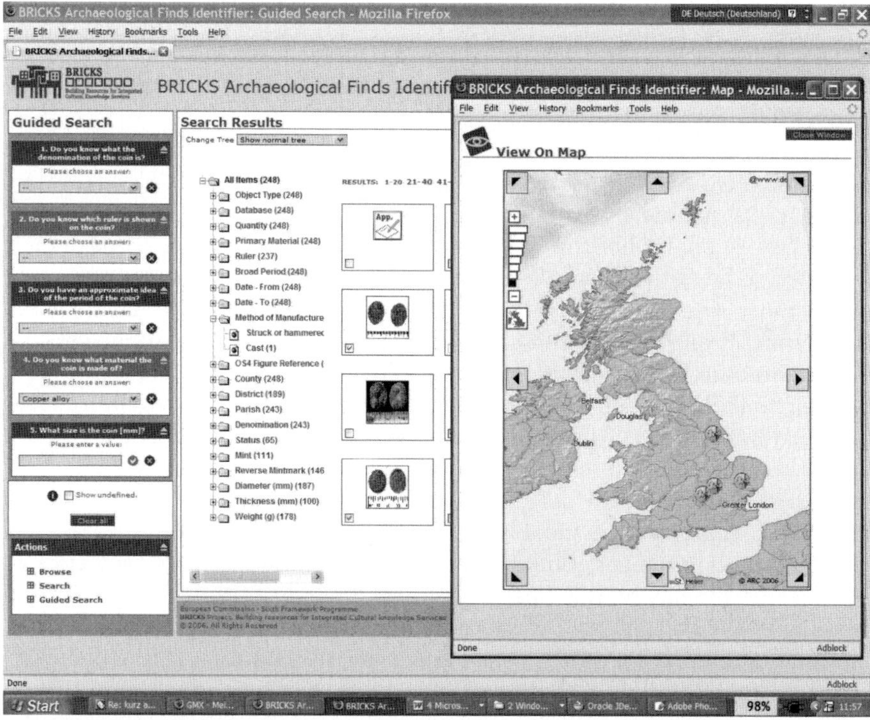

Fig. 7. Finds Identifier Web Front-End. GPS habitat metadata are resolved to maps

4 Summary and Conclusion

In this chapter we have described the technical details of the BRICKS digital library infrastructure and presented three applications that were developed on top of it. The main architectural difference between BRICKS and other digital library systems is its distributed nature: rather than managing contents and metadata in a centralized system, institutions have the possibility to install a BNode for bringing in their contents and metadata into the BRICKS network. Each BNode instance provides a set of services which cover the major functionalities (e.g. DRM, User Management) required by each institution.

A clear advantage of the BRICKS infrastructure is its openness and modularity. One can easily reuse existing BNode (Web) services or develop additional ones in order to provide additional, not yet supported features. Further work must be invested in performance-tuning and scalability. Due to the distributed nature of BRICKS, it is a difficult task to reach the same performance level as a centralized digital library software.

Semantics in Greenstone

Annika Hinze, George Buchanan, David Bainbridge, and Ian Witten

1 Introduction

This chapter illustrates the impact on a well–known digital library system – Greenstone – when it is moved from fixed modules and simple metadata-based structures, to open semantic digital library modules. This change has profound effects on the tools available to end-users to retrieve relevant content from the library, and an equally significant impact on the digital library (DL) architecture. Most current DL systems contain protocols for internal communication that define information exchange solely in terms of searching, browsing, and document retrieval. These communications reflect traditional user interactions in the library. However, this regimented approach results in inflexible systems that are difficult to extend to support other retrieval techniques. Furthermore, simple field-based metadata limits the ability of the DL to connect or disambiguate key items of information, impeding the precision of retrieval.

Greenstone, an open source digital library toolkit that has developed over the last 10 years [226], forms the basis for the work described here. The software comes in two flavours: Greenstone 2 and Greenstone 3. The former exemplifies the classic form of digital library, with the added twist that (through UNESCO involvement) it is capable of running on primitive computing platforms that are common in developing countries (e.g., Windows 3.1 using Netscape 4). The latter is a reimplementation that is backwards compatible with the earlier version but far more ambitious in its goals. Particularly germane to the present work is the fact that it adopts an open protocol that works in tandem with a dynamic, componentised architecture [15].

In this article we describe the semantic aspects of the Greenstone 3 design and compare it with the earlier version, as a representative example of the archetypal approach. To illustrate key design elements, we draw upon three examples – an alerting service, ontology-enhanced representation and retrieval, and interoperability with a tourist information system – where many of the required user tasks and system features cannot be achieved through traditional digital library capabilities alone. These build upon the Greenstone 3 infrastructure. The details are developed in two steps:

1. *Semantics of documents and collections.* In the first step, we describe and analyse typical user tasks in the Greenstone Alerting Service. These tasks call for a semantic model for digital library collections and content. We show how this requirement can be met by providing an ontology-based extension to the Greenstone Librarian Interface, an interactive subsystem for creating and maintaining digital library collections.
2. *Semantics for services and collaboration.* In the second step, we address the semantic issues of collaboration within a software framework. We study interoperability between the mobile Tourist Information Provider (TIP) information system and Greenstone, which together provide location-based access to digital library documents. This example shows how the software architecture of Greenstone 3 supports different semantic models.

The structure of the chapter is as follows. We begin with an introduction to the Greenstone system. Then we detail Greenstone's solutions for semantic issues, both at the collection level (see Sect. 3) and for collaborating modules and systems (see Sect. 4). We conclude with a general discussion about semantic support in general-purpose digital library software and the cost of providing rich semantic information (see Sect. 5).

2 Greenstone Digital Library Software

Greenstone is an open source digital library toolkit [225]. Used out of the box it provides the ability to create collections of digital content, to display the content in a web browser and to access and search the collections that have been built. Through UNESCO sponsorship the software is fully documented in English, French, Spanish, and Russian; in addition, its web interface has been translated into over 40 languages through volunteer efforts.

Countless digital libraries have been built with Greenstone since its public release on SourceForge in 2000: from historic newspapers to books on humanitarian aid; from eclectic multimedia content on pop-artists to curated first editions of works by Chopin; from scientific institutional repositories to personal collections of photos and other document formats. All manner of topics are covered: the black abolitionist movement, bridge construction, flora and fauna, the history of the Indian working class, medical artwork, and shipping statistics are just a random selection.

A wide variety of formats are accommodated, including HTML, PDF, OpenOffice, Word, PowerPoint, and Excel document formats; MARC, Refer, Dublin Core, LOM (Learning Object Metadata) and BibTeX metadata formats; as well as a variety of image, audio, and video formats. Greenstone also

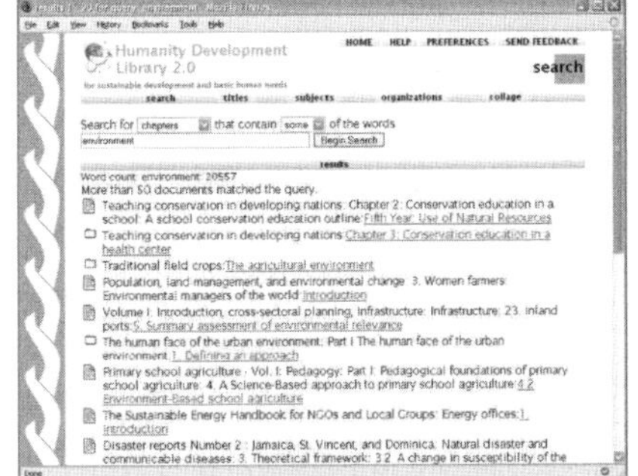

(a) Query interface and match list

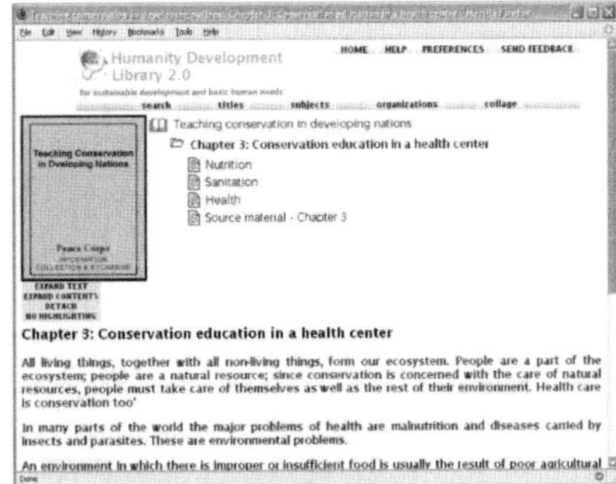

(b) Full text document view

Fig. 1. Screenshots of Greenstone readers' interface

supports numerous standards including OAI-PMH (Open Archives Initiative Protocol for Metadata Harvesting), Z39.50 and METS (Metadata Encoding and Transmission Standard) to to assist interoperability. Export options include Fedora, DSpace and MARC. See our web-site `www.greenstone.org` for more details.

An end-user's experience of Greenstone is through a web interface, such as the one shown in Fig. 1, taken from the Human Info NGO's *Humanity Development Library.*[1] Documents in this collection can be searched by chapter title, in addition to full text searching by chapter or entire document. Alternatively, users might choose to browse alphabetically by title, or hierarchically by subject or organisation. In Fig. 1a the user has searched within chapters for the word "environment" with a ranked listed of matches displayed; in Fig. 1b the user is viewing the document that results from selecting the second matching item: Chapter 3 of *Teaching conservation in developing nations.*

Figure 2 shows the Greenstone Librarian Interface (GLI), a graphical application for creating and maintaining collections such as the *Humanity Development Library.* Through a system of tabbed panels accessed along the top of the interface, the digital librarian decides what files to include in the collection, what metadata is manually assigned (in addition to that automatically extracted by Greenstone from the source files), the collection's searching and browsing capabilities, and the customisation of presentation details.

Both Greenstone 2 and 3 provide the above capabilities – the archetypal digital library – but differ radically in implementation. Version 3 is fully built on open standards technology. Its predecessor was designed before many standards (such as XML and SOAP) existed, and although it has kept pace with developments, this has involved building onto a framework that was never designed for such dramatic extensions. Additionally, Greenstone 2 follows a traditional client server model, the protocol of which, as noted earlier, is fixed. In contrast, Greenstone 3 is based upon a distributed network of

[1] `http://www.nzdl.org/hdl`

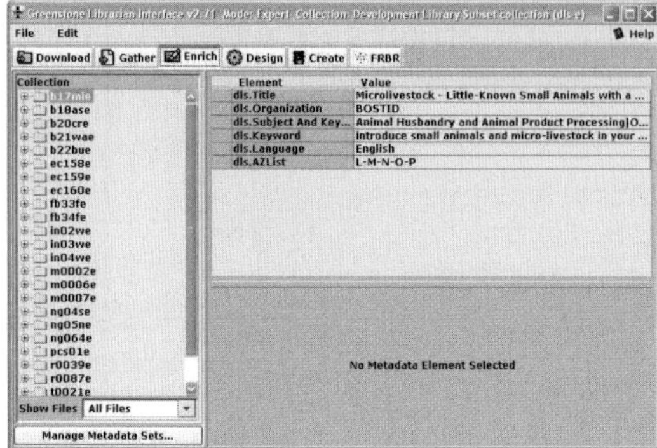

Fig. 2. Screenshot of the Greenstone Librarian Interface, including the FRBR ontology-based extension

modules and uses SOAP to stream XML messages between them, with the option of customisation of messages at any point through the use of XSL Transforms. Dynamically loadable modules are layered on top of this communication channel. A "describe-yourself" call is a mandatory fixture that allows service discovery in a heterogeneous world of communicating applications.

Figure 2 is actually a Greenstone 3 version of the Greenstone Librarian Interface, built using this very capability. Notice the rightmost tab (labelled "FRBR") which indicates that GLI has been initiated with the *Functional Requirements for Bibliographic Records* [176] extension loaded – the ontology enhanced feature discussed in Sect. 3.2. Further technical details of the two architectures are discussed in Sect. 4.2. Henceforth we use "Greenstone" to denote the semantic-capable version of the software, and write "Greenstone 2" when it is necessary to refer to the earlier version.

3 Semantic Model for Documents and Collections

In terms of a semantic model for documents and collections, we first describe the issues that were identified when implementing the Greenstone alerting service. Then we explain how these issues are addressed by the FRBR ontology support that has been introduced into the Greenstone Librarian Interface.

3.1 Greenstone Alerting Service

Users of digital libraries often have ongoing information needs: a doctor may need to track new publications in their field of speciality; an academic may wish to identify new articles on an individual whose biography they are writing. In either case, "stored" searches, using filtering or event-based technologies, are a critical addition to the digital library tool-set.

The Greenstone Alerting Service (Greenstone-AS) is a generic event-based alerting system that is provided as an optional extra to the Greenstone toolkit package [37, 90]. The system implements alerting across several libraries, including Fedora [136] and DSpace [202]. It supports the creation of profiles that represent a user's information needs. These profiles are subsequently used to match the user's needs against new or modified documents that are added to any DL server across a federated and/or distributed network of heterogeneous DL servers. In other words, in a network of DL servers the user can keep track of any document changes on any server. Furthermore, Greenstone-AS supports the notification of other types of events – such as the creation of a new classification within a topic heading, or the addition of an entirely new collection of material on an existing server.

The following examples are typical tasks that a user may be interested in. They can be defined as profiles that can be registered with the alerting service.

1. A new *electronic document* has been made available, for example, an electronic document about climate change. A user wants to be notified once the document is entered into a DL collection and available via the digital library.
2. A new physical work has been published, e.g., the latest Harry Potter book. A related task is a user keeping track of new issues of a journal (again in physical form).
3. An old manuscript is newly digitised by scanning, in a higher resolution, or in a different format. A music recording has been re-sampled in a new audio file.
4. Another edition of the same book is published.
5. An electronic document has been *newly published in the digital library.* The document is not new but has been newly added to the collection.
6. A document is deleted from the digital library. This event may be of interest, for instance, to a professor who wants to keep track of the DL documents available to students.
7. An electronic document has changed: for example, online software documentation may be continually written and adapted. Similar properties hold for blogs and wikis.

These different user profiles have implications for the semantic model used by the digital library. For illustration, we show the semantic hierarchy of our example items as perceived for alerting in Fig. 3a. We see the view of a book (in the example, a volume of "Harry Potter") from the perspective of an alerting system. The circled numbers correspond with the alert types listed immediately above. On the right, in Fig. 3b, is a depiction of a simple FRBR data model of the same needs. The figures are compared in detail in Sect. 3.2 below.

Different media types (e.g., text, music, film, maps) require and allow different tasks to be carried out (e.g., scan, sample, change after digitising)

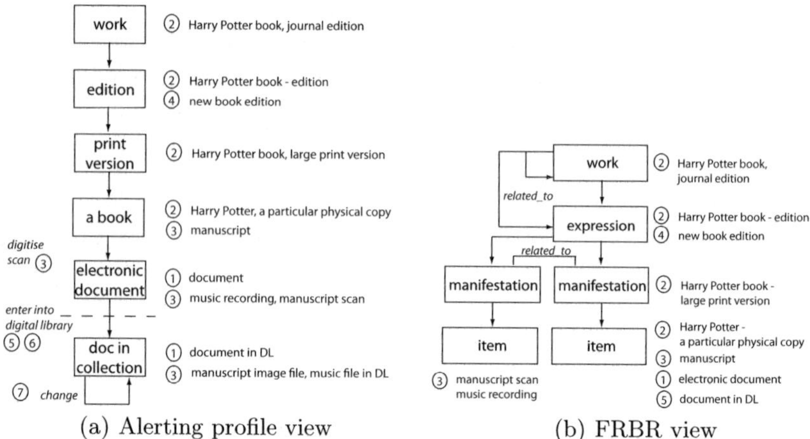

(a) Alerting profile view (b) FRBR view

Fig. 3. Semantic hierarchies of documents and DL items. Numbers refer to the enumerations of profile tasks on the previous page

and allow for different types of profiles (see above). We need to distinguish actions within the digital library and actions outside; both types may need to be captured. For example, the concept of a new document may carry the following semantics: new 'real world' document, scanning (i.e., making an electronic document), adding the document to the library.

There are several semantic consequences from this. Across the DL network involved, all items (works, editions, documents, scans) must have a consistent identifier over time. A new version of an item may be assigned a new identifier while the old one retains its identifier. Alternatively, the new document may take the identify of the previous version, while the old document is archived (and obtains a new identifier) or is deleted. In addition, both the new and old version could be assigned new identifiers. Semantically, the abstraction of the work and edition from a document or recording is crucial to the successful execution of alerts.

3.2 FRBR in Greenstone

The recommendation on Functional Requirements for Bibliographic Records (FRBR) [176] is an important and relatively recent recommendation for the enriched description of creative works in digital indexes. FRBR can be used to improve the features and functionality of the reader's experience of using a digital library [34]. As an example of a simple ontology developed by the Library of Congress, FRBR is highly significant to the DL research community.

The FRBR model is based upon four entities: *works, expressions, manifestations* and *items.* A work is a unique creative product (e.g., James Joyce's "Ulysses" or the latest Harry Potter book), available in one or more *expressions* (commonly termed editions or versions). Each expression has a particular selection of content, and may be produced in several different *manifestations*. For example, a book may be printed in a number of different bindings (paperback, hardback), or electronically (in PDF). An *item* is a single copy of a particular manifestation – the file on your computer, or the volume on the library shelf. This simple framework creates a tree for each work.

Beyond the core entities, there are others for expressing the identities of people and organisations concerned with the creation of the work or expression, such as authors, performers and publishers. Similarly, the subject of books can be encoded, including again people and organisations, but also events, places, and so forth. Works can also be related. For example, "West Side Story" can be encoded to identify that it is derived from William Shakespeare's "Romeo and Juliet".

Figure 3b illustrates some potential examples. In the case of a music manuscript, both the physical print and the electronic scan reflect the same *expression* of the same work. However, the printed version and the related scan are best modelled as different *manifestations* of this expression. Both the printed and scanned manifestations may have a number of different actual instances, or *items*. In contrast, the user's view of a scanned copy, when defining an alert, is probably different. Looking left to Fig. 3a, the scanned copy is seen as a derivative of the physical (printed) copy it was taken from. Whilst in both cases the logical modelling could be altered, or represented in a different manner, digitisation often throws up such possibilities for different outcomes to arbitrary decisions, and a good DL system should include the ability to resolve these – particularly when including material hosted elsewhere. Referring to our example alerting tasks, we observe that the manuscript as well as the scanned manuscript are items to different manifestation that refer to each other. Note that tasks 6 and 7 (actions within the DL) are not represented in FRBR. Similarly, the relationship between a manuscript and its electronic representation (see alerting task 3) can be made explicit by relating the two manifestations (see Fig. 3b).

The initially simple framework of FRBR provides powerful tools for resolving some common user requirements. As we noted in Sect. 3.1, users often want to track accessions to a library, such as the arrival of a new issue of an important journal. Whilst traditional metadata can track some relatively simple requirements, complexities in the wider world or in the user's needs often mean that metadata-only methods lack critical levels of precision. To take some simple examples, if a journal that is being tracked for new issues changes its title, alerting may fail; authors with common names may be difficult to disambiguate; translations of a work may have entirely different titles. These are just some cases where only a richer semantic approach can hope to support the user's actual information goals.

Collaboration

Users of digital libraries often use several different digital libraries to fulfill their information needs. Developing the dataset to support a rich information environment such as a sizable FRBR repository may similarly require the inclusion of material from several different sources. As any given *work* may appear in dozens or hundreds of individual *items*, FRBR is quite capable of including the content of several libraries. Such an approach also offers the opportunity to support the discovery of content from traditional DLs that are built on regular metadata. Thus, much of the semantic-technology benefits of FRBR can be extended to older DL architectures as well.

Greenstone FRBR Implementation

FRBR support in Greenstone includes several different facets: the encoding of FRBR information using the Greenstone Librarian Interface (see Fig. 2); the discovery of material from metadata-based DLs; the support of pure "FRBR" retrieval; novel user interactions and improved alerting. Space precludes a full discussion of these different aspects, so here we will focus on GLI's support for ingest, searching metadata-based DLs through FRBR, and alerting. For each aspect, we first discuss its semantic challenges and then discuss the details of Greenstone's approach.

FRBR Ingest

The use of any ontology or semantic model, such as FRBR, requires the population of the model with actual data. Interactionally and architecturally, adding FRBR support to the GLI is not trivial as the application was originally developed to support a metadata-driven build process, albeit with a configurable workflow and the ability to handle any chosen metadata standard (e.g., MARC, Dublin Core). However, most metadata schemes have little or no hierarchical aspects, and none take the object-oriented, ontological approach of FRBR.

The differences are easily highlighted when one compares the ingest of a new document. One key step is the addition of author metadata to the document. Using Dublin Core in a traditional DL architecture, one would simply add data to the DC.creator field. However, in FRBR one creates a relationship between a *work* and a *creator*. The creator will often be a specific person, who is represented by a specific object in the FRBR repository. Thus, what in one approach is represented by a metadata field is in the other represented by an object-to-object relationship. The former simply requires text input, whilst the latter requires a query to be executed against the FRBR repository, and perhaps a new object to be created.

These differences have clear impacts on the Greenstone 3 system and interaction design. For example, an author query will result in the system selecting one or more matching author objects and their corresponding documents, whilst in Greenstone 2 a simple search against the metadata of all documents is sufficient. In interaction terms, a traditional DL architecture has no system concept of the author as an object, the author cannot be represented in the interface directly. In contrast, Greenstone with FRBR explicitly represents the author in a data object. Consequently, a specific page can be created for each author with a list of their works and biographical details. An analogue of this could be created in a traditional architecture but the biographical details, etc. must be encoded in a document in the collection and similarly named authors would have to be distinguished by careful manual creation of the author document. Worse, author biographies for collection access would now now mixed with original material in a collection.

FRBR is only one example of ontological support. Other schemes could provide further or complementary advantages. Ontologies can also support traditional metadata libraries: for example, ingest of new documents can be assisted by extracting relevant data from an ontology. Once a particular *expression* or *manifestation* of a FRBR work is associated with a new digital document, FRBR data can be ingested into a metadata-based library through the simple step of outputting the FRBR data in a compatible metadata format such as MARC. Further, library specific, data can subsequently be added, such as subject classification and accession date. The Greenstone–FRBR module provides such a facility for Greenstone 2.

FRBR Retrieval

Interactive retrieval lies at the heart of any digital library system. Traditional metadata-based digital libraries, such as Greenstone 2 and DSpace, provide document retrieval through the document metadata and/or full text. As in the case of FRBR ingest in Greenstone, however, this simple mechanism alters. Whilst the syntax can appear to be similar – e.g., retrieval of a document by author name – the corresponding operations underneath have changed. Furthermore, the range of possible retrieval operations expands beyond what is simply expressed by traditional search.

A semantic approach also simplifies the index encoding issues for more complex retrieval tasks. A search for books by "Winston Churchill" may seem straightforward. However, there were in fact two well-known Winston Churchills who were nearly contemporaneous: Sir Winston Leonard Spencer–Churchill, the wartime Prime Minister of the United Kingdom, and American novelist Winston Churchill. In fact, there are a number of other Winston Churchills of other dates who have written well-known texts. Using document metadata alone, all that can be done is to maximise the data encoded about any individual document – giving as much author information as possible. However, doing so consistently is problematic, and identifying possible confusions fraught with potential misunderstandings or simple lack of knowledge. Worse, some authors write under more than one name (Agatha Christie also published as Mary Westmacott, for example) or with various spellings of their name (a common problem with Russian writers translated into English). Using a document-by-document approach produces many problems of scale (multiple inputting) and validity (e.g., ensuring consistent encoding of all documents by an author). A structured, semantic approach yields immediate benefits.

However, how can this be achieved when a considerable investment has already been made in an existing metadata-based DL, such as Greenstone 2? Using a separate FRBR database, documents in Greenstone 2 are stored as particular FRBR *items* in the FRBR database, connected to Greenstone 2 by their unique document identifiers. Subsequently, the FRBR database can be used as a supplementary tool to disambiguate metadata through the FRBR system, rather than endeavouring to use complex encoding in the metadata features of the DL. With Greenstone an installation can be customised using its open architecture, to provide this functionality directly within the running DL system. Alternative or additional further ontologies can be supported in by exactly the same method: for instance, a bespoke ontology in Greenstone has been created for a commercial collection of 18th century literature.

Alerting

In Sect. 3.1 we looked at a number of the difficulties that can emerge when a user attempts to define an ongoing alert requirement. As with many metadata-centred methods, particular requirements can be difficult to express precisely in the original Greenstone-AS alerting system. The use of FRBR or an equivalent ontological method provides one technique for increasing precision or recall for many alerting tasks. Simple alerts directly correspond to the retrieval requirements identified above, but are triggered whenever the Greenstone ingest process performs changes on a collection. Though additional data is required to distinguish current and prior state of the DL to establish when a change occurs, these simply provide a second filter to reduce the final result set. Greenstone with FRBR covers all of the alerting tasks detailed in Sect. 3.1.

However, the vocabulary and language of potential alert requirements is vast. Alerts are not necessarily only the product of readers' information needs about documents. Alerts could correspond with subject classifications, and may be the product of managing the library content, rather than use of the library content. In other words, *librarians* themselves have information needs that do not correspond with traditional document retrieval. For example, a librarian may wish to know when a subject classification exceeds a particular size, suggesting that it may require new sub-classifications to be added.

Any one ontological model is unlikely to cover all possible requirements, and FRBR contains no direct representation of subject hierarchies, though particular information on the subject of individual documents (e.g., of people, places or topic) is supported. Just as FRBR can provide a method for better modelling the connection of documents, authors and publishers, classification hierarchies in turn can better model structured maps of document topics.

Semantic Challenges

In developing FRBR support and alerting in Greenstone, further semantic challenges have emerged. Some reflect significant issues in the modelling of library content. One such challenge is the question of *aggregate works*. Aggregates are publications – such as an anthology of poetry – that contain a number of separate *works*. Researchers from library science argue for different approaches to modelling aggregates in FRBR. One such approach is to identify an aggregate as a particular *manifestation* of many different works. In consequence, the aggregate can only then be identified as a relationship between the many manifestations of different works that constitute it. In other words, as a distinct entity, it becomes implicit. There are serious shortcomings to this and other approaches that attempt to model aggregates within the existing FRBR model. Our approach was to model aggregates as a separate entity type, and support for this new type was added to Greenstone [36].

4 Semantics for Collaboration

The collaboration of Greenstone with the TIP service for location-based access identifies further semantic challenges. We describe the Greenstone 3 architecture and explain how its open framework addresses a variety of these challenges.

4.1 Location-based Access to Greenstone

The TIP/Greenstone Bridge [89] provides location-based access to documents in a digital library. TIP is a mobile tourist information system that gives context-aware access to information about sights that are in the vicinity of the user. In a typical interaction, a user starts from a TIP information page, e.g., about the University of Waikato, and decides to look up the digital library collections that refer to their current location. When they switch to the page from the TIP/Greenstone Bridge, the system will display nearby regions and places that they might want to search for in the collection repository provided by Greenstone. This reflects their location at the University of Waikato, in the city of Hamilton, in the Waikato region, on the North Island of New Zealand, etc. All these locations could be used to search the library; the user can guide the selection.

Based on the user's selection, the system triggers a location-based search of the DL collections. The user is presented with a list of all collections that refer to the selected region. After selecting a collection (e.g., Hamilton Gardens) and a document they are interested in (e.g., a description of the Chinese Garden), the user is presented with the digital library document with the place name highlighted. These names serve as anchor points that can link to further

(a) highlighted text (context world) (b) back link pop-up (context world) (c) gazetteer (context New Zealand)

Fig. 4. Overview of example interaction with TIP/Greenstone [89]

documents within the Greenstone collection, to a gazetteer of placements, and to TIP pages. An overview of the interactions is given in Fig. 4.

For location-based access, documents must be pre-processed in order to identify any locations that they mention. Our current implementation of the TIP/Greenstone bridge uses a gazetteer to identify place names annotated by country. A simple location-aware mark-up of the documents is used in the software version described in [89]; a design using more complex access via spatial indexes is described in [179].

In either case, the challenge lies in identifying location or place names. For example, a document may be about Hamilton New Zealand, or Hamilton Canada. The term Hamilton may also refer to Captain Hamilton, after whom the city was named, or to any other person with the first name or surname Hamilton. Similar challenges apply for other contextual semantic information, such as the distinction between documents *by* Shakespeare and documents *about* Shakespeare.

Different systems collaborating with the digital library may have different notions of semantic information. For example, the digital library bridge combines Greenstone, TIP, and the Gazetteer. Collaboration requires the semantics of place names to be made explicit: correct hyper-links to related pages within the three systems (as shown in Fig. 4(b)) are only possible if the respective concepts are aligned. In addition, the semantic context needs to be considered: in Figs. 4(a) and 4(b), all place names are identified; whereas in Figs. 4(c), only place names in New Zealand are taken into consideration.

4.2 Open Framework in Greenstone

In the earlier version of Greenstone, communication between the underlying services and the user interface was provided through the Greenstone protocol [13]. This was a closed protocol, in common with other contemporary DL protocols such as SDLIP and Dienst. In Greenstone 3, each service (module) can provide its own interface, and the operational DL system can be composed from the desired mix of individual services and modules. To support simple adoption of the standard features, an analog to the earlier Greenstone protocol is provided. However, this is no longer the only method of providing communication, and it is this very mechanism that was used to implement the TIP/Greenstone bridge.

Suleman [209] has produced a powerful argument for modularising digital library systems. Greenstone 3 follows this philosophy (which is already present in many areas of Greenstone 2) throughout its entire architecture, from the ingest of new material to runtime services. This openness, which naturally embraces semantic technologies, also brings pointed challenges. For instance, co-ordinating multiple services at runtime becomes difficult when new services can readily be added or existing ones removed.

Certain elements must remain constant to provide sufficient rigour and regularity for implementation to remain reliable and efficient. The protocols of Greenstone 2, Dienst and SDLIP share common features that mean that coupling a client of one protocol with a server of another is relatively straightforward [13]. These similarities apply at both document and service levels: all protocols use unique document identifiers, and all protocols support query-based retrieval.

5 Discussion

Ontologies and semantic models provide more powerful levers for information retrieval than do classical metadata-based digital libraries. The simple metadata structures such as Dublin Core (or MARC) used by standard digital library systems provide only limited means of expressing particular information needs. Greenstone 3 allows for the creation of a simple metadata-based digital library collection. It supports the use of rich semantic data and corresponding services that transcend traditional metadata. Thought this semantic framework complex ontological methods can be built to annotate documents, classifiers and the collections that contain them.

As discussed in this chapter, documents in a digital library can play a critical role in the retrieval process. The semantics that occur *within* documents can be expressed simply as flat text, but at the cost of precision during retrieval. Just as FRBR can disambiguate between different authors of the same name, detailed mark-up and semantic modelling of document content can distinguish places of the same name in a text, or between a place name and a personal name.

Supporting a richer range of retrieval methods requires corresponding runtime services and ingest time indexation. Greenstone has responded to both these challenges by extending the use of open standards within its architecture and implementation. At ingest time, the system provides the opportunity to tailor the accession process, including the use of additional indexers, applying metadata and content validation and running data extraction processes such as summarisation. At runtime, the system retains the provision of a simple Greenstone 2-like protocol, but in addition each module and service can define its own messaging options, and the entire communication between user interface and runtime services can be fully componentised.

The application of semantics to digital library systems is not cost free. Considerable time investment is required to achieve richer mark-up, and costs on metadata creation are already high. Such costs also apply to the installation and configuration of a digital library system: whilst the configuration of Greenstone 2 for a collection of Dublin–Core encoded XML documents for later retrieval by metadata and full text is straightforward, the task of preparing a Greenstone 3 collection for retrieval using FRBR for cross-document retrieval and internal semantic modelling within documents requires an entirely different level of commitment. The process of configuring an ontology-enabled Greenstone 3 collection is more complex, requires more effort, and is resource intensive. Providing API-style access at runtime to the first system is also simple, whilst the latter is open to much greater variation between installations. Currently, such complexities directly challenge the widespread adoption of the richer retrieval technologies that semantic DLs can provide. A considerable body of further research is required to lower these costs, both at installation and runtime.

Part V

Building the Future – Semantic Digital Libraries in Use

Hyperbooks

Gilles Falquet, Luka Nerima, and Jean-Claude Ziswiler

The first part of the chapter presents a synthesis of recent works in the domain of hyperbooks and introduces a general hyperbook model. In this model, a hyperbook is made of a knowledge structure, a set of informational fragment, links between the fragments and the knowledge structure, and a user interface specification. This specification is used to generate the actual reading interface which is a hypertext whose nodes and links are derived from the knowledge and fragment structures. The knowledge structure provides a mean to interconnect different hyperbooks in a semantically consistent way, so as to create digital libraries of hyperbooks.

The second part explains in more details the knowledge structure alignment process that is at the heart of the semantic interconnection of hyperbooks. The presentation is based on a real-world example, in the domain of agriculture. It also provides experimental results about the performance, in terms of precision and recall, of this process.

1 Introduction

Hyperbook, or hypertext book, is a term that is commonly used to refer to a hypertext that has some of the characteristics of a printed book. In particular, a hyperbook is generally organized as a set of elements that are grouped together to form larger entities such as chapters or sections. Moreover, the content of a hyperbook should be autonomous and have a clearly identified topic or objective (in this sense, an encyclopedia is not a (hyper)book).

There is presently no consensus about a common hyperbook model. Nevertheless, most of the models proposed in the literature and actually implemented are comprised of a first order hypertext [189], which corresponds to the book content and the logical orgnization of its entities, and a second order structure that represent knowledge about the book's domain. This structure can range from a simple network of concepts, with semantic links, to a formal domain ontology. These two levels already existed in early hypertext systems such as KMS [10] and MacWeb [162]. In addition, some models and systems provide a way to specify the generation of user interface documents. In this case, the hyperbook is a kind of virtual, or potential, document, in the sense of [190] and its user interface is made of actual documents generated from the hyperbook's contents.

In the rest of this introduction we briefly present a list of systems and models that are typical of the hyperbook or virtual document approach.

The Woven Electronic Book Systems (WEBSs) [183] is an electronic book management system for the creation and organiszation of documents (texts, figures, logic-mathematical models, indexes, etc.). The documents, or blocks within documents, can be interconnected through a network of semantic links. It is also possible to create hierarchical structures (similar to table of contents), called browser documents. The WEBSs has a powerful scripting language used to define new user interface components such as browsers or indexes.

The InterBook project [33] presents an e-learning platform that includes two basic models: the domain model and the student model. The domain model is a network of domain concepts. The student model describes the student knowledge as well as the student learning goals, both expressed in terms of the concepts of the domain model. The system uses this model to adaptively generate the content the student can access at a certain point, depending on his or her knowledge and goals. At a hight leve, several books can be integrated in a bookshelf. The interconnection of several books is realized by a shared domain model. In [229], the authors propose a similar model of adaptive hypertext which includes a domain model, a user model and adaptation rules. The domain model is a semantic network consisting of domain concepts and relations between concepts. This model serves essentially to define adaptation rules, depending, for instance, on the concepts known or understood by the user.

The KBS hyperbook system [164] is also dedicated to e-learning, with a constructivist approach. It makes use of the O-Telos modelling language to create a rich semantic description of the book's domain. An interesting feature of this system is the possibility to create different semantic abstractions over the same information units in order to represent different viewpoints.

Crampes and Ranwez [48] propose two models of virtual documents. Both of them use domain ontologies for indexing informational fragments (the resources). In the first case, a "conceptual backward chaining" strategy can construct reading paths corresponding to the user objectives (described in terms of conceptual graphs). In the second case, a pedagogical ontology defines teaching rules, which guide the assembling of fragments to produce documents with respect to a predefined pedagogical approach. These rules determine the order of appearance of the different types of learning material in the documents. An inference engine generates documents that satisfy these rules.

Garlatti, Iksal and colleagues [96,97] propose a comprehensive and detailed model of virtual documents. It is based on four ontologies for modeling the domain, the metadata, the application and the user. These ontologies allow a fully declarative approach of document composition.

In the e-learning context, we can find similar approaches for instance in [193]. The authors present an ontology-based hyperbook model where the modeling of relations is of particular interest. Links between concepts in the domain ontology are not represented directly in the interface documents, but generated implicitly around concepts of interest. The idea is to avoid users (mostly students) getting confused by seeing too many of the top-level concepts of the ontology. The Learning Object Model (LOM) is fully integrated into the system so that people using other learning systems can reuse their tutoring and student models. They have to adapt only the knowledge base by working out the concepts of the ontology. The authors also provide an example ontology about concepts in computer sciences.

Bocconi [25] describes a hypertext generation system to automatically select and compose scholarly hypermedia. The presented content is generated through a domain ontology containing the concepts and their relations and a discourse ontology containing different roles and narrative units describing different genres. The discourse ontology holds a very detailed and highly formalized description of the points of interest that a user can have about a domain.

In the next section we will present a hyperbook model that synthesizes and generalizes the main concepts introduced in the above-mentioned approaches. Then, in Sect. 3, we will show how to extend this model to create semantic digital libraries of hyperbooks. Section 4 details the automated hyperbooks' alignment process and provides a concrete example together with experimental results.

2 A Conceptual Model of Hyperbooks

The hyperbook model we present here is comprised of a fragment repository, a domain ontology, and an interface specification (see Fig. 1). The fragments and the ontology, together with their interconnecting links, form the structural part of the hyperbook while the interface specification is intended to dynamically generate the actual documents and hyperlinks that form the reading interface. This model has been introduced in [67] and it can be seen as a synthesis of the above mentioned approaches.

2.1 The Hyperbook Structure

The basic informational contents of the hyperbook are made of reusable fragments, which can be texts, images, sounds, mathematical formulae, etc. Fragments can be connected by structural links, for instance from fragments to sub-fragments, to form compound fragments. These typed links indicate the roles played by the different fragments in the compound fragment. For instance

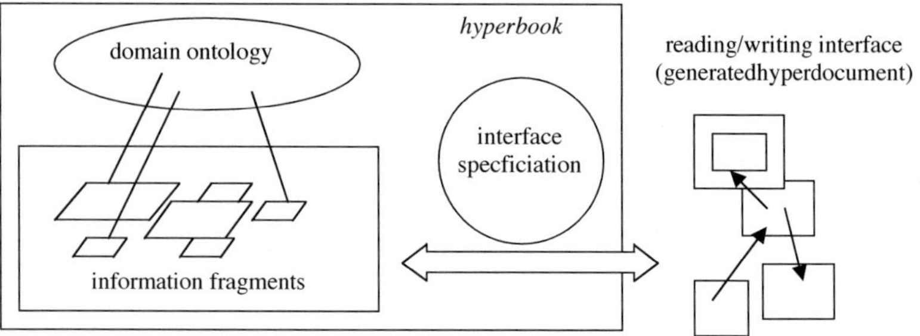

Fig. 1. Components of the virtual hyperbook model

an exercise could be made up of a question fragment, one or more answer fragments, and a discussion. Compound fragments can have different purposes, they can represent pedagogical or narrative/rhetoric units (exercise, elaboration, summary, reinforcement, etc.), argumentative units (an issue related to positions, arguments, contradictions, etc.), or even hyperbook management units (group discussions or weblogs). For instance, a discussion structure can be made up of topic and message fragments connected through about and reply-to links. In fact, this structure corresponds to what Rada [189] calls the first order hypertext, it also roughly corresponds to the kind of structure that is supported by markup languages such as XML (considering not only the hierarchic decomposition in elements but also "transverse" links).

The domain ontology of a hyperbook is intended to hold a formal representation of the domain's concepts. Since the hyperbook authors are not supposed to be knowledge engineers or ontologists, the ontology model must be kept simple. For this reason, the ontology is a directed graph whose nodes represent concepts and whose labelled links represent semantic relations. Among these relations, the is a relation (or generalization/specialisation) plays a particular role since it provides a taxonomic structure of concepts. This relation must form a directed acyclic subgraph of the ontology.

The connection between the ontology and the fragments is provided by semantic annotation links. These links not only index each fragment with one or many concepts but they also indicate the role played by a fragment with respect to a concept. Typical link types are:

- Instance, example, illustration: The fragment describes a particular instance of the referred concept
- Definition: The fragment contains a textual (or audio, or graphical) definition of the concept
- Property: The fragment describes a property of the concept
- Reference, use: the fragment refers to the concept (it is necessary to know the concept to understand the fragment)

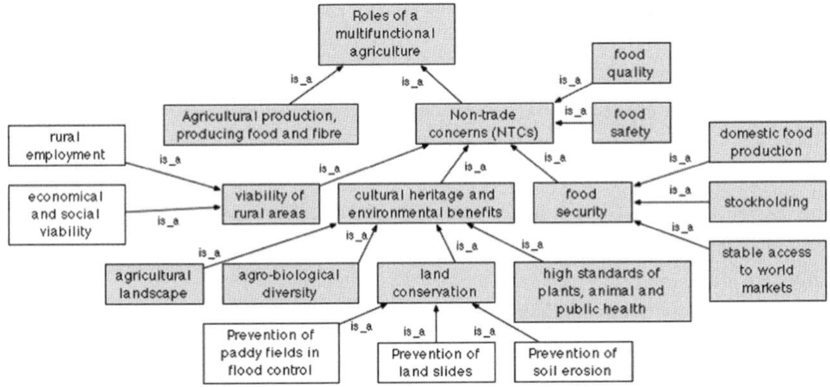

Fig. 2. The domain ontology of the hyperbook about multifunctional agriculture

Other link types may exists in specific contexts. For instance, a scientific hypertextbook may have links such as theorem, exercise, algorithm, historical note, etc. Figure 2 presents an example of a hyperbook ontoloy Gray boxes indicate concepts that are connected to fragments.

In the previous section we have seen that the ontological or domain knowledge level may have different purposes such as providing a semantic index of the hyperbook, guiding the production of pedagogical documents, adapting the displayed content to the user, etc. In this section we will emphasize the role of the ontology in the inference of semantically relevant links between fragments and between interface documents; in the following section we will show that hyperbook ontologies play a central role to integrate different hyperbooks into a digital library.

2.2 The Model-based Hyperbook Interface

Following the virtual document approach, we define the user interface of a hyperbook as a navigable hypertext, made of documents and hyperlinks that are derived from the hyperbook structure. The aim is to present the informational content of the hyperbook to the user and to help him or her read, understand, and write the hyperbook's content in different ways and under multiple perspectives.

To reach this aim, the interface documents must be composed by selecting and assembling several fragments that make up semantically coherent units of presentation. Given the richness of the static hyperbook model, it is impossible to design a single "optimal" reading and writing interface. This is why the interface model is designed to support the specification of various views on the hyperbook content, thus enabling the hyperbook designer to adapt the interface to each particular hyperbook [65]. In particular, it is necessary to adapt the hyperbook structure to different pedagogical styles or to specific practice or rules of a domain.

An interface specification consists of a set of hypertext node schemas that will be instantiated on demand to produce the actual interface documents [67]. Hence, the interface nodes (the documents the user sees) are instances of node schemas. A node schema is comprised of

- A selection expression: what objects (fragments/concepts) to select
- A content description: how to organize the selected objects within the nodes
- A link description: what kind of links to generate to which nodes

The link model is richer than what exists in hypertext systems such as the Word-Wide Web. In addition to the "jump" links (the usual Web links), it is possible to specify *inclusion* and *expand-in-place* links. Inclusion links are intended to build complex hierarchical nodes by including the content of other (sub)nodes. Expand-in-place links enable the user to dynamically create a document by including the content of selected nodes in the current node. Figure 3 shows an interface document of the above-presented hyperbook about multifunctional agriculture. It is an instance of the concept[C] node schema, shown (in abbreviated form) in Fig. 4, with C set to Cultural heritage and environmental benefits. It includes, among others, an instance of the concept_definitions node schema that displays the contents of the fragments connected to C through a definition link.

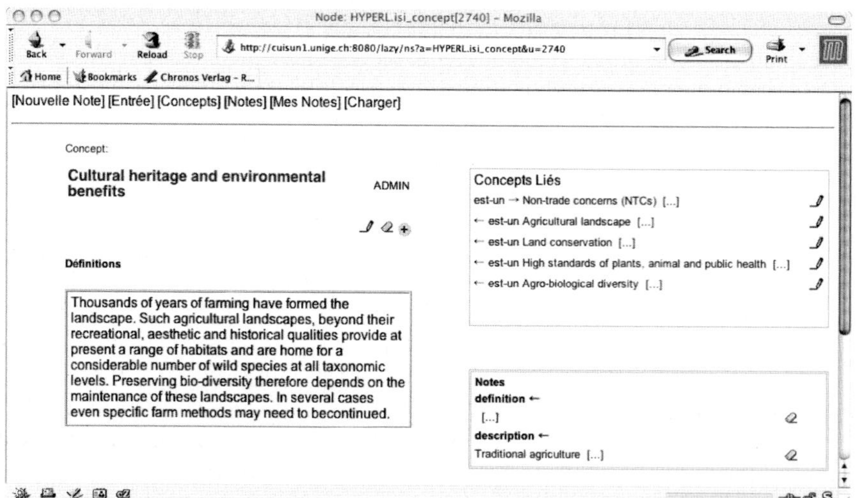

Fig. 3. A user interface node of the hyperbook about multifunctional agriculture

```
node concept[C]
{
  <left-column>(
      C.content,  /* display the concept name */
      include concept_definitions[C]  /* and all its definitions */
  </left-column>
  <right-column>
      include related_concepts[C],
      include related_notes[C]
   </right-column>
}
from C

node concept_definitions[C]
{
   F.content
}
from  C (definition)> F
/* select all the fragments connected to C
   throug a "definition" link */

... other node schemas ...
```

Fig. 4. Node schemas for producing the node shown in Fig. 3

2.3 Link Inference

Inferred links correspond to paths starting from a fragment, going through one or more concepts in the ontology, and ending on another fragment. Inferred links are preferred to direct links because authors are generally able to establish correctly typed links from the fragments they write to the relevant concepts, whereas, when they are asked to link their fragments directly to other fragments, they have difficulties finding relevant fragments to link to and deciding on what type of links to establish [66].

Since the hyperbook ontology has a graph structure, an interesting property of the model is that semantically meaningful links can be obtained by simple inference rules that consist of path expressions. If we consider the global labeled graph formed by the domain ontology, the fragment collection, and the concept of fragment links, a path expression is an alternated sequence of nodes and arc specifications. A node specification is composed of a node type (concept or fragment), a category name (for fragments) or a term (for concepts). An arc specification is composed of a link type, a traversal direction. In addition, each node and arc can be associated to a variable. An instance of a path expression is a path in the hyperbook graph that satisfies all the specifications of the path expression. Figure 5 shows an extract of the domain ontology about political sciences, links (1) are instance of the above-described path expression.

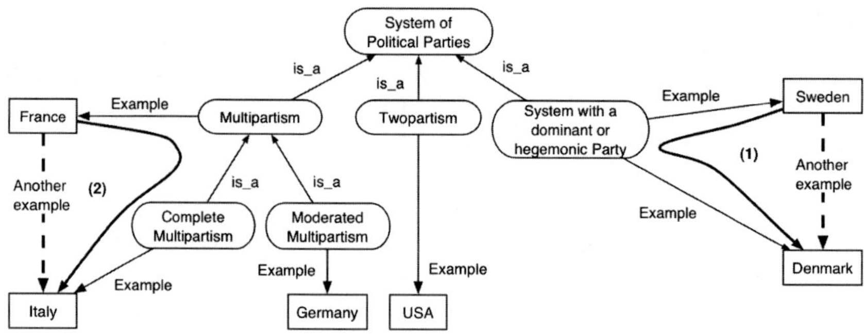

Fig. 5. Link inference through the domain ontology (rectangles are fragments and rounded rectangles are concepts)

Depending on the link types and fragment categories of the hyperbook, it will be possible to define link inference paths that have a precise and useful meaning for the reader. The following expressions show examples of link inferences that typically occur in a hyperbook.

```
F1 (Another Example)> F2 :-
F1 <(Example) C1 <(is-a*) C2 (Example)> F2.
```

Generates a link, with type Another Example from fragment F1 to fragment F2 if F1 is an example of a concept C1 , and C1 has a sub-concept C2 , which has an example F2 The <(is-a*) notation represents the traversal of zero, one or more is-a taxonomic links in the generic to specific direction.

```
F1 (has property)> F2 :-
F1 (uses)> C (is-a*)> D (property)> F2
```

If fragment F1 refers to concept C , create a link, with type has property to every fragment F2 that describe properties of a concept D that is more generic than C. For instance, If F1 is an exercise, this will link it to all properties of the concepts required by the exercise.

An interesting property of this link inference method is its robustness with respect to the hyperbook's evolution. Since the domain ontology is usually more stable than the hyperbook's fragments, a link to a concept will probably have a longer lifetime than a link to a fragment. Moreover, inferred links are, by definition, always up to date.

3 Semantic Digital Libraries of Hyperbooks

In this section we will explore the construction and development of digital libraries made of hyperbooks instead of traditional electronic documents (such as PDF or HTML files). The main distinction between a traditional digital library and a virtual document library is the disappearance of the monolithic nature of a book or an article.

In a digital library of hyperbooks, a document reading system should be able to compose new documents from all the available informational fragments of the library, according to the readers' objectives. We can also consider that a hyperbook, once inserted into a library, will automatically enrich itself by connecting to fragments of other books, For instance, a hyperbook that has fragments related to a concept C can be augmented by finding fragments about an equivalent concept C' in another hyperbook. This implies, of course, that there exists a mean to find a concept that is "considered as equivalent" to C in another hyperbook ontology.

3.1 Establishing Links Between Hyperbooks

Once several hyperbooks have been (partly) written, the characteristics of the hyperbook model allow aligning the different hyperbooks by semantic links (Fig. 6). The links are realized in a way similar to the semantic relations we have inside a hyperbook ontology. The link can be defined by hand with the advantage that a specific type can be added. As this might become a time consuming task in a bigger environment, we introduce the possibility to establish similarity links in an (semi-) automatic way by applying known ontology alignment methods to our hyperbook model. The technical details are described in the next section that comes also with a sight to experiences we conducted during the last years. The final result might be several connected hyperbooks that are linked by different types of link: Some of them might be set up by hand and can be considered as precise semantic relations between concepts of the hyperbooks' ontologies. Others might be generated just on the fly in the interface level if a user wants to browse through the content of different hyperbooks. These links typically might be generated automatically and don't have a type other than "similar". Finally, we can imagine to establish link verification by social navigation, or that the automatic generation process helps

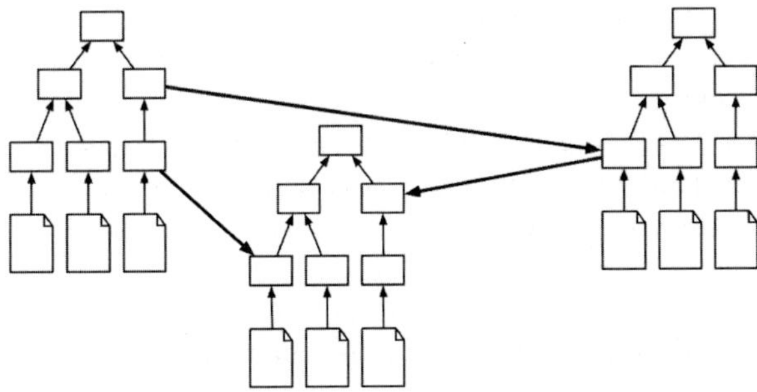

Fig. 6. A semantic digital library made of hyperbooks and semantic links between hyperbook concepts

user to detect links that they finally establishes by hand and by giving them a more specific type.

The so created structure is not a fully integrated hyperbook, but a semantic digital library that takes the form of a network of semantically inter-connected hyperbooks. As mainly the user interface plays an important role on how the user will browse in the digital library and how she or he considers the semantic relations between hyperbooks, we particularly consider the re-using of hyperbook interface specification in the following.

3.2 Reusing Interface Specifications and Creation of New Global Books

Another interesting characteristic of the virtual hyperbook model and of the integration model is the possibility of re-using specifications of virtual interface documents to create global reading interfaces.

A first technique for building a global interface consists in re-using the specification of a hyperbook interface, but to apply it to the whole information space of the library, i.e. to the fragments and ontologies of all the hyperbooks and their interconnections through similarity inks. If we consider that a hyperbook represents a point-of-view (semantic or narrative), we will obtain a vision of the whole library according to the point-of-view of this hyperbook. In other words, we extend a hyperbook with the help of the others. The most direct manner to extend a hyperbook consists in using the similar concepts found in the other hyperbooks and links issued from these concepts. For example, the path

```
F<(example)  C -(example)> G
```

becomes

```
F<(example) C -(similar_to)> C' (example)> G
```

A fragment `f` that contains an example for concept `C` will be connected to a fragment `G` if `G` is an example of a concept `C'` that is similar to `C` (the set of examples of a hyperbook is extended thanks to the example found in other hyperbooks). In the same way, it is also possible to make present other definitions of concept c.

It should be noted that the effectiveness of this approach depends on the quality of ontology integration; This means that we must find the same link types and fragment categories in these ontologies. This last problem, although non-trivial, is nevertheless simpler than the integration of domain ontologies because the number of concerned concepts is quite limited. Another way of re-using an interface specification consists in applying this specification to another hyperbook. In this case, we will see the informational content of one hyperbook with the interface of another. It is the dynamic part of the narration of a book that is applied to another content. This kind of re-use does not require any rewriting of interface node schemas, but it implies that the hyperbook ontologies have been well integrated.

Another case concerns the creation of new "global" books. We suppose that an author wants to create a new book starting from information already existing in the digital library. This is a second level author, who will not create information, but invent new narrations and presentations. This task can be achieved either by creating new interface node schemas, or by re-using schemas of different hyperbooks. As we have already seen, each interface node schema can be applied to any hyperbook. As a consequence, a second level author can create new schemas that include or refer to existing schemas, without having to modify the latter.

4 Automatic Hyperbook Integration

This section discusses how different hyperbooks can be aligned to build a digital library. Concretely, our aim is to establish semantic links between concepts of different hyperbooks. We explain in the following how we compute different semantic similarity values between concepts and how we decide which of the calculated similarity values have the right quality to indicate candidates for semantic relations between concepts.

4.1 Determining Semantic Similarity

An approach to determine semantic similarity, to which our problem is close, is the one of Rodrguez and Egenhofer [191]. Their aim is to calculate semantic similarity between concepts of heterogeneous and disconnected ontologies. In their approach, calculating semantic similarity between concepts means calculating semantic similarity between "entity classes" through three different basic components: a set of synonym words (synsets) that denotes the entity class, a set of semantic interrelations among these entity classes, and a set of distinguishing features that characterizes entity classes. In order to determine the similarity between entity classes, they first define similarity functions for synonym sets, semantic neighbourhoods and distinguishing features (parts, functions and attributes). Then, a matching process over the calculated similarities establishes semantic similarity links between the entity classes (concepts).

We are concerned with small-scale domain ontologies where concepts are described by their relationships and by textual fragments, so we can't apply Rodrguez and Egenhofer's algorithm as such. They apply their algorithm to larger top-level ontologies like WordNet or SDTS. In our application, an author will not define several synonyms of a term and all their semantic relationships and features. Determining similarity between different synonym sets is becoming a comparison between two single terms (Word matching WM).

Rodrguez and Egenhofer outline that the more complete and detailed the entity classes' representation, the better the algorithm will work. In the hyperbook structure, we have a rich semantic representation of the concepts, but in a less formal way. Thus, we propose to substitute feature matching that indicates common and different characteristics between concepts with fragment matching (FragM). Instead of comparing concepts' features, we compare their textual fragments.

Only the third similarity measure, which compares concepts and their associated features/fragments in the semantic neighbourhood (NeighM), can be applied as in the original method.

In order to calculate the three mentioned similarities, we have to determine the distance from the concepts to the immediate super-class that subsumes them, or in other words, their common least upper bound. In the case of independent ontologies, this means to connect them by making each of their roots a direct descendant of an imaginary and more general root "anything". The path distance $\alpha(a,b)$ is determined as

$$\alpha(a,b) = \begin{cases} \frac{depth(a)}{depth(a)+depth(b)} & \text{if } depth(a) \leq depth(b) \\ 1 - \frac{depth(a)}{depth(a)+depth(b)} & \text{if } depth(a) > depth(b) \end{cases} \quad (1)$$

where $depth(a)$ and $depth(b)$ stand for the shortest path from concept a (resp. b) to the imaginary root "anything".

The basic similarity function is based on set theory involving both common and different characteristics of concepts:

$$S(a,b) = \frac{|A \cap B|}{|A \cap B| + \alpha(a,b)|A - B| + (1 - \alpha(a,b))|B - A|} \quad (2)$$

where, in the case of WM, A and B stand for the sets of words found in the term designating concept a (resp. b) of the respective ontologies (after stopword filtering). In the case of FragM, A (resp.) B stands for the terms found in all the fragments linked to concept a (resp. b) in the corresponding hyperbooks (after stopword filtering). NeighM applies these two similarity measures recursively to all concepts within a preliminary defined radius.

To compute the final similarity value $S_{final}(a,b)$ between two entity classes (concepts), Rodrguez and Egenhofer weight the three matching values.

$$S_{final}(a,b) = w_1 S_{WM}(a,b) + w_2 S_{FragM}(a,b) + w_3 S_{NeighM}(a,b) \quad (3)$$

with $w_1 + w_2 + w_3 = 1$.

The difficulty is to indicate how to assign the weights w_i for WM, FragM, and NeighM. We will discuss different settings in the next section where we present our experimental results with the matching algorithm.

4.2 An Example from the World of Agriculture

We illustrate the outcomes of the algorithm with the above-presented hyperbook about multifunctional agriculture (HMA). The aim is to establish semantic similarity links towards a second hyperbook about agriculture politics of the World Trade Organization WTO (HWTO). The matching algorithm compares each concept of HMA (36 concepts) with each concept of HWTO (54 concepts). In this way, we established in total 1944 comparisons (36×54). Out of them, we manually identified 79 reference comparisons that imply a real similarity relation between two concepts.

We discuss now the influence of the different matching components by analyzing different settings of the above-presented algorithm. Figure 7 shows the interpolated precision and recall values for the different settings. Interpolation of the precision on recall i is defined as the maximum precision for all recall equal or higher than i. The first setting, we consider is WM only, or in other words: $1.0 \times WM + 0.0 \times FragM + 0.0 \times NeighM$. Usually, two problems are enumerated if using isolated word matching. The first point concerns polysemy. This happens when a word has different meanings, for instance *bank*, which can denote either a financial institution or a sloping land (a riverbank). In our example, we didn't find a lot of polysemous terms, mostly because we work at the level of domain ontologies and we are not dealing with cross-domain or top-level ontologies where experts might use the same terms to express different concepts. This results in high precision for WM. The second problem concerns synonyms. Synonyms are different words or word sequences

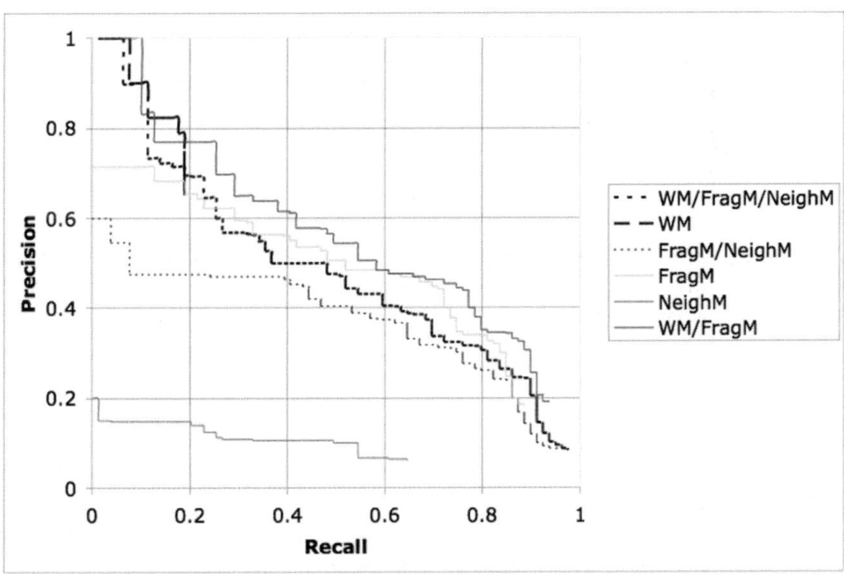

Fig. 7. Interpolated precision and recall values for different settings

that denote the same or very similar concept. Consider for instance *stadium* and *sports arena*. A comparison function based only on the syntactical analysis of words cannot detect similarities well enough, which results in low recall. In our example, WM cannot reach more than 20% recall.

Other problems appear if only adjectives match. We found for instance a high WM value (0.43) between the concepts *Agricultural Training Services* and *Agricultural Landscape*. Stopword filtering is in general known as an effective help to reduce matching between functional words, which do not carry meaning. We apply stopword filtering, but in a domain-specific environment, we are concerned with expressions that are functional and noisy in the range of the domain, but not in general. Using commonly known stopword filters does not resolve this problem. We conclude that even though there is no word ambiguity problem, word matching alone isn't sufficient to evaluate concept similarity.

To provide evidence that our function runs well, we tested WM with different comparison functions. On of the most popular is the Levenshtein distance, which calculates the minimal number of operations needed to transform one string into another, where operation is an insertion, deletion, or substitution of a single characters. This statistical approach is an alternative way to the identification of word stems. In the example, we calculated the distance with equivalent costs to insert, delete or substitute a single character, but found similar results to the applied comparison of words.

Next, we discuss settings that concentrate on FragM or on NeighM especially with the aim to increase recall. We consider FragM only, NeighM only and FragM in conjunction with NeighM ($0.0 \times WM + 0.5 \times FragM + 0.5 \times NeighM$). We preliminary has to mention that not all concepts are illustrated with fragments, only 18 concepts of HMA come with fragments, respectively, 31 concepts of HWTO. Especially at the leave level of the hyperbook ontology, the hyperbook authors did not detail all concepts through fragments.

As we expected, we can observe in Fig. 7 that recall goes up at the price that precision decreases. Further, we detect that the precision of WM is reinforced. If WM gives unexpectedly high values, FragM and NeighM sorts a low value. In the above-mentioned comparison between *Agricultural training service* and *Agricultural landscape*, we found 0.43 for WM while the corresponding values for FragM and NeighM are considerably lower, at 0.044 and 0.036.

We also discovered that FragM enhances results much better than NeighM. This can be explained by the fact that the structure of the hyperbook ontologies is relatively weak and too small to obtain good results with NeighM. NeighM runs better if the ontologies have a certain number of concepts that forms a well-described environment of a concept.

Due to the fact that the structure of the hyperbook ontologies are weak and NeighM results in low values for precision and recall, we finally proceed to the most promising setting we found for this example: WM in conjunction with FragM or $0.5 \times WM + 0.5 \times FragM + 0.0 \times NeighM$. Experiments

Table 1. Results with WM and FragM

Source concept	Target concept	WM+FM
Public stockholding programmes for food security purposes	Food security	0.473
Domestic food aid	Domestic food production	0.453
Domestic food aid	Food safety	0.411
Domestic food aid	Food security	0.374
Public stockholding programmes for food security purposes	Stockholding	0.374
Domestic food aid	Food quality	0.363
Public stockholding programmes for food security purposes	Food quality	0.362
Public stockholding programmes for food security purposes	Food safety	0.344
Public stockholding programmes for food security purposes	High standards of plants, animal and public health	0.308
Domestic support in agriculture	Domestic food production	0.267
Public stockholding programmes for food security purposes	Domestic food production	0.241

show that considering all three components is not necessarily the best way to find similarity between two ontology-based hyperbooks. This observation is consistent with the results of the Ontology Alignment Evaluation Campaign (OAEI held in 2006. In [141], the authors of one of the best alignment methods (RIMON) explain that their algorithm first compares a linguistic based and a structure based alignment technique and then decides which one will be dominant in the final alignment. They also mention that in some cases, one of the two methods alone can be better than the combination of both of them.

Table 1 shows the highest scores for WM in conjunction with FragM. Rows in gray indicate relations that we do not consider as real similarities. Table 1.

The example shows that it is difficult to maintain high precision. We preserve 100% precision only up to 10% of recall. After, we quickly fall down to 75% of precision at 20% of recall, and to 65% of precision for 40% of recall. For instance, 20% of recall means losing 4 of 5 relations. If a concept in hyperbook A has 5 relations to concepts of hyperbook B, we find only one. And if a concept of hyperbook A is similar to only one concept of hyperbook B, the chance to find this relation is only 20%. The situation looks better when we focus on recall. For 75% of recall, we still have 40% of precision. Concretely, this means that a user will find 75% of the similar concepts and almost half of the propositions indicate really a correct similarity relation. Analyzing precision and recall, we see that this setting is a compromise of the above-discussed situations. Word matching increases precision, while FragM increases the recall of the comparison.

4.3 Using the Similarity Links in an Interactive Interface

The right boundary between precision and recall depends on the application and on the user. If we consider for instance users who use the hyperbook much in the sense of a glossary or a lexicon, they would probably prefer a high recall or in other words as much generated links as possible. Initially considering one concept and exploring others in its surrounding thanks to generated similarity links is an argument for higher recall. On the other side, if we consider users who want to explore a whole book, we must move towards higher precision to avoid cognitive overload. A clearly structured content with selected similarity links might be much better than a proliferation of links that lead to less relevant information.

One way to solve this issue consists in letting the user set the similarity threshold (for instance with a graphical slider in the user interface). When the user considers the number of generated similarity links as too high (or too low) or the quality as too low, he or she can raise the threshold and interactively see the effect on the hyperbook interface.

Another argument for a user-determined setting of precision and recall is the problem of the graphical representation of the similarity relations in a hyperbook. We compare precision and recall settings in hyperbooks with settings in Information Retrieval (IR). Search engines graphically present the results in lists, ordered by the similarity value and often presented in pages with ten or twenty hits. The first page contains the hits with the highest score, or in other words, the results with the highest precision. The more the user browses through the following pages, the more recall will rise and precision decrease. Considering the graphical user interface of a hyperbook, it is obvious

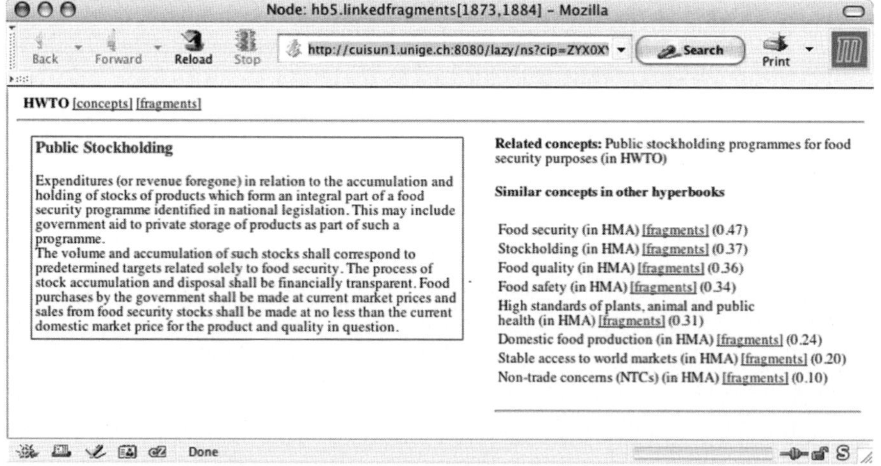

Fig. 8. A graphical interface with generated similarity links

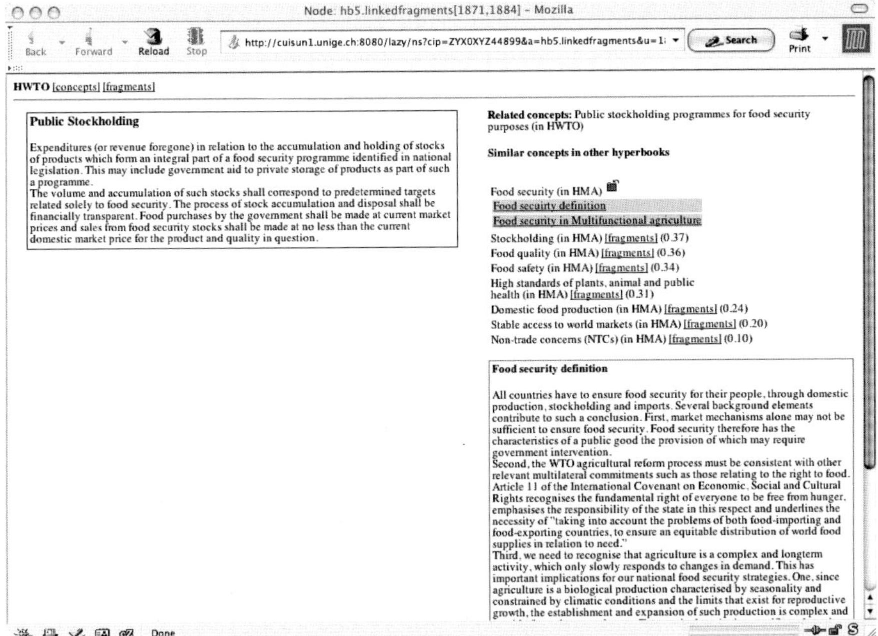

Fig. 9. An opened link with the fragments of the related concept *Food security*

that we can't reproduce a similar list, even less if we think that such a list might spread over several pages.

Figure 8 presents a user interface that includes generated similarity links (on the right). When clicked, these links expand to a list of related fragments of the corresponding hyperbook (Fig. 9, top right). The fragments contents are shown (bottom right) when their name is clicked.

5 Conclusion

In this chapter we have presented a semantic hyperbook model that integrates concepts developed over these last years in the domain of hyperbooks and virtual documents. We have particularly emphasized the user-interface aspect of the model to show that a specification-based approach, relying on node schemas and link inference, is well suited to easily generate reading interfaces that are well adapted to the author and reader aims. In addition, this approach readily handles the generation of "global books" within a digital library of integrated hyperbooks.

In order to create semantic digital libraries of hyperbooks we propose to take advantage of the knowledge structure (the domain ontology) of each hyperbook to integrate them in a semantically consistent way. Thus, a digital library of hyperbooks is not a mere collection of hyperbooks, it provides a semantic interconnection structure among the hyperbooks.

This approach is realistic because, as we have shown, the integration process can be automated, even when the hyperbook ontologies are not fully formalized. This process is based on known ontology alignment techniques that we have extended to the specific case of hyperbooks and tested on a real-world example.

Semantic Digital Libraries for Archiving

Bill McDaniel

Digital libraries offer several benefits for archiving unstructured or semi-structured data for long term use. Archival systems which follow a typical document access curve typically leverage online, near line, and offline storage mechanisms to efficiently store and retrieve documents. The nature of storage which is always online, such as large document conglomerations, such as Wikipedia or Google, changes the access curve for digital documents of the future. Semantic enablement over these corpora offers benefits for improved retrieval accuracy, timeliness, and relevance. This paper will discuss the advantages and disadvantages of semantically powered digital libraries in the archival arena.

1 Introduction

Digital libraries in the sense of document repositories have been around for several decades pre-dating the web by at least ten years. They were originally called virtual libraries or electronic libraries. They have evolved over the years but still retain basic traits such as the fact that they have a dedication to a collection of material, are usually organized around a large hardware data store, and offer search and retrieval features through a user interface that represents the contents as documents or books.[1]

Many are standardized and available commercially and are in heavy use in enterprise environments. More are becoming common in large academic and national libraries. However, traditional digital libraries use data structures which assume a specific document access curve with the bulk of access

[1] For the purposes of this paper, I will use the term document for any object catalogued into a digital library regardless of origin, media, content, purpose, or nature. This can include temporal collections and even living beings such as people.

attempts falling in the beginning of the document life cycle, followed by a tapering period. Many libraries encourage or force documents to go to nearline storage and ultimately to offline storage, following the traditional document access curve.

The emergence of large document corpora online at all times and searchable by accident through the use of engines such as Google and Wikipedia changes access curve significantly. The result is a higher than optimal level of stress on the document retrieval systems supporting these large document libraries. Since nearline and offline have become somewhat obsolete concepts with respect to web searches and particularly to Web2.0 applications with their greater levels of interaction, the benefits of an archival system which could distinguish more attributes of a document are increasing.

2 Document Retrieval Cycle

Documents follow a typical retrieval cycle once archived [146]. The access curve, plotting retrieval activity over time, looks like the diagram below (see Fig. 1).

Archivists have always relied on this usage curve to plan movement from online to nearline and ultimately to offline storage as documents age. However, the advent of digital libraries and generic large scale search engines such as Google, tend to play havoc with traditional retrieval scenarios since less and less is being relegated to near and offline status. Consequently, any document is as likely to be retrieved as any other and yet the actual relevance of documents retrieved will tend to follow the same curve. The curve above indicates rather, the intentional access of documents, meaning document retrieval that is precisely targeted, usually by name or catalogue id.

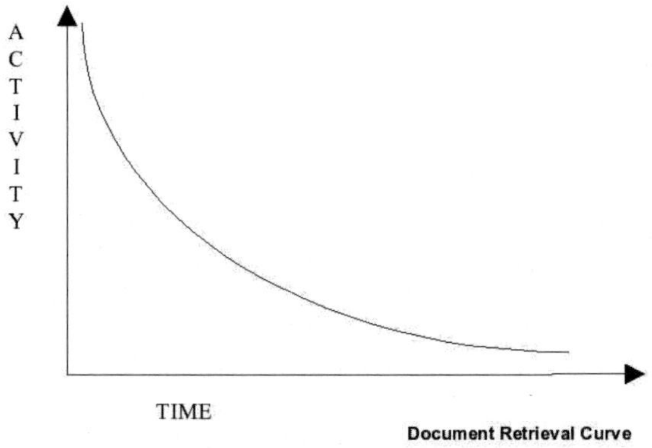

Fig. 1. Document retrieval curve

The Semantic Web as outlined by [20] and knowledge augmentation systems (electronic libraries) as outlined by [63] come together in the form of semantic digital libraries. Such libraries augment the capabilities of normal electronic libraries with facilities and functions highly useful to archivists.

Semantic Digital Libraries offer several features which help improve the accuracy and precision of retrieval and of search. These features improve the access to documents making it less important for documents further along the retrieval curve to be rotated to near and offline storage. Consequently, semantic digital libraries make the trend toward keeping all documents online all the time more tenable since improved search precision causes the documents to continue to fall on the traditional curve and not be retrieved accidentally.

3 Semantic Archiving Features

Enter Semantic Digital Libraries. Semantic Digital Libraries provide a set of services and constructs which improve access to objects stored within the library. A short description of Semantic Digital Library features which aid archivists is in order here

Semantic digital libraries do not have to deal with any single entry type. Specifically, they may catalogue and manage abstract objects. These objects consist of anything which can be addressed by a Universal Resource Identifier (URI). In theory this includes objects that consist of other abstract collections and even of transient collections such as exhibitions of art, performances, or meetings of people.

Semantic digital libraries provide

- Faceted search
- User tagging
- Folksonomic search
- Ontological search
- Annotation

3.1 Faceted Search

Semantic digital libraries allow for faceted classification systems inherently which means each entry can belong to a number of classification schemes. Semantic Libraries allow these classification schemes to be expanded by the addition of new tags added to the classification schema.

Faceted classification allows each object in the library to participate in multiple classifications simultaneously [17]. This provides the necessary infrastructure for faceted search where an object my be searched for by specifying the classification attributes it has attached to it. This results in highly efficient filtering as well as allowing objects to be located by user-specified terminology.

3.2 User Tagging

Such user tagging as extensions to the classification schema is a property specific to semantic libraries. Extending the schema is possible because the Resource Description framework language used to describe such relations is non-relational in structure. It is formed as an acyclic graph which allows for any number (theoretically) of relationships (attributes, properties, or facets) to be defined.

3.3 Folsonomic Search

User tagged classification systems, which do not constrain the user to a specific set of tags, create what are known as folksonomies. Folksonomies are usually associated with social networks such as MySpace or Flickr. The facility which allows users to add their own tags to objects in the network (people, themselves, blog entries, photos, etc.) allows for socially relevant groupings to emerge in an organic fashion.

On the face of it, such a facility would seem anathema to a formal digital library structure. The random and somewhat chaotic nature of folksonomies seems at odds with a librarians desire to clearly classify documents, books, media, and other objects. From an archivists point of view, however, this facility is priceless.

Archivists are faced with the difficulty of not only classifying documents (for the purposes of storage and retrieval) but of finding the documents later, often much later. The retrieval curve of archived documents traditionally shows a high retrieval rate shortly after archival, followed by a tapering off of access to the archived material as time passes.

The concomitant problem is that the classification mechanism may have changed over time by the time later retrievals are needed. In particular, digital documents to be located via keyword search may become virtually inaccessible when indexed only with the formal classification of the current day.

Folksonomies, on the other hand, allow documents to be classified in an organic manner which reflects the very natural way users think of the contents. This is particularly true of non-literary documents such as photos. How users perceive an image, what tags they assign to it, how they come to consensus of opinion about its relevant content, all these things are very difficult to classify formally, yet yield rich tagging metadata when users are allowed to build their own folksonomies.

Such folksonomies permit future researchers to have a far better chance of locating relevant documents because they will be able to search for the documents using folksonomic terminology and principles.

3.4 Ontological Search

Folksonomic searches and indeed the formal classification search can be aided by the provision of ontological search facilities. Ontological search, another defining feature of semantic digital libraries, makes the retrieval of catalogued documents more precise and accurate by taking into account the different specification of search concepts and terminologies [81]. Different classification systems may use different terms. Ontological search resolves the differences between ontologies as well as providing concept similar search in addition to traditional keyword search.

Archivists discover that over time ontologies and vocabularies used in classification change. Consequently ontological search which can resolve disparate ontologies provides an invaluable resource for retrieval during the long tail phase of a documents archival. Coupled with the ability to extend the classification via folksonomic additions, the ability to perform ontological and semantic search, faceted search, makes the likelihood of being able to retrieve an archived document much later in its life cycle much higher.

3.5 Annotation

Semantic digital libraries also add annotation abilities to the objects catalogued within them. Annotation implies the ability to share; that is annotation adds a social networking component to the notion of digital libraries [197]. This opens the door to significant new capabilities for managing, sharing, and classifying documents in a digital library. Annotations which are shared through a social network allow for catalogued works to be extended and new information added, discussed, integrated or discarded.

The annotations themselves can become catalogued objects in the library. The recursive nature of data to metadata to data is one of the more powerful features of semantic digital libraries. The transformation of metadata such as annotations into document objects themselves provides a natural and organic growth process. This process allows shared semantic digital libraries to extend themselves by virtue of being used as well as by virtue of precise augmentation through archival of documents under formal classifications.

4 Conclusion

In this chapter I have examined the applications of Semantic Digital Libraries to digital document archival and retrieval. The emphasis in this paper has been on noting how the semantic features and functions alter and aid the standard retrieval curve of a digital archive.

Semantic digital libraries provide a set of functions and features which improve the usability and efficacy of digital libraries when used in a document archival application.

Acknowledgement

This material is based upon works supported by Enterprise Ireland under Grant No. ILP/05/203 and by Science Foundation Ireland Grant No. SFI/02/CE1/I131.

Evaluation of Semantic and Social Technologies for Digital Libraries

Sebastian Ryszard Kruk, Ewelina Kruk, and Katarzyna Stankiewicz

Libraries are the tools we use to learn and to answer our questions. The quality of our work depends, among others, on the quality of the tools we use. Recent research in digital libraries is focused, on one hand on improving the infrastructure of the digital library management systems (DLMS), and on the other on improving the metadata models used to annotate collections of objects maintained by DLMS. The latter includes, among others, the semantic web and social networking technologies. Recently, the semantic web and social networking technologies are being introduced to the digital libraries domain. The expected outcome is that the overall quality of information discovery in digital libraries can be improved by employing social and semantic technologies. In this chapter we present the results of an evaluation of social and semantic end-user information discovery services for the digital libraries.

1 Introduction

Libraries are the tools we use to learn and to answer our questions. The quality of our work depends, among others, on the quality of the tools we use. The research and development in digital libraries has a long established tradition; Recent research in digital libraries domain is focused, on one hand on improving the infrastructure of the digital library management systems (DLMS); on the other, on improving the metadata models used to annotate collections of objects using the semantic web [118, 131, 136] and social networking technologies [117].

Semantically-rich and carefully crafted metadata support expressive and powerful information discovery solutions. User profiling, in the context of online communities, can improve the overall usability of information discovery and sharing. Through the community-based interactions the users become active producers of the metadata; hence digital library can provide more focused and more accurate search results through, e.g., recommendations techniques.

It is expected that *the overall quality of information discovery in digital libraries can be improved by employing social and semantic technologies.* So far the evaluation studies were conducted to show the value added of separate social and semantic components [121, 126, 127]. We believe that it is important to evaluate a number of known solutions setup together through user experience in information discovery.

2 State of Art – Evaluation of Digital Libraries

Fuhr et al. [75] present a comprehensive study on evaluation frameworks for digital libraries. They determine the *attractiveness* of the collections and the *ease of use* of the technologies as key factors in assessing the quality of digital libraries. They suggest that currently used *relevance* metrics are not enough, since they do not take into account user satisfaction, the quality of information, the relations between the documents, or the reliability of information. The authors emphasize the importance of the user satisfaction. The authors [75] present the *interaction triptych model*, which defines three components of the digital library environment: the system, the content, and the user. They identify three axes of evaluation: *Usability* of user interaction with the system, *Usefulness* of the content for the user, *Performance* of managing the content by the system. Fuhr et al. define *usability evaluation* as the act of measuring the usability attributes of a system or device with respect to particular users, performing particular tasks in a particular context. To evaluate the *usefulness* of the content the authors suggest information behavior, content-related studies, and user studies.

Evaluating of the usability of the semantic digital library system has to take into account also the human computer interaction research. Shneiderman and Plaisant [199] identified five usability measures: *time to learn*, *speed of performance*, *rate of errors by users*, *retention time*, and *subjective satisfaction.* Hornbæk and Effie [91] present the meta-analyses of various usability measures. They analyze the relation between usability and effectiveness, efficiency, and satisfaction. Chin et al. [44] present the Questionnaire for User Interface Satisfaction (QUIS) setup. They identify various measures for user satisfaction related to *overall reaction to the software*, *terminology and system information.* For each measure they use a set of metrics presented in the questionnaire with a ten point scale between two antagonistic, e.g., terrible-wonderful or difficult-easy.

3 Social and Semantic Information Discovery Solutions

JeromeDL [118,131] is a semantic digital library which aims to deliver an out-of-box digital library equipped with a number of social and semantic solutions. The high level architecture of JeromeDL identifies three conceptual tiers of metadata and services: legacy, semantic, and social [118]. JeromeDL services and semantic object model on the *legacy* layer support *the behind-the-scene* management of resources and collections, and the interoperability with other systems. In this article, however, we present the evaluation results related only to the end-user information discovery features. In this section we will briefly introduce each of those solutions that were used during the evaluation.

Semantic Features

In addition to dynamic collections and SQE which were not used in the evaluation, JeromeDL provides four core semantic information discovery features based on semantic web technologies.

- *Natural Language Query Templates (NLQ)* component allows library administrator to specify a number of query templates that answer, complex questions which might be added by the users library [127].
- *TagsTreeMaps (TTM)* allow to filter information space using tags (keywords) associated with information objects [124,126]. Unlike TagClouds, TTM represents a clustered, hierarchically organized tags rendered using treemaps layout algorithm [200].
- *MultiBeeBrowse (MBB)* is a faceted navigation component, which exploits previously not specified relations between information items [121]. Adaptive hypermedia techniques have been implemented into MBB to facilitate the process of selecting graph concepts and presenting results.
- *Exhibit* is one of the components developed by MIT within the SIMILE project [94]. It allows to easily filter a set of information objects. Exhibit allows to easily visualize information space using, e.g., timeline or Google Maps.

Social Features

Social interactions are a key concept of next generation of digital libraries. In order to facilitate them we have provided a number of social features in JeromeDL.

- *Bookmarks Sharing and Collaborative Filtering* is delivered by the component called Social Semantic Collaborative Filtering (SSCF) [117]. It allows users to maintain and share securely private bookshelf with hierarchical classification of bookmarks folders.
- *Collaborative Browsing* is a solution which enables to share and reuse MBB queries through the notion of bookmarks in SSCF.

- *Blogging* in JeromeDL is realized by a component which allows to leave comments related to certain resources. Each comment (encoded in SIOC [30]) can be annotated with tags [122].
- *Resources Ranking* allows users to easily rank resources and check an average ranking within the given degree of separation in the social network.

Recommendations

Although recommendations are effectively a semantic services, we have decided to threat them separately, since they usually do not require *any* input from the user. JeromeDL provides two solutions:

- *Recommendations Based on the Resource Description* are computed using information like classification, keywords/tags, title, authors, etc. To get these recommendations user has to request the web page with the view of the information object.
- *Recommendations Based on SSCF Profile* are computed based on information in the FOAF profile [116] and semantic annotations on SSCF folders. These recommendations come from farther parts (2–3 degrees of separation) of the social network. Next, the engine attempts to include the suggested folders directly in the current structure of SSCF bookmarks.

4 Evaluation Setup

In this section we describe in details the setup of the evaluation procedure and the apparatus. The evaluation aims to measure three (*time to learn*, *rate of errors by users*, and *subjective satisfaction*) out of five metrics identified by Shneiderman and Plaisant [199].

The procedure and the apparatus were designed to answer following questions: 1. Do the social and semantic services increase the quality of the answers provided by the users in response to given problems? 2. Do the social and semantic services increase the accuracy of the references provided by the users to answer given questions? 3. Do the social and semantic services increase overall satisfaction of using the digital library? 4. Which services, i.e., semantic, social, or recommendations, are found to be most useful by the end users?

4.1 Evaluation Apparatus

For the purpose of the evaluation a dedicated system has been designed, and set up online (`http://q.digime.name/`). The main objective were: (1) To control access to digital libraries, (2) To control flow of the evaluation scenario (see Sect. 4.2), (3) to enable/disable contain features of the semantic digital library, (4) to facilitate question-answering tasks, (5) to other opinions through questionnaires. Our goal was to provide the evaluation environment which could mimic the real-life conditions, and of the same time to record users actions and and control flow of the evaluation scenario.

To compare results from participants using the classic and the semantic digital library we have selected a popular, open source digital library – DSpace [169] and an open source semantic digital library – JeromeDL [131]. Both libraries were installed in their *vanilla versions* (JeromeDL version 2.1-beta-build-3627 and DSpace version 1.4.2). Both libraries and the evaluation service were installed on the 8-core Intel Pentium Xeon server, with 3GB RAM and 75GB SAN disks.

Set of Questions

For the purpose of the question-answering tasks (see Sect. 4.2) we have prepared seven questions. The questions were related to the domain of the Internet psychology. The rationale was to have questions which would not be too obvious to the participants and required some time to find the answer. We expected a certain level engagement, i.e., the participants would be interested to find the answers to these questions.

Building the Database

Both digital libraries contained 529 articles from `http://library.deri.ie/` and from `http://books.deri.ie/` (*noise*) and a set of 35 articles (*reference database*) which provided correct answers to the aforementioned questions.

4.2 Evaluation Scenario

The evaluation consisted of a number of tasks, each accompanied with a questionnaire measuring user satisfaction. There where two additional questionnaires: one before the whole evaluation (*pre-evaluation*) and one directly after completing the whole evaluation (*post-evaluation*).

- *Pre-evaluation questionnaire.* Prior to the actual evaluation we wanted to determine: (1) general demographics (2) general level of computer/Internet/Web 2.0 literacy, and (3) most popular workflows to find literature required to complete university assignments.
- *Initial Task: Getting to know the digital library.* The participants were asked to register to one of the digital library systems. In the questionnaire, after the task, the participants were asked about their first impression of the system (*solution satisfaction metrics* – see Sect. 5.2) and their comments on the tasks they were asked to perform (*task evaluation metrics* – see Sect. 5.2).

- *Question-answering tasks.* These tasks (3 in total) provided the core results for the evaluation. During each task users were asked to answer one of randomly selected questions (see *Set of questions* in Sect. 4.1). They had 45 min to find the articles, which would help them to answer the question. The participants were asked to provide an answer of up to 300 words and a list of references (URLs to the related articles).
- *Networking task.* Directly after the first QA task, participants using JeromeDL were asked to create social network connections with other users registered in the system.
- *Post-evaluation questionnaire.* After completing the third task we asked the participants to fill in the post-evaluation questionnaire. The questions were set to capture the overall impression about the digital library system (*solution satisfaction metrics*). We asked the JeromeDL users to indicate their most and least favorite and useful features, express their opinion on social and semantic features (*complex satisfaction metrics*), and list features they missed or thought required further improvement. All participants were asked if they would like to continue using the library, and why.

4.3 Measuring Results of the Evaluation

In order to answer the aforementioned questions for the evaluation we compared: (1) *The quality of answers* given by the users during the question-answering tasks (see Sect. 4.2); (2) *The standard information retrieval metrics*, i.e., recall and precision, applied to the list of references returned with each question; (3) *User satisfaction metrics* – a set of criteria used to measure participants arbitrary opinion.

We have identified three sets of satisfaction metrics: (1) Solution-related satisfaction metrics – a set of six metrics applied to measure users satisfaction of the features offered by the digital library system: *easy to use* vs *hard to use, complex, mind boggling* vs *simple,clearly organized, hard to master, unintuitive* vs *intuitive, straight forward, boring* vs *interesting, ugly, unattractive* vs *attractive, useless* vs *useful, handy.* (2) Task-related satisfaction metrics – a set of three metrics applied to measure users opinion on the task they had to perform: *hard to understand* vs *easy to understand, hard to execute* vs *easy to execute, hard to master, unintuitive* vs *intuitive, straight forward.* (3) Overall satisfaction metrics – a combination of solution and task metrics.

5 Evaluation Results

The evaluation has been advertised on various online communities ranging from general-purpose social networking sites, such as, Orkut, to thematic (digital libraries, semantic web) online communities and discussion channels. The evaluation site has been opened between Dec 18th, 2007 and Feb 7th,

2008. For most comparison metrics we also calculate percentage difference $\Delta = \frac{v_{JDL} - v_{DS}}{|v_{DS}|}$ by which JeromeDL was found better (or worse) than DSpace.

Participants

During the evaluation, 59 people have registered to the evaluation; 26 of them completed it. Most of the participants where 21–25 years old postgraduates or under graduate students; they major subject of education was informatics and computer science. Most of the participants had a fairly good understanding of evaluated technologies: *social tagging* (75%), *Web 2.0* (92%), and *Semantic Web* (85%). Almost half of them (42%) where using *online social bookmarking*; most of the participants (88%) were registered to at least one *online social network*. Most of the participants visit a university library or a university digital library more seldom than once a month (61.54 and 73.08% respectively).

5.1 Evaluation Results

This section presents the core results of our evaluation. First we analyze the results based on the quality of the answers user provided during the three query-answering (QA) tasks. Later, we analyze the results based on the references provided by the participants in the QA tasks.

Results Based on the Quality of Users' Answers

Each answer provided during the QA task was assigned 0 to 5 points.

Average, normalized results for each task show negligible differences between those achieved using JeromeDL ($JDL_{task.1} = 3.85$, $JDL_{task.2} = 4.38$, $JDL_{task.3} = 4.38$) and those of DSpace ($DS_{task.1} = 4.08$, $DS_{task.2} = 4.23$, $DS_{task.3} = 4.15$); although, JeromeDL overage results ($JDL_{avg} = 4.21$) where slightly better ($\Delta_{avg} = 1.24\%$) than those of DSpace users ($DS_{avg} = 4.15$).

Results Based on the Accuracy of Provided References

We used scale between -2 and 2 score each reference provided together with the answer to the QA task. For each question (q) a reference (ref) from *our reference database* (DB_{Ref}) which presented an answer to the question ($Answer_q$) was assigned two (2) points; auxiliary articles which could also help in answering the given question (Aux_q, where $Aux_q \bigcap Answer_q \equiv \emptyset$) were scored with one (1) point. Since only the resources in DB_{Ref} provided answers to given questions, and all questions were related to one domain of interest, we scored articles which were not in $Answer_q$ or Aux_q with zero points. References which did not belong to the reference database DR_{Ref} were scored minus two (-2) points.

In the following sectors we define *precision* and *recall* metrics for information discovery. We use variations of the aforementioned scoring function; we compute these metrics on the set of references provided by the participants (A_{ref}).

Precision of Information Discovery Features

The *precision* is the percentage of retrieved documents that are relevant to given search. In our case, this would be a percentage of references which are relevant to the question being answered by the participants. We have defined two precision-based metrics: $Prec_{[0\div1]}$, which is a direct interpretation of the original definition; $Prec_{[0\div2]}$ which takes into account difference between references that are correct ($Answer_q$) and auxiliary (Aux_q) references to the given question q, using aforementioned scoring function without negative values.

Average values of either $Prec_{[0\div1]}$ ($JDL = 31.44\%$, $DS = 30.97\%$, $\Delta = 1.54\%$) or $Prec_{[0\div2]}$ ($JDL = 33.18\%$, $DS = 33.49\%$, $\Delta = -0.91\%$) bare no significant difference for either library.

Comparing results from both precision metrics shows that DSpace users were providing references with better precision ($\Delta(Prec_{[0\div1]})$ and $\Delta(Prec_{[0\div2]})$) during the first task; their results where much worse than JeromeDL users' during the third QA task. The growing precision of JeromeDL users' answers was very likely influenced by two factors. They were learning more about how to use this complex system; they were also able to use the more of semantic and social features offered by the library.

Recall of Information Discovery Features

In information retrieval the *recall* (*sensitiveness*) is defined as the percentage of the documents, which are relevant to the query, that has been successfully retrieved. In the context of our experiment we define *recall* as the sum of the *Score* values for references provided by the participants divided by the complete sum of non-negative *Score* for the given question. We defined three versions of recall metrics: (1) $Rec_{[-2\div2]}$, which is uses aforementioned *Score* function. (2) $Rec_{[0\div2]}$, which takes into account distinction between correct answers ($Answer_q$) and auxiliary references (Aux_q). It is similar to $Rec_{[-2\div2]}$ but does not assign negative scores for non-relevant references; (3) $Rec_{[0\div1]}$, which does not distinguish between correct ($Answer_q$) and auxiliary (Aux_q) references.

The average results of the recall metrics for each library, unlike the precision-based metrics, show significant gain of using semantic and social technologies; the results for JeromeDL ($Rec_{JDL[-2\div2]} = 7.32$, $Rec_{JDL[0\div2]} = 17.50$, $Rec_{JDL[0\div1]} = 15.84$) users are always much better than those for DSpace users ($Rec_{DS[-2\div2]} = 4.62$, $Rec_{DS[0\div2]} = 16.22$, $Rec_{DS[0\div1]} = 14.15$). In case of the metric $Rec_{[-2\div2]}$ the difference was above **50%** in favor for JeromeDL.

Similar to the *precision* metrics, JeromeDL users were providing less *sensitive* results for the first task; however, only in case of the $Rec_{[-2\div2]}$ the difference was significant. Again, the references provided by the participants using JeromeDL during the last task were far better ($\Delta_{[0\div1]} = \mathbf{33\%}$). For $Rec_{[-2\div2]}$ metric the differences in average values for the second and the third task were above 10% in favor of JeromeDL; in case of second QA task the difference went off the scale – due to negative *recall* value for DSpace. In case of $Rec_{[0\div2]}$ and $Rec_{[0\div1]}$ values for the third QA task, the differences in favor of JeromeDL were above 20%. The differences for the first and the second QA task, although in favor of DSpace, were almost equal 0%.

5.2 Discussion of Satisfaction Measures based on the Questionnaire Results

In this section we present, compare, and analyze the data gathered through the questionnaires completed after each task.

Satisfaction Metrics

We have identified three types of user satisfaction measures (see Sect. 4.3): *task-related satisfaction*, *solution-related satisfaction*, and *overall satisfaction*. To facilitate processing the gathered results we have defined three *weighted satisfaction* measures: *Task-related satisfaction measure* ρ_t, *Solution-related satisfaction measure* ρ_s, *Overall satisfaction measure* ρ_o [125]. In the questionnaire, users were able to choose a value (see Sect. 4.1) between -50 and $+50$ to express their opinion on each aforementioned metrics.

Tasks-based Satisfaction

After each task the participants were asked to express their opinion about these tasks.

The first tasks i.e., registration, simple and advanced search, were much better perceived by the DSpace users. However, only for the registration task the percentage difference $|\Delta_{\rho_t(registering)}|$ was reported to be 10% lower by the JeromeDL users. For both search tasks the ρ_t measure is similar for both libraries; it is slightly higher for DSpace, though. The simple search was claimed to be more (**28%**) intuitive in JeromeDL implementation; the advanced search was perceived to be easier to understand by the JeromeDL users.

The task-based satisfaction metrics and the ρ_t measure for the QA tasks is coherent with the *quality of the answers* provided by the users (see Sect. 5.1). The DSpace users were more satisfied during the first task ($|\Delta_{\rho_t(task.1)}| = 37.87\%$); but JeromeDL users were much more satisfied during the remaining two tasks ($\Delta_{\rho_t(task.2)} = 398.12\%$ and $\Delta_{\rho_t(task.3)} = 119.75\%$).

Search-related Satisfaction

After each QA task we have ask the participants about their opinion a information discovery features in the digital library. Only during the first task the DSpace users' satisfaction regarding *ease of user*, *simplicity*, and *intuitiveness* was higher then JeromeDL users. Other satisfaction metrics for all tasks, as well as, the overall satisfaction measure ρ_s for all tasks, was scored higher by the participants using JeromeDL; the percentage differences were quite significant for the first task ($\rho_{s,\,JDL,\,task.1} = 14.86$, $\rho_{s,\,DS,\,task.1} = 13.41$, $\Delta_{\rho_s(task.1)} = 10.78\%$) and very large for following tasks ($\rho_{s,\,JDL,\,task.2} = 21.99$, $\rho_{s,\,DS,\,task.2} = 1.88$, $\Delta_{\rho_s(task.2)} = \mathbf{1{,}070.66\%}$ and $\rho_{s,\,JDL,\,task.3} = 22.69$, $\rho_{s,\,DS,\,task.3} = 9.39$, $\Delta_{\rho_s(task.3)} = \mathbf{141.57\%}$).

Satisfaction from Social and Semantic Features

After each QA task we have asked the participants to express their opinion about social and semantic features that were enabled during the given question-answering task. After the first task we measured satisfaction metrics for NLQ ($\rho_s(NLQ) = 6.42$), TTM ($\rho_s(TTM) = 3.62$), Exhibit ($\rho_s(Exhibit) = 9.72$), and MBB ($\rho_s(MBB) = 2.68$); after the second task: SSCF ($\rho_s(NLQ) = \mathbf{17.76}$), Collaborative Browsing (($\rho_s(Coll.Browse) = 10.28$)), Blogging ($\rho_s(Blogging) = 13.44$), and Ranking ($\rho_s(Ranking) = 12.47$). And after the last task we recorded users' opinion on recommendation services ($\rho_s(Res.\ Recommend) = \mathbf{19.32}$, $\rho_s(SSCF.Recommend) = 15.83$).

Based on average values of each of six solution-based metrics and the overall ρ_s measures, we can conclude that the participants found SSCF and the resource-based recommendations to be the most satisfying. Additionally, the SSCF-based recommendations of bookmarks were found to be the most *easy* and one of most *simple* to use. The participants considered blogging feature to be one of the most *intuitive* features, and NLQ to be the most *interesting* one. MBB was considered one of the most *attractive*, and Exhibit one of the most *useful* solutions [125]. Overall, the social and recommendation solutions had been scored with the highest satisfaction values ρ_s.

We have also asked the participants about their overall satisfaction related social and semantic features. Similar to aforementioned solution-based satisfaction metrics, the social features have received much higher scores ($\rho_o(social) = 21.27$) than the semantic ones ($\rho_o(semantic) = 8.65$). Only the *interestingness* and *usefulness* metrics for the semantic solutions came close, but did not exceed, the values of the social ones.

Overall Impression of the Digital Library

Before the first and directly after the third QA task we have measured users' overall impression about the digital library they were using, we used *solution-based satisfaction metrics* to calculate the measure $\rho_s(impression)$ for each library.

It is worth noticing that overall impression $\rho_s(impr)$ grew more positive for both libraries through the evaluation; JeromeDL: from $\rho_s(pre, impr) = 15.10$ to $\rho_s(post, impr) = 16.99$, DSpace: from $\rho_s(pre, impr) = 4.21$ to $\rho_s(post, impr) = 6.46$. The overall impression of JeromeDL was much higher ($\Delta_{pre} = 258.34\%$, $\Delta_{post} = 162.90\%$) than DSpace, both before and after the evaluation however.

Intention to Continue Using the Digital Library

Finally, we have asked all participants if they would like to continue using the digital library they were using during the evaluation. After all aforementioned results, it came as no surprise that almost twice as many JeromeDL (84.62%) than DSpace (46.15%) users declared they would like to continue using it.

5.3 Answering the Questions for the Evaluation

In Sect. 4 we have presented four questions, which we wanted to find answers for with this evaluation.

Question 1. Do the social and semantic services increase the quality of the answers provided by the users in response to given problems? The answers provided by the DSpace users were of higher quality only during the first QA task; the quality of answers for the remaining two QA tasks and the average quality were slightly higher for JeromeDL. Hence we can conclude that social and semantic services slightly increase the quality of provided answers.

Question 2. Do the social and semantic services increase the accuracy of the references provided by the users to answer given questions? The accuracy of references is a function of *precision* and *recall*[1] (see Sect. 5.1). DSpace users were providing more accurate references during the first one or two tasks; however, the overall measures indicated higher accuracy for JeromeDL. The average *precision* measures were only slightly better for JeromeDL; the differences in the *recall* measures were much higher, even up to *58%* when compared to DSpace. Based on the aforementioned results, we can conclude that social and semantic services do increase the accuracy of the references provided to answer given questions.

Question 3. Do the social and semantic services increase overall satisfaction of using the digital library? To answer this question we have analyzed the satisfaction metrics for each stage of the evaluation, and additional ones gathered before and after the whole evaluation (see Sect. 5.2). The overall impression before and after using each system was higher for JeromeDL, with $\Delta_{\rho_s(impression)} > \mathbf{150\%}$. DSpace users were slightly more satisfied after the initial tasks; with only significant difference in case of registration task ($|\Delta_{\rho_t(registering)}| = 14.52\%$). Also after the first question-answering task the overall user satisfaction was higher for DSpace ($|\Delta_{\rho_t(task\ 1)}| = 37.87\%$). In case of bookmarking task and the second and third question-answering tasks, i.e., in later stages of the evaluation, the participants using JeromeDL were much more satisfied; respectively $\Delta_{\rho_t(bookmarking)} = 254.61\%$, $\Delta_{\rho_t(task\ 2)} = 398.12\%$, and $\Delta_{\rho_t(task\ 3)} = 119.75\%$. We have also compared user satisfaction related to the information discovery (searching) features in each library after each question-answering task. In all three cases JeromeDL users rated information discovery features higher than DSpace users, $\Delta_{\rho_s(task\ 1)} = 10.78\%$,

[1] Detailed report [125] presents additionally analyzes of *fall-out* and *f-measure*.

$\Delta_{\rho_s(task\ 2)} = 1070.66\%$, and $\Delta_{\rho_s(task\ 3)} = 141.57\%$ respectively. Based on this results we can conclude that the social and semantic services do increase the overall satisfaction of using the digital library.

Question 4. Which services, i.e., semantic, social, or recommendations, are found to be most useful by the end users? The three features with highest satisfaction measures were resource-related recommendations ($\rho_s = 19.32$), SSCF ($\rho_s = 17.76$), and bookmarks recommendations ($\rho_s = 15.83$). Among other features, all *social* were ranked higher than *semantic* ones. Hence we can answer that the type of features the users found most useful were the *recommendations*, followed by the *social/collaborative* solutions.

6 Conclusions and Future Work

Results gathered during this evaluation (see Sect. 5) show the advantage the enhanced information discovery features can offer to digital libraries. Not only users' satisfaction is higher than when using non-semantic digital library; also the quality of the knowledge they gather and use is of higher quality.

The users are more eager to depend results of their search process on the automated solutions, such as recommendations, and on their trust in the information provided by their friends. Therefore, the meaning of semantics in the digital libraries should heavily include the social (*soft*) semantics. Future research on semantic features should concentrate more on improving accuracy of automated recommendations services and usability of existing solutions.

The results of the evaluation presented in this article will help to focus on most important issued during our further research on the semantic digital libraries. We intend to further develop, tailor, and customize the solutions implemented in JeromeDL to improve their usability and user satisfaction.

Acknowledgement

This material is based upon works supported by Enterprise Ireland under Grant No. ILP/05/203 and by Science Foundation Ireland Grant No. SFI/02/CE1/I131.

Conclusions: The Future of Semantic Digital Libraries

Sebastian Ryszard Kruk and Bill McDaniel

Through out this book we showed that Semantic Digital Libraries are no longer an abstract concept; we have presented both underlying technologies, examples of semantic digital libraries, and their applications. However, the bright future of this technology only begins, and we expect more and more genuine applications of semantic digital libraries to emerge.

In this section we will spotlight on three of, in our opinion, the most promising fields of applications: semantic museums, eLearning 2.0, and semantic digital libraries in enterprises.

1 Semantic Museum

Libraries and digital libraries are, we could say, worlds apart; the former exist in the physical world, the latter in the digital one. Although there are strong tights between both type of system, this distinction remains pretty accurate. With the evolution of web technologies we have noticed a move towards building "digital" museums. What many museums do, at the moment, is building their existence on the Internet. Technologies, such as VRML [218], SecondLife[1] or 2LIP [102], allow to render 3D objects on web sites; we can imagine aforementioned virtual tours to come to existence. Virtual tours allow users to browse not only through the metadata but also through virtual exhibitions. For example, National Gallery of Art allows to stroll virtually through the exhibition of works of Alexander Calder.[2] What is interesting about museums, is that new technologies should support visitors in the real life as well. Mainly because the physical presence at the museum gives much better experience

[1] SecondLife: `http://www.secondlife.com/`

[2] Alexander Calder virtual tour at National Gallery of Art: `http://www.nga.gov/exhibitions/calder/realsp/roomenter-foyer.htm`

than the virtual tour which can be used for, e.g., getting quick overview of current exhibitions and location of the presented items.

Let's consider a simple scenario, where current educational purpose of museum exhibitions can be enhanced with semantic web and mobile technologies.

Many people, when visiting a museum, usually try to be very focused on reading and listening to all auxiliary material delivered to assist with the exhibition. Depending on particular solution provided by the museum, they can usually read short, sometimes very short, descriptions of, e.g., paintings they are looking at. Sometimes, the audio guide, synchronized with their tour, will give them better understanding of what they are looking at, at the moment. And usually this is where all support from the auxiliary materials end. Unless, visitors have a very broad and deep knowledge of the topic, and can track most of important exhibitions related to the one they is at the moment, there is no way they can get any further with their visit. To some extent, most of the interesting information seems to be veiled before them.

Now imagine, that instead of just an audio guide the museum provides an ubiquitous guide. Visitors could it access this guide with their own mobile device or with the one provided by the museum. The sensors, such as camera, GPS, or accelerometer, build in or delivered along with this device can track their current position and their current subject of interest. Now, looking at an item and moving their smart phone camera in front of it, visitors can see regions of interest (ROI), similar to those we know from Flickr,[3]) overlaid on the view presented by the device. These ROIs can be heavily annotated with all information the visitor can be interested in. If the mobile device holds visitor's profile, it can even filter out those that he/she would not be interested in, or those he/she already know. These additional information bits can also allow visitors to start a virtual tour from the place where they are at the moment; they can browse through, e.g., *a picture of a dog*, which was represents an allegory of *fidelity*, to other paintings where the same allegory is used. Their personal guide, running on their mobile device, can also tell the visitors if any of these paintings are being now on display anywhere near to where they are at the moment. They can also share their thoughts, knowledge, ideas with others that will come across this painting in the future.

Semantic Web, Web 2.0, adaptable interfaces, ubiquitous computing, all these technologies come handy to develop a service as described in our scenario. Providing accurate information based on user context is where semantic technologies can help; the context can range from current position, item being viewed at the moment, user's interests, or previous history of museum visits. The social technologies, like tagging and blogging, allow users to share their knowledge and opinion with others. Semantic indexes, such as Sindice[4] will bind together the formal and informal information coming from the museums and other sources.

[3] Flickr: `http://www.flickr.com/`

[4] Sindice: `http://www.sindice.com/`

2 Semantic Digital Libraries for E-Learning

Libraries were always a source of valuable information for the scholars and the students. We came to understanding that digital libraries need to evolve in order to continue fulfilling this mission.

Our scenario finds John, a high school teacher, preparing a new course on biology for his class. This class, however, is distributed over a number of villages. Students attend classes over the Internet, and they only meet twice a year for the exams (see Fig. 1).

John's course on biology consists of 15 lectures; each lecture is assisted with a collection of reading material. John would like to easily distribute the reading material related to each lesson a week in advance, no sooner, no later; he would like to make sure his students will read and understand delivered information. Furthermore he would like to pre-assess students based on their reading assignments and their comprehension of given material; additionally, he would like to pass the knowledge gathered by current students to next year's students.

John finds that most of the materials he would like to deliver to students comes either from the university library, wikipedia, or other online sources. He also discovers that some of the bookmarks sharing systems can help him with the materials delivery process. John decides to use a blogging platform to gather student opinions, references, etc. on the reading material; he will assess his students reading assignments based on their activity; the blogs will also gather students' knowledge, which will be passed to next year's students.

John is pretty pleased with his solution; however, he notices that operating on three different systems (digital library, bookmarks sharing, blog) is quite time-consuming; he needs to discover the resources using different search features, bookmark them locally; then he copies bookmarks to a shared space in the Internet bookmarking service which he decided to use. Finally, he needs to create a blog entry for each reading material item. John wishes there was an easier and more productive way to do that. In this thesis we will show how

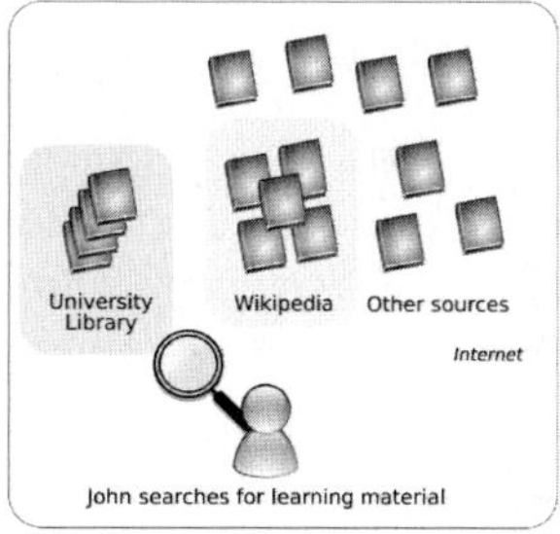

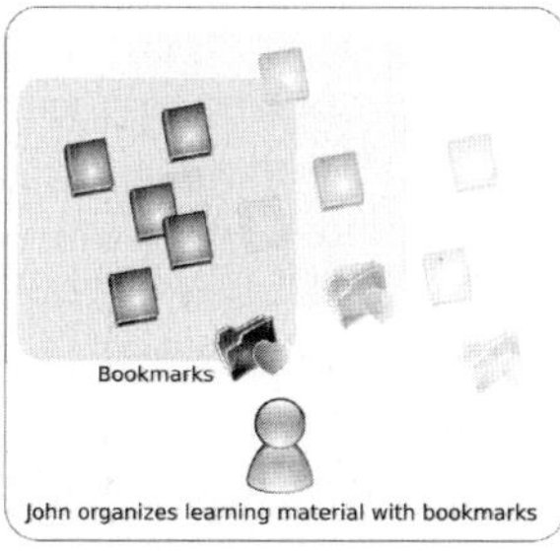

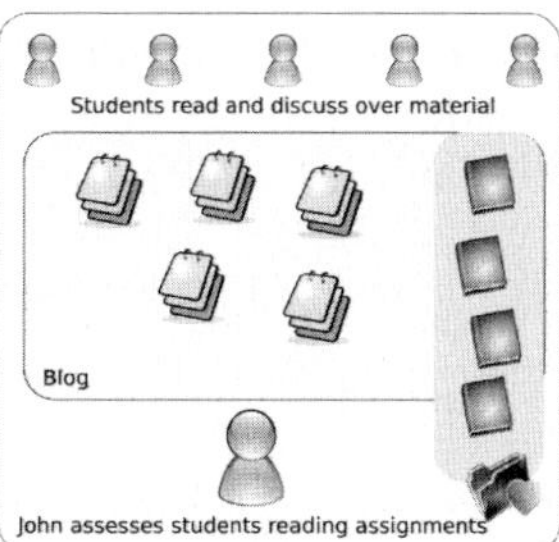

Fig. 1. E-learning use case scenario for semantic digital libraries

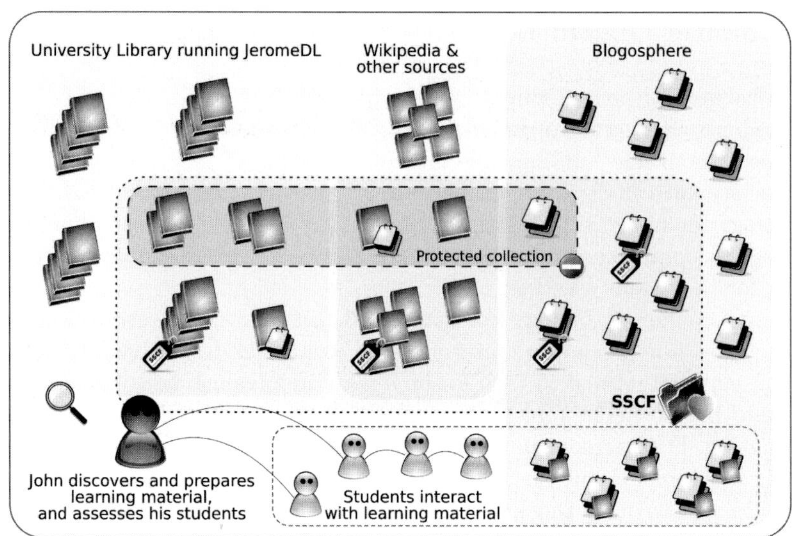

Fig. 2. John prepares lectures with SSCF and a semantic digital library

social and semantic services in digital libraries can help John in his work, and John's students in their studies.

With social and semantic services every library user can bookmark interesting books, articles or other materials. Users can share their knowledge with others within a social network (see Fig. 2).

A semantic digital library provides an answer to the problem stated in the aforementioned scenario. It is a platform that joins three separate applications: digital library, blog and bookmarking application. A semantic digital library is a service where he can keep the resources needed for his biology course and any additional materials which can help him. In systems like JeromeDL [118] or FEDORA [69], every resource can become a blog, so John can track his students' opinions and progress. SSCF incorporated into JeromeDL, allows John and his students to easily discover and retrieve resources, and later create, share and import bookmarks. John can even contact library administrators, and suggest a set of natural language query templates which will help him and his students to find resources much more easily. With Social Semantic Collaborative Filtering components (see Chapter "*JeromeDL – the Social Semantic Digital Library*") and SIOC (see Chapter "*Social Semantic Information Spaces*") integration community based materials can also be added and browsed with the SSCF interface.

To summarize, a semantic digital library can become a service that allows users to utilize old and create new knowledge, it is a tool that can be very helpful in many domains, especially in e-Learning. It can be a place where community meets and individuals influence each other.

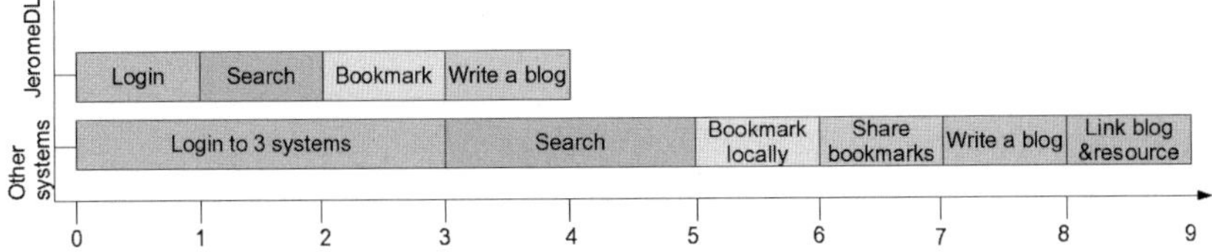

Fig. 3. Theoretical comparison of time required for performing a task with semantic digital library and other systems

Finally, we have compared an effort required to complete John's scenario using a classic approach and a semantic digital library for eLearning scenario. Performing real-world experiments is quite cumbersome in this case and prone to noise from the human factor; therefore, simply compared times required to perform a sequence of activities, defined in our scenario, by John, in order to prepare the course (see Fig. 3). John finds out that working with an integrated platform such as a semantic digital library is less time consuming. He spends less time on logging-in to different systems and searching through them. John can immediately bookmark resources and start a blog about them, without copying or linking to other systems. This observation is coherent with the results of the evaluation of semantic digital libraries (as presented in Chapter "*Evaluation of Semantic and Social Technologies for Digital Libraries*").

3 Semantic Digital Libraries in Enterprises

Semantic technologies are emerging into the enterprise as the semantic web becomes more and more real. The use of semantic search and semantic annotation in intra-enterprise communications is growing rapidly. Products such as Twine[5] and OpenCalais[6] are being installed or used in corporate environments.

One particularly popular application is product catalogue searches. Semantically powered faceted search applications make it possible to browse product catalogs in a variety of ways without the usual overhead of planning and constructing all possible views of the data source. Data mining applications also are emerging which use semantic knowledge representations to discover new knowledge hidden in enterprise document repositories.

Enterprises traditionally retain documents, papers, notes, books, and other printed material for long periods. Many of these paper systems have been replaced with back office databases holding the same information in structured format. The trend in stored data from computing environments, however, is toward less structured documents, more memos, proposals, contracts, and

[5] Twine: `http://www.radarnetworks.com`

[6] OpenCalais: `http://www.opencalais.com`

other non- or semi-structured. Enterprises are already drowning in a sea of documents [172] and solutions are being sought. Large document management systems, such as Documentum™ and content management systems such as Sharepoint™ provide some solution, but the need of enterprise to mine and sift the information and knowledge in these document databases is growing and exceeding the capabilities of traditional systems, even those which offer some measure of semantics.[7]

Semantic Digital Libraries offer a mechanism for enhancing the traditional document repository. Many existing repositories support some level of metadata, but few provide the dynamic collections, threaded lookup and ontologically mediated viewpoints.

Searching through most enterprise document libraries is a straightforward, but not terribly efficient or productive activity. Most document library systems present in the enterprise today provide for keyword search, full text search on a variety of formats and keyword searching of a few metadata fields.

Semantic digital libraries can add to this by providing networked knowledge discovery. Resident within document sets, within libraries, are implicit networks of information and knowledge. These networks consist of such things as the subset of documents authored by colleagues, subnets of documents pertaining to similar concepts but using different terminologies or even languages. Traditional, keyword driven library systems are not able to support finding such subnets if the alternative terminologies are not known.

Semantic digital libraries allow dynamic and expansive tagging of documents so that folksonomic searches can be carried out. These allow the user community, the business teams and departments, to add their own linguistic flavour to documents, generally as they are shared and used. Semantic digital libraries also offer the opportunity to locate documents which fit an ontological pattern such as documents which contain references to one concept, but which are related to documents containing information pertaining to other,parent or child concepts.

Indeed, the relationships discoverable with semantic digital libraries are richer than that. Searches such as, show me all the documents pertaining to our mid east oil partners which cover production yields of their distribution partners can be easily resolved. Such a query over a semantically linked digital library would also locate documents which referenced both Venezuelan oil production (a member of the largely mid-eastern organization, OPEC) in relation to production as well as documents discussing light sweet crude instead of oil. Ontology mediated searches would allow synonymous and grammatically related knowledge networks to be illuminated.

Faceted search capabilities implemented over digital libraries will provide business researchers, such as those in legal departments or new product

[7] Documentum™is a product of EMC Corporation and Sharepoint™is a product of Microsoft Corporation

development teams to find documents pertaining to a variety of topics and points of view.

Semantic digital libraries offer a method for enterprise organizations to discover new knowledge in their document repositories, reference libraries, email archives, and other communications logs. By treating such things as books to be catalogued and managed in a semantic manner, semantic digital libraries can offer significant value add to the enterprise. By augmenting other semantic technologies such as internal wikis, blogs, chats, collaborative forum and project rooms, semantic digital libraries add a great deal of value to an enterprises document repository.

4 Conclusions

Often, in research, subtle changes in perception or point of view lead to dramatically new and improved ideas. The process is non-linear and chaotic. But, at that edge of well understood order and the jumbled mess of chaos, significant insights lie.

Semantic digital libraries offer expanded facilities for knowledge discovery, data mining of semi-structured text, and mechanisms for linking and searching related concepts. In sometimes obscure ways, new knowledge emerges from large collections of data, large volumes of text, and large aggregates of information. Research areas from pharmaceuticals to anti-terrorism benefit from linkages and interrelationships that are subtle and often hard to explain.

Semantic digital libraries as repositories for semantically empowered objects such as books, papers, images, and other collections of information provide a powerful means for sorting, searching, identifying, and deriving new knowledge from the vast jumble of information organizations, enterprises, and individuals collect. Such libraries provide a far easier way to change the point of view and to alter the perceptions of information. Thus, they offer an easier way to discover new insights to both the past that generated them and the future that will use them.

The future of such libraries is bright because they offer a better way to use the knowledge our species is doubling so rapidly.

Without these advanced techniques, many insights and alternative points of view might be missed.

With them, whole new vistas of opportunity emerge.

Acknowledgement

This material is based upon works supported by Enterprise Ireland under Grant No. ILP/05/203 and by Science Foundation Ireland Grant No. SFI/02/CE1/I131.

References

1. Faceted metadata search and browse (searchtools.com/info/faceted-metadata.html).
2. FOAF Vocabulary Specification: http://xmlns.com/foaf/0.1/.
3. Sesame: An architecture for storing and querying rdf data and schema information.
4. ISO 14721:2003. Space data and information transfer systems open archival information system – reference model. 2003.
5. C. Thomas A. Sheth, C. Ramakrishnan. Semantics for the semantic web: The implicit, the formal and the powerful. *International Journal on Semantic Web and Information Systems*, 1(1):1–18, 2005.
6. K. Aberer and P. Cudré-Mauroux. Semantic overlay networks. In K. Böhm, C.S. Jensen, L.M. Haas, M.L. Kersten, P.-A. Larson, B.C. Ooi, editors, *VLDB*, page 1367. ACM Press, 2005.
7. M. Agosti, L. Bischofs, L. Candela, D. Castelli, N. Ferro, W. Hasselbring, N. Moumoutzis, H. Schuldt, G. Weikum, M. Wurz, P. Zezula. Evaluation and Comparison of the Service Architecture, P2P, and Grid Approaches for DLs. Deliverable 1.1.1, DELOS, January 2006.
8. M. Agosti and N. Ferro. An information service architecture for annotations. In Agosti et al. [9], pages 115–126.
9. M. Agosti, H.-J. Schek, C. Türker, editors. *Digital Library Architectures: Peer-to-Peer, Grid, and Service-Orientation, Pre-proceedings of the Sixth Thematic Workshop of the EU Network of Excellence DELOS, S. Margherita di Pula, Cagliari, Italy, 24–25 June, 2004*. Edizioni Libreria Progetto, Padova, 2004.
10. R. Akscyn, D. McCracken, E. Yoder. Kms: a distributed hypermedia system for managing knowledge in organizations. *Communications of the ACM*, 31:820–835, 1988.
11. J. Andrews and D.G. Law. *Digital libraries: Policy, planning and practice.* Ashgate, Burlington, VT, 2004.
12. W. Arms. *Digital libraries.* MIT, Cambridge, MA, 2000.
13. D. Bainbridge, G. Buchanan, J. McPherson, S. Jones, A. Mahoui, I.H. Witten. Greenstone: A platform for distributed digital library applications. In *ECDL'01: Proceedings of the 5th European Conference on Research and Advanced Technology for Digital Libraries*, pages 137–148, London, UK, 2001. Springer-Verlag.

14. D. Bainbridge, K.J. Don, G. Buchanan, I.H. Witten, S. Jones, M. Jones, M.I. Barr. Dynamic digital library construction and configuration. In R. Heery and L. Lyon, editors, *ECDL*, volume 3232 of *Lecture Notes in Computer Science*, pages 1–13. Springer, 2004.
15. D. Bainbridge, K.J. Don, G.R. Buchanan, I.H. Witten, S. Jones, M. Jones, M.I. Barr. Dynamic digital library construction and configuration. In *Research and Advanced Technology for Digital Libraries*, pages 1–13, 2004.
16. J.A. Barnes. Class and Committees in a Norwegian Island Parish. volume 7, pages 39–58. Human Relations, 1954.
17. H. Bast and I. (n.d.). Weber. When You're Lost for Words: Faceted Search with Autocompletion.
18. P. Bausch, M. Haughey, M. Hourihan. *We Blog: Publishing Online with Weblogs*. Wiley, New York, 2002.
19. M.K. Bergman. Untapped Assets: The $3 Trillion Value of U.S. Enterprise Documents, 2005.
20. T.H. Berners-Lee. The semantic web. scientific american. May 2001.
21. A.P. Bishop, N.A. Van House, B.P. Buttenfield. *Digital library use: Social practice in design and evaluation.* MIT, Cambridge, MA, 2003.
22. C. Bizer and T. Gauss. RDF Book Mashup – Serving RDF descriptions of your books, November 2006.
23. Rebecca Blood. *The Weblog Handbook: Practical Advice on Creating and Maintaining Your Blog.* Perseus Books Group, July 2002.
24. J. Blyberg. Library 2.0 websites: Where to begin? http://www.blyberg.net/2006/03/12/library-20-websites-where-to-begin/, December 2006.
25. S. Bocconi. Automatic presentation generation for scholarly hypermedia. In *Proc. of the 1st International Workshop on Scholarly Hypertext at the Hypertext 2003 conference*, Nottingham, U.K., 2003.
26. U. Bojars, J.G. Breslin, A. Passant. Sioc browser – towards a richer blog browsing experience, October 2006. Accepted for the 4th Blogtalk Conference (Blogtalk Reloaded), Vienna, Austria.
27. C.L. Borgman. *From Gutenberg to the Global Information Infrastructure: Access to Information in the Networked World.* MIT, Cambridge, MA, 2000.
28. D.M. Boyd. Friendster and Publicly Articulated Social Networking. In *Conference on Human Factors and Computing Systems (CHI 2004)*, http://www.danah.org/papers/CHI2004Friendster.pdf, 2004.
29. J.G. Breslin, S. Decker, A. Harth, U. Bojars. SIOC: An Approach to Connect Web-Based Communities. *The International Journal of Web-Based Communities*, 2(2):133–142, 2006.
30. J.G. Breslin, A. Harth, U. Bojars, S. Decker. Towards semantically-interlinked online communities. volume 3532, pages 500–514, June 1993. Proceedings of the 2nd European Semantic Web Conference (ESWC'05), Heraklion, Greece.
31. G. Brettlecker, H. Schuldt, H.-J. Schek, G. Brettlecker, H. Schuldt, H.-J. Schek, C. Türker, G. Zini, O. Nee, M. Eichelberg, U. Steffens. Evaluation of mobile information and information dynamics with special emphasis on applications in e-health. Deliverable 1.3, DELOS, 2004.
32. D. Brickley and L. Miller. FOAF Vocabulary Specification. http://xmlns.com/foaf/0.1/.
33. P. Brusilovsky, J. Eklund, E. Schwarz. Web-based education for all: A tool for developing adaptive courseware. *Computer Networks and ISDN Systems*, 30:291–300, 1998.

34. G. Buchanan. FRBR: enriching and integrating digital libraries. In *JCDL'06: Proceedings of the 6th ACM/IEEE-CS joint conference on Digital libraries*, pages 260–269, New York, NY, USA, 2006. ACM Press.
35. G. Buchanan, D. Bainbridge, K.J. Don, I.H. Witten. A new framework for building digital library collections. In *JCDL'05: Proceedings of the 5th ACM/IEEE-CS joint conference on Digital libraries*, pages 23–31, New York, NY, USA, 2005. ACM Press.
36. G. Buchanan, J. Gow, A. Blandford, J. Rimmer, C. Warwick. Representing aggregate works in the digital library. In *Proceedings of the ACM/IEEE JCDL*, pages 247–256, 2007.
37. G. Buchanan and A. Hinze. A generic alerting service for digital libraries. In *JCDL'05: Proceedings of the 5th ACM/IEEE-CS joint conference on Digital libraries*, pages 131–140, New York, NY, USA, 2005. ACM Press.
38. L. Candela, D. Castelli, P. Pagano, C. Thanos, I. Pisa, Y. Ioannidis, G. Koutrika, G. Athens, S. Ross, H.J. Schek, Others. Setting the Foundations of Digital Libraries: The DELOS Manifesto. *D-Lib Magazine*, 13(3/4), 2007.
39. L. Candela, D. Castelli, N. Ferro, Y. Ioannidis, G. Koutrika, C. Meghini, P. Pagano, S. Ross, D. Soergel, M. Agosti, M Dobreva, V Katifori, H. Schuldt. The DELOS Digital Library Reference Model – Foundations for Digital Libraries. Technical report, DELOS, November 2007.
40. L. Candela, D. Castelli, P. Pagano, M. Simi. Moving digital library service systems to the grid. In Agosti et al. [9], pages 13–24.
41. L. Candela, P. Manghi, P. Pagano. An architecture for type-based repository systems. In *Castelli and Y. Ioannidis, editors, Proceedings of the Second Workshop on Foundations of Digital Libraries, in conjunction with 11th European Conference on Research and Advanced Technologies on Digital Libraries (ECDL 2007)*, Pisa, Italy.
42. S. Cayzer. Semantic blogging and decentralized knowledge management. *Communications of the ACM*, 47(12):47–52, 2004.
43. Chimra. http://www.ksl.stanford.edu/software/chimaera/.
44. J.P. Chin, V.A. Diehl, K.L. Norman. Development of an instrument measuring user satisfaction of the human-computer interface. In *CHI '88: Proceedings of the SIGCHI conference on Human factors in computing systems*, pages 213–218, New York, NY, USA, 1988. ACM Press.
45. G.G. Chowdhury and S. Chowdhury. *Introduction to digital libraries.* Facet Publishers, London, 2003.
46. CIDOC Documentation Standards Group. CIDOC Conceptual Reference Model (CRM) – ISO 21127:2006, December 2006.
47. The OWL Services Coalition. Owl-s: Semantic markup for web services, 2003.
48. M. Crampes and S. Ranwez. Ontology-supported and ontology-driven conceptual navigation on the world-wide web. In *Proceedings of the ACM Hypertext 2000 Conference, San Antonio, USA*, 2000.
49. N. Crofts, M. Doerr, T. Gill, S. Stead, M. Stiff. Current Official Version of the CIDOC CRM version 4.2 of the reference document. Definition of the CIDOC Conceptual Reference Model. June 2005.
50. G. Csanyi and B. Szendroi. Structure of a large social network, 2003.
51. D. Connolly, F. van Harmelen, et al. Daml+oil reference description, w3 consortium. Technical report, March 2001. http://www.w3.org/TR/daml+oil-reference.

52. M. Dahl, K. Banerjee, M. Spalti. *Digital Libraries: Integrating content and systems.* Chandos Publishing, Oxford, 2006.
53. Daml ontology library. http://www.daml.org/ontologies/.
54. R. Daniel, C. Lagoze, S.D. Payette. A metadata architecture for digital libraries, pages 276–288, 1998.
55. I. Davis and R. Newman. Expression of Core FRBR Concepts in RDF. Working draft, 2005.
56. Dublin Core Metadata Initiative (DCMI). http://www.dublincore.org/.
57. J. de Bruijn and A. Polleres, editors. OWL-, WSML Working Draft. Technical report, May 2005. http://www.wsmo.org/TR/d20/d20.1/v0.2/20050515/.
58. L. Dempsey and B. Lavoie. Dlf service framework for digital libraries. progress report, DLF Steering Committee, 2005.
59. M. Dewey. A Classification and Subject Index for Cataloguing and Arranging the Books and Pamphlets of a Library – Dewey Decimal Classification. Technical report, Gutenberg.net, 2004.
60. E.W. Dijkstra. A note on two problems in connexion with graphs. *Numerische Mathematik*, 1:269–271, 1959.
61. L. Dodds. An Introduction to FOAF. http://www.xml.com/pub/a/2004/02/04/foaf.html, February 2004.
62. DOE - The Differential Ontology Editor. http://opales.ina.fr/public/.
63. D.C. Engelbart. *A Conceptual Framework for the Augmentation of Man's Intellect.* Spartan Books, 1963.
64. U. Sattler F. Baader, I. Horrocks. *Description Logics, Handbook on Ontologies.* Springer, Berlin, 2004.
65. G. Falquet, L. Nerima, J. Guyot. Languages and tools to specify hypertext views on databases. In P. Atzeni, A. Mendelzon, G. Mecca, editors, *Porc. of The World Wide Web and Databases*, volume 1590 of *LNCS*, Berlin, 1999. Springer.
66. G. Falquet, L. Nerima, J.-C. Ziswiler. Utilisation des ontologies dans les environnements d'écriture collaborative d'hyperlivres, expériences et perspectives. *Revue STICEF*, 11:333–350, 2004.
67. G. Falquet and J.-C. Ziswiler. A virtual hyperbooks model to support collaborative learning. *AACE International Journal on E-Learning (IJEL)*, 4:39–56, 2005.
68. T. Fanjiang, L. Congrong, D. Wang. Evolving information filtering for personalized information service. *Journal of Computational Science Technology*, 16(2):168–175, 2001.
69. Fedora Development Team. Fedora open source repository software: White paper. Technical report, Cornell University, 2005.
70. C. Fellbaum. WordNet – An Electronic Lexical Database, 1998.
71. E.A. Fox and G. Marchionini. Toward a worldwide digital library. *Communications of the ACM*, 41(4):29–32, 1998.
72. P. Doreian and T. Snijders, (Eds). Social Networks. Elsevier Science Publishers, 1979.
73. M. Freeston. Towards a global infrastructure for georeferenced information. In Agosti et al. [9], pages 175–182.
74. I. Frommholz, P. Knezevic, B. Mehta, C. Niederée, T. Risse, U. Thiel. Supporting information access in next generation digital library architectures. In Agosti et al. [9], pages 49–60.

75. N. Fuhr, G. Tsakonas, T. Aalberg, M. Agosti, P. Hansen, S. Kapidakis, C.-P. Klas, L. Kovas, M. Landoni, A. Micsik, C. Papatheodorou, C. Peters, I. Solvberg. Evaluation of digital libraries. Appeared online in International Journal of Digital Libraries, 2007. http://www.springerlink.com/content/w2w0j4h272k26812/.
76. V. Geroimenko. A semantic web primer. *Computer Journal*, 48(1):126, 2005.
77. N. Gioldasis, N. Pappas, F.G. Kazasis, G. Anestis, S. Christodoulakis. A P2P and SOA Infrastructure for Distributed Ontology-Based Knowledge Management. In Agosti et al. [9], pages 93–104.
78. R.J. Glushko and T. McGrath. *Document Engineering.* MIT, 2005.
79. D. Greenstein and S.E. Thorin. *The Digital Library: A Biography.* Digital Library Federation, 2002.
80. S. Griffin, C. Peters, C. Thanos. Towards the new-generation digital libraries: recommendations of the NSF/EU-DELOS working groups Guest editor introduction. (4):253–254, August 2005.
81. T. Gruber. Ontology of Folksonomy: A Mash-up of Apples and Oranges. International Journal on Semantic Web and Information Systems. 2007.
82. T. Gruber. Ontology of Folksonomy: A Mash-up of Apples and Oranges, 2005.
83. T. Gruber. TagOntology – a way to agree on the semantics of tagging data, 2005.
84. M. Halbert. The OCKHAM library nework. Technical report, ockham.org, 2003.
85. S. Harum and M. Twidale. *Successes and failures of digital libraries.* Urbana-Champaign, IL: Graduate School of Library and Information Science, University of Illinois, Urbana- Champaign, 2000.
86. M.A. Hearst. Design recommendations for hierarchical faceted search interfaces. In *Proceedings of the International ACM SIGIR Workshop on Faceted Search*, Seattle, WA, August 2006.
87. M.L.N. Herbert. Resource harvesting within the oai-pmh framework. *D-Lib Magazine*, 10(12), 2004.
88. A. Hinze and G. Buchanan. A distributed alerting service for open digital library software. In *ICDCSW'05: Proceedings of the Fourth International Workshop on Distributed Event-Based Systems (DEBS) (ICDCSW'05)*, pages 444–450, Washington, DC, USA, 2005. IEEE Computer Society.
89. A. Hinze, X. Gao, D. Bainbridge. The TIP/Greenstone Bridge: A Service for Mobile Location-Based Access to Digital Libraries. In *Proceedings of ECDL 2006*, pages 99–110, 2006.
90. A. Hinze, A. Schweer, G. Buchanan. An integrated alerting service for open digital libraries: Design and implementation. In *Proceedings of the 13th International Conference on Cooperative Information Systems (CoopIS 2005)*, volume 3760 of *Lecture Notes in Computer Science*, pages 484–501. Springer, 2005.
91. K. Hornbaek and E.L.-C. Law. Meta-analysis of correlations among usability measures. In *CHI'07: Proceedings of the SIGCHI conference on Human factors in computing systems*, pages 617–626, New York, NY, USA, 2007. ACM Press.
92. http://learningcircuits.blogspot.com/. Should all learning professionals be blogging?
93. http://www.w3.org/TR/rdf. Resource Description Framework (RDF). W3C Recommendation, 1999.

94. D.F. Huynh, D.R. Karger, R.C. Miller. Exhibit: lightweight structured data publishing. In *WWW'07: Proceedings of the 16th international conference on World Wide Web*, pages 737–746, New York, NY, USA, 2007. ACM Press.
95. IFLA Study Group on the Functional Requirements for Bibliographic Records. *Functional Requirements for Bibliographic Records: Final Report*, volume 19 of *UBCIM Publications-New Series*. K.G.Saur, München, 1998.
96. S. Iksal and S. Garlatti. Spécification declarative pour les documents virtuels personalisables. In S. Garlatti and M. Crampes, editors, *Actes du congrès Documents virtuels personalisables (DVP2002)*, 2002.
97. S. Iksal, P. Tanguy, F. Ganier. Semantic composition of special report on the web: A cognitive approach. In *Proceedings of the H2PTM'01 Conference*, Valenciennes, France, 2001.
98. ISO 21127:2006 Information and documentation. A reference ontology for the interchange of cultural heritage information. December.
99. Y. Ioannidis, H.-J. Schek, G. Weikum, editors. *Future Digital Library Management Systems: System Architecture and Information Access*, April 2005.
100. S. Choudhury and J. Hunter. A semi-automated digital preservation system based on semantic web services, 2004.
101. S. Choudhury and J. Hunter. Semi-automated preservation and archival of scientific data using semantic grid services, 2005.
102. J. Jankowski and S.R. Kruk. 2LIP: The Step Towards The Web3D. In *17th International World Wide Web Conference*, Beijing, China, April 2008.
103. Jena – A Semantic Web Framework for Java. http://jena.sourceforge.net/.
104. G. Jennifer, B. Parsia, J. Hendler. Trust Management for the Semantic Web. In *Proceedings of Cooperative Intelligent Agents*, http://www.mindswap.org/papers/CIA03.pdf, 2003.
105. M. Kaczmarek, S.R. Kruk, A. Gzella. Collaborative building of controlled vocabulary crosswalks. In *11th European Conference on Research and Advanced Technology for Digital Libraries*, Budapest, Hungary, September 2007.
106. D. Soergel, B. Lauser, A. Liang, F. Fisseha, J. Keizer, S. Katz. Reengineering thesauri for new applications. The agrovoc example. *Journal of Digital Information*, 4(4), 2004.
107. J. Kessler. *Internet Digital Libraries: The International Dimension.* Artech House, Boston, MA, 1996.
108. Z.A. Khan, M. Odeh, R. Mcclatchey. Digital libraries: From process modelling to grid-based service oriented architecture, Feb 2006.
109. J. Kleinberg. Small-world phenomena and the dynamics of information, 2001.
110. N. Knouf. BibTeX Definition in Web Ontology Language (OWL) Version 1.0, Working Draft. Technical report, Massachusetts Institute of Technology (MIT).
111. I. Koffina, G. Serfiotis, V. Christophides, V. Tannen, A. Deutsch. Integrating xml data sources using rdf/s schemas: The ics-forth semantic web integration middleware (swim). In Ioannidis et al. [99].
112. G. Kokkinidis, L. Sidirourgos, T. Dalamagas, V. Christophides. Semantic Query Routing and Processing in P2P Digital Libraries. In Ioannidis et al. [99].
113. G. Koutrika and A. Simitsis. An enhanced search interface for information discovery from digital libraries. pages 87–98. 2006.
114. D. Kresh. *The whole digital library handbook.* American Library Association, Chicago, 2007.

115. S.R. Kruk and H. Krawczyk. Intelligent Resources Search in Virtual Libraries. In Trojanowski Klopotek, Wierzchon, editor, *Intelligent Information Processing and Web Mining*, pages 439–444. Polish Academy of Science, Springer, 2004. Proceedings of the International IIS: IIPWM'04 Conference held in Zakopane, Poland, May 17–20, 2004.
116. S.R. Kruk. FOAF-Realm – control your friends' access to resource. In *Proceedings of FOAF Workshop 2004*, Galway, Ireland, September 2004.
117. S.R. Kruk and S. Decker. Semantic social collaborative filtering with foafrealm. In S. Decker, J. Park, D. Quan, L. Sauermann, editors, *Proc. of Semantic Desktop Workshop at the ISWC, Galway, Ireland, November 6*, volume 175, November 2005.
118. S.R. Kruk, S. Decker, L. Zieborak. JeromeDL – Adding Semantic Web Technologies to Digital Libraries. In K.V. Andersen, J.K. Debenham, R. Wagner, editors, *DEXA*, volume 3588 of *Lecture Notes in Computer Science*, pages 716–725. Springer, 2005.
119. S.R. Kruk, S. Grzonkowski, A. Gzella, T. Woroniecki, H.-C. Choi. D-FOAF: Distributed Identity Management with Access Rights Delegation. In *Proceedings to ASWC'2006*, 2006.
120. S.R. Kruk, S. Grzonkowski, A. Gzella, T. Woroniecki, H.-C. Choi. D-FOAF: Distributed Identity Management with Access Rights Delegation. In R. Mizoguchi, Z. Shi, F. Giunchiglia, editors, *ASWC*, volume 4185 of *Lecture Notes in Computer Science*, pages 140–154. Springer, 2006.
121. S.R. Kruk, A. Gzella, F. Czaja, W. Bultrowicz, E. Kruk. Multibeebrowse – accessible browsing on unstructured metadata. In R. Meersman and Z. Tari, editors, *OTM Conferences (1)*, volume 4803 of *Lecture Notes in Computer Science*, pages 1063–1080. Springer, 2007.
122. S.R. Kruk, A. Gzella, D. Jaroslaw, B. McDaniel, T. Woroniecki. E-learning on the social semantic information sources. In *Second European Conference on Technology Enhanced Learning*, September 2007.
123. S.R. Kruk, B. Haslhofer, P. Nussbaumer, S. Payette, T. Woroniecki, editors. *Tutorial on Semantic Digital Libraries at ESWC'2007*, June 2007.
124. S.R. Kruk, E. Kruk, M. Dabrowski. Tag Clouds and TreeMaps – Results of an Extensive Usability Experiments. eLITE Deliverable 1.5.302, DERI, NUIG - Ireland, 2007.
125. S.R. Kruk, E. Kruk, S. Katarzyna. Results of the Evaluation of the Semantic and Social Technologies for Digital Libraries. Technical Report 1.1.12, DERI NUI Galway; eLITE Project; Lion Project, March 2008.
126. S.R. Kruk, K. Samp, E. Kruk. TagsTreeMaps 1.0 Research Report. Technical Report 1.5.302, DERI NUI Galway; eLITE Project, 2006.
127. S.R. Kruk, K. Samp, C. O'Nuallain, B. Davis, B. McDaniel, S. Grzonkowski. Search Interface Based on Natural Language Query Templates. In *Proceedings of IADIS International Conference WWW/Internet 2006*, Murcia, Spain, October 2006.
128. S.R. Kruk, M. Synak, K. Zimmermann. MarcOnt – Integration Ontology for Bibliographic Description Formats. In *Proceedings to Dublin Core Conference 2005*, September 2005.
129. S.R. Kruk, M. Synak, K. Zimmermann. MarcOnt Initiative – Mediation Services for Digital Libraries. In *Proceedings to Demo and Poster session at ECDL 2005*, September 2005.

130. S.R. Kruk, M. Synak, K. Zimmermann. MarcOnt Initiative. Bibliographic Description and Related Tools Utilising Semantic Web Technologies. Technical Report 3.01, DERI, NUI Galway; Lion Project, June 2005.
131. S.R. Kruk, T. Woroniecki, A. Gzella, M. Dabrowski. JeromeDL – a Semantic Digital Library. In *Semantic Web Challenge Colocated with The 6th International Semantic Web Conference and the 2nd Asian Semantic Web Conference the 2nd Asian Semantic Web Conference*, November 2007.
132. S.R. Kruk, K. Zimmermann, B. Sapkota. Semantically Enhanced Search Services in Digital Libraries. In *Telecommunications, 2006. AICT-ICIW'06. International Conference on Internet and Web Applications and Services*, 2006.
133. N. Ferro Y. Ioannidis G. Koutrika C. Meghini P. Pagano S. Ross D. Soergel. With M. Agosti Dobreva V. Katifori H. Schuldt L. Candela, D. Castelli. *The DELOS Digital Library Reference Model. Foundations for Digital Libraries. version .098.* ISTI CNR, Pisa, Italy, December 2007.
134. C. Lagoze. Fedora Tutorial 1 – Introduction to Fedora. Technical report, Fedora Commons, 2005.
135. C. Lagoze and J.R. Davis. Dienst: an architecture for distributed document libraries. *Communications of the ACM*, 38(4):47, 1995.
136. C. Lagoze, S. Payette, E. Shin, C. Wilper. Fedora: an architecture for complex objects and their relationships. *International Journal on Digital Libraries*, V6(2):124–138, 2006.
137. L. Lamport. *LaTeX: A Document Preparation System.* Addison-Wesley, Reading, MA, 1986.
138. M. Lesk. *Practical Digital Libraries: Books, Bytes and Bucks.* Morgan Kaufmann, San Francisco, CA, 1997.
139. M. Lesk. *Understanding digital libraries. 2. ed.* Elsevier, Boston, MA, 2005.
140. D.M. Levy and C.C. Marshall. Going digital: a look at assumptions underlying digital libraries. *Communications of ACM*, 38(4):77–84, 1995.
141. Y. Li, J. Li, D. Zhang, J. Tang. Result of ontology alignment with rimom at oaei'06. In *Proc. of the International Workshop on Ontology Matching (OM-2006), Nov. 5, 2006, Athens, Georgia, USA*, 1998.
142. R. Lorie. The uvc: A method for preserving digital documents, proof of concept, 2002.
143. P. Lyman and H. Varian. How much information, 2003.
144. C. Lynch, S. Parastatidis, N. Jacobs, H.V. de Sompel, C. Lagoze. The OAI-ORE effort: progress, challenges, synergies. In *JCDL'07: Proceedings of the 7th ACM/IEEE joint conference on Digital libraries*, pages 80–80, New York, NY, USA, 2007. ACM Press.
145. C.A. Lynch. The Z39.50 information retrieval protocol: an overview and status report. *SIGCOMM Computer Communication Review*, 21(1):58–70, 1991.
146. C.P. (n.d.). M. Buckland. Selecting libraries, selecting documents, selecting data.
147. G. Lausen and M. Kifer. F-logic: A higher-order language for reasoning about objects, inheritance, and scheme. In *Proceedings of the 1989 ACM SIGMOD international conference on Management of data.*
148. S. Decker and M. Sintek. Triple – a query, inference and transformation language for the semantic web. In *International Semantic Web Conference*, Sardinia, June 2002. http://triple.semanticweb.org/doc/iswc2002/TripleReport.pdf.

149. D-Lib Magazine. http://dlib.org.
150. M.A.Goncalves, E.A. Fox, L.T. Watson, N.A. Kipp. Streams, Structures, Spaces, Scenarios, Societies (5S): A Formal Model for Digital Libraries. In *ACM Transactions of Information Systems (TOIS)*, number 2, pages 270–312, 2004.
151. F. Manola and E. Miller, editors. *RDF Primer.* W3C Recommendation. World Wide Web Consortium, February 2004.
152. C. Meghini and T. Risse. BRICKS: A Digital Library Management System for Cultural Heritage. *ERCIM News*, (61), April 2005.
153. C. Meghini and N. Spyratos. Information access in digital libraries: Steps towards a conceptual schema. In Ioannidis et al. [99].
154. A. Micsik, L. Kovács, R. Stachel. Collaboration of loosely coupled repositories using peer-to-peer paradigm. In Agosti et al. [9], pages 85–92.
155. P. Mika. Ontologies Are Us: A Unified Model of Social Networks and Semantics. In *International Semantic Web Conference*, LNCS, pages 522–536. Springer, 2005.
156. S. Milgram. The Small World Problem. *Psychology Today*, pages 60–67, May 1967.
157. D.R. Millen, J. Feinberg, B. Kerr. Dogear: Social bookmarking in the enterprise. In *CHI'06: Proceedings of the SIGCHI conference on Human Factors in computing systems*, pages 111–120, New York, NY, USA, 2006. ACM Press.
158. M. Mlivoncic, C. Schuler, C. Türker. Hyperdatabase infrastructure for management and search of multimedia collections. In Agosti et al. [9], pages 25–36.
159. K. Moeller, U. Bojars, J.G. Breslin. Using semantics to enhance the blogging experience. In *ESWC*, pages 679–696, 2006.
160. D.L. McGuinness N.F. Noy. Ontology development 101: A guide to creating your first ontology. http://protege.stanford.edu/publications/ontology_development/ontology1 01-noy-mcguinness.html.
161. M.A. Musen and N.F. Noy. Prompt: Algorithm and tool for automated ontology merging and alignment. In *the Proceedings of the Seventeenth National Conference on Artificial Intelligence (AAAI-2000).*
162. M. Nanard and J. Nanard. Should anchors be typed too? an experiment with macweb. In *Proceedings of the ACM Hypertext '93 Conference*, 1993.
163. National Information Standards Organization (NISO). Understanding metadata, 2004. http://www.niso.org/standards/resources/Understanding Metadata.pdf.
164. W Nejdl and M. Wolpers. Kbs hyperbook – a data-driven information system on the web. In *WWW8 Conference, Toronto*, 1999.
165. M. Newman. Models of the Small World: A Review.
166. D. Novak and P. Zezula. Indexing the distance using chord: A distributed similarity search structure. In Ioannidis et al. [99].
167. N.F. Noy and M. Klein. Ontology evolution: Not the same as schema evolution. *Knowledge Information System*, 6(4):428–440, 2004.
168. Open Archival Information System (OAIS). http://en.wikipedia.org/wiki/Open_Archival_Information_System.
169. J.M. Ockerbloom. Towards the next generation: Recommendations for the next dspace architecture. Technical report, DSpace, January 2007.
170. DELOS Network of Excellence on Digital Librarie. delos.info.

171. OILed Ontology Editor. http://oiled.man.ac.uk/.
172. M. Ojala. Drowning in a sea of documents. *eContent*, 2002.
173. Task Force on Archiving of Digital Information. Preserving digital information: Final report and recommendations, 1996.
174. International Journal on Digital Libraries. dljournal.org.
175. Joint Conference on Digital Libraries (and predecessors) 1994. jcdl.org/past-event-conf.shtml.
176. Study Group on the Functional Requirements for Bibliographic Records. *Functional requirements for bibliographic records.* K.G. Saur, 1998.
177. Ontolingua. http://www.ksl.stanford.edu/software/ontolingua/.
178. Ontology inference layer (oil). http://www.ontoknowledge.org/oil/.
179. Wendy Osborn and Annika Hinze. Issues in location-based indexing for co-operating mobile information systems. In *Proceedings on Workshop of Context-aware Mobile Systems in conjunction in OTM workshops (Part I)*, volume 4805 of *Lecture Notes in Computer Science*, pages 226–235, 2007.
180. OWL Web Ontology Language Guide. http://www.w3.org/TR/owl-guide/.
181. OWL Web Ontology Language Overview. http://www.w3.org/TR/owl- features/.
182. OWL Web Ontology Language Reference, W3C Recommendation. http://www.w3.org/TR/owl-ref/.
183. J. Pasquier-Boltuck and G. Collaud. An object-oriented approach to conceptualizing and programming an interactive system for the creation and consultation of electronic book. In J. Pasquier-Boltuck, G. Collaud, J. Monnard, R. Ingold, D. Armangil, editors, *Electronic Books and their Tools. The WEBS Prototype and the OSCAR Project*, University of Fribourg Series in Computer Science, pages 23–39, Bern, 1992. Peter Lang European Academic Publishers.
184. O. Patashnik. Bibtexing, February 1988.
185. S. Payette and T. Staples. The mellon fedora project. In *ECDL'02: Proceedings of the 6th European Conference on Research and Advanced Technology for Digital Libraries*, pages 406–421, London, UK, 2002. Springer-Verlag.
186. F. Pentaris and Y.E. Ioannidis. Query trading in digital libraries. In Agosti et al. [9], pages 205–212.
187. J. Perez, M. Arenas, C. Gutierrez. Semantics and complexity of sparql. *ISWC06.*
188. Protegé OWL Library. http://protege.stanford.edu/ontologies/ontologies.html.
189. R. Rada. Hypertext writing and document reuse: the role of a semantic net. *Elec- tronic Publishing*, 3:125–140, 1990.
190. S. Ranwez and M. Crampes. Conceptual documents and hypertext documents are two different forms of virtual document. In *Proceedings on Virtual Documents Hypertext Functionality and the Web workshop of the 8th Intl. World Wide Web Conference*, Toronto, Canada, 1999.
191. M.A. Rodrguez and M.J. Egenhofer. Determining semantic similarity among entity class from different ontologies. *IEEE Transactions on Knowledge and Data Engineering*, 15, 2003.
192. R. Rogers. Poignancy in the us political blogsphere. *Aslib Proceedings*, 57(4):356–368, 2005.
193. M. Ronchett and S. Paramjeet. Knowledge management in an e-learning system. In *Proceedings of the 4th IEEE International Conference on Advanced Learning Technologies (ICALT2004)*, Joensuu, Finland, 2004.

194. J. Rothenberg. Digital information lasts forever – or five years, whichever comes first, 1997.
195. J.A. Rydberg-Cox. *Digital libraries and the challenges of digital humanities.* Chandos Publishing, Oxford, 2006.
196. A. Seaborne. Rdql – a query language for rdf. Technical report, W3C Member Submission. http://www.w3.org/Submission/RDQL/.
197. A. (n.d.). Seldow. Social Tagging in K-12 Education: Folksonomies for Student Folk.
198. Sesame user guide, aduna b.v. http://www.openrdf.org/doc/sesame/users/.
199. B. Shneiderman and C. Plaisant. *Designing the user interface: strategies for effective Human-Computer Interaction.* Addison-Wesley, 4th edition, 2004.
200. B. Shneiderman and M. Wattenberg. Ordered treemap layouts. In *INFO-VIS'01*, 2001.
201. J. Skvoretz. Complexity theory and models for social networks. *Complex.*, 8(1):47–55, 2002.
202. M. Smith, M. Bass, G. McClella, R. Tansley, M. Barton, M. Branschofsky, D. Stuve, J.H. Wakler. DSpace: An open source dynamic digital repository. *D-Lib Magazine*, 9(1), 2003.
203. D. Soergel. A framework for DL research: Broadening the vision. In *D-Lib Magazine 8*, December 2002.
204. D. Soergel. Information organization. In *D. Bainbridge, editor, Berkshire Encyclopedia of Human-Computer Interaction*, pages 355–360, Great Barrington, MA: Berkshire, July 2004.
205. D. Soergel. Information retrieval. In *D. Bainbridge, editor, Berkshire Encyclopedia of Human-Computer Interaction*, pages 363–371, Great Barrington, MA: Berkshire, July 2004.
206. SPARQL Query Language for RDF, W3C Working Draft. http://www.w3.org/TR/rdf-sparql-query/.
207. L. Stoilova, T. Holloway, B. Markines, A.G. Maguitman, F. Menczer. Givealink: mining a semantic network of bookmarks for web search and recommendation. In *LinkKDD'05: Proceedings of the 3rd international workshop on Link discovery*, pages 66–73, New York, NY, USA, 2005. ACM Press.
208. H. Suleman. Analysis and evaluation of service oriented architectures for digital libraries. In Agosti et al. [9], pages 163–174.
209. H. Suleman and E.A. Fox. Designing protocols in support of digital library componentization. *Proceedings of the European Conference on Digital Libraries*, 2458:568–582, 2002.
210. M. Synak. MarcOnt Ontology – Semantic MARC21 Description for L2L and L2C Communication. Master's thesis, WETI, Gdansk Univeristy of Technology, 2005.
211. The DARPA Agent Markup Language Homepage. http://www.daml.org/.
212. The protegé ontology editor and knowledge acquisition system. http://protege.stanford.edu.
213. Y.L. Theng. *Design and usability of digital libraries: Case studies in the Asia Pacific.* Information Science Publishers, Hershey, PA, 2005.
214. J. Scheffczyk L. Schmitz U.M. Borghoff, P. Rödig. Long-term preservation of digital documents, principles and practices, 2005.
215. M. Uschold. Where are the semantics in the semantic web? *Boeing - AI Magazine*, September 2003.

216. Z.W. Hendrikse and V.B. Gundersen. Bibtex as xml markup. http://www.eeng.dcu.ie/local-docs/btxdocs/btxdoc/btxdoc/btxdoc.html.
217. E.v. Vlist, D. Ayers, E. Bruchez, J. Fawcett, A. Vernet. *Professional Web 2.0 Programming (Wrox Professional Guides).* Wrox, November 2006.
218. W3C. VRML Virtual Reality Modeling Language. http://www.w3.org/MarkUp/VRML/, April 1995.
219. W3C Semantic Web Activity – RDF Core Working Group. Resource Description Framework (RDF), 2004. http://www.w3.org/RDF/.
220. W3C Semantic Web Activity – RDF Data Access Working Group. SPARQL Query Language for RDF, 2006.
221. W3C Semantic Web Activity – Web Ontology Working Group. Web Ontology Language (OWL), 2004. http://www.w3.org/2004/OWL/.
222. P. Warren, I. Thurlow, D. Alsmeyer. Applying semantic technology to a dl. In *Semantic Web Technologies: Trends and Research in Ontology-based Systems*, Wiley, 2006.
223. D.J. Watts, P.S. Dodds, M.E.J. Newman. Identity and Search in Social Networks. *Science*, 296. no. 5571:1302 – 1305, May 2002.
224. I.H. Witten. *How to build a digital library.* Morgan Kaufmann, San Francisco, CA, 2003.
225. I.H. Witten and D. Bainbridge. *How to Build a Digital Library.* Elsevier Science Inc., 2002.
226. I.H. Witten and D. Bainbridge. A retrospective look at greenstone: lessons from the first decade. In *JCDL'07: Proceedings of the 2007 conference on Digital libraries*, pages 147–156, New York, NY, USA, 2007. ACM Press.
227. M. Wozniak. Service oriented architecture for collaboration and negotiation ontology management portal. Master's thesis, Gdansk Univeristy of Technology, Poland, 2006.
228. M. Wozniak, S.R. Kruk, P. Piotrowski, P. Szczecki. MarcOnt Portal Ubiquitous Collaborative Ontology Life-cycle Management. In *Proceedings to Demo session at ESWC2006*, 2006.
229. H. Wu, E. de Kort, P. De Bra. Design issues for general-purpose adaptive hypermedia systems. In *Proceedings of the ACM Hypertext 2001 Conference*, pages 141–150, Århus, Denmark, 2001.
230. W.G. Wu and J. Li. Rss made easy: a basic guide for librarians. *Medical Reference Services Quarterly*, 26(1):37–50, 2007.
231. Xsb, a logic programming and deductive database system. http://xsb.sourceforge. net/.
232. M. Zhang, D. Yang, Z. Deng, S. Wu, F. Li, S. Tang. Webgis-rbdl – a rare book digital library supporting spatio-temporary retrieval. pages 255–265. 2004.

Index

Printing: Krips bv, Meppel, The Netherlands
Binding: Stürtz, Würzburg, Germany